Men at the Crossroads

BOOKS BY BERYL D. COHON

Introduction to Judaism
  A Book for Jewish Youth

The Prophets: Their Personalities and Teachings

Feasts of the Lord
  A sacred pageant

Judaism—In Theory and Practice (3d ed.)

From Generation to Generation

Jacob's Well: Some Jewish Sources and Parallels
  to the Sermon On the Mount

Out of the Heart: Intimate Talks from a Jewish
  Pulpit on the Personal Issues of Life

God's Angry Men
  A Student's Introduction to the Hebrew Prophets

My King and My God: Intimate Talks
  On the Devotions of Life

Vision and Faith: Confirmation Services for
  Jewish Congregations

Men at the Crossroads

Between Jerusalem and Rome

Synagogue and Church

THE LIVES, TIMES, AND DOCTRINES
OF THE FOUNDERS OF TALMUDIC JUDAISM
AND NEW TESTAMENT CHRISTIANITY

by

Beryl D. Cohon

THOMAS YOSELOFF
South Brunswick ● *New York* ● *London*

Thomas Yoseloff, *Publisher*
Cranbury, New Jersey 08512

Thomas Yoseloff Ltd
108 New Bond Street
London W1Y OQX, England

SBN 498 07339 4
Printed in the United States of America

To. Sally

ואהבת עולם אהבתיך

Jeremia 31. 2.

Contents

Preface   11

Part I
ROME AND JERUSALEM

1. *Herod—Idumean King of the Jews*   19
   Herod is Proclaimed King—How Judea Became a
   Roman Province—How Herod Established Him-
   self in Power—Herod's Character and Idumean
   Origin—How Herod Removed Opposition—
   Herod As Administrator—Herod's Will: Judea
   Dismembered.

2. *Hillel and Shammai: Pharisaic Sages*   36
   A Babylonian in the Jerusalem Academy—Folk-
   lore—Aphorisms—Scholar and Jurist—Hillel and
   Shammai—"Prosbul"—Hillel, Shammai, Herod.

Part II
BIRTHPANGS OF THE MESSIAH

3. *Sadducees and Pharisees*   49
   Two Classes: Their Positions in Society—"Scribes,
   Pharisees, Hypocrites"—Written and Oral Torah
   —Interpretation and Reinterpretation—Beliefs and
   the Synagogue.

4. *The Essenes*   55
   Testimonies of Josephus,—Philo,—Dead Sea
   Scrolls

5. *Zealots*   60
   Dagger Men—John of Gishchala—Simon bar
   Giora—Josephus Testifies.

6. *Apocalyptists and Messiahs*   63
   Visions and "The End of Days."

7. *Procurators: Pontius Pilate*   66

Part III
THE BIRTH OF CHRISTIANITY

8. *John the Baptist: A Voice Crying in the Wilderness*   73
    Legends—Elijah Reborn—In the Desert—Baptism—Martyrdom

9. *Jesus of Nazareth: Palestinian Rabbi or
    Resurrected Christ?*   80
    Jesus the Palestinian Rabbi: A Word on the Sources
    —Childhood and Youth—Baptism—Jesus the
    Pharisee; Social and Religious Conditioning and
    Teaching—Ethics, Social Action—Prayer—Miracles—"Good Tiding to the Afflicted"—Passover in
    Jerusalem— Trial and Crucifixion—What Manner
    of Man? *Jesus the Resurrected Christ*: Transfiguration and Transubstantiation.

10. *Paul of Tarsus: Slave of Christ, Apostle to
    the Gentiles*   121
    Sources—The Facts of His Life, Environment and
    Personality—The Stoning of Stephen and the Road
    to Damascus—Missionary Journeys—Jerusalem
    Again—Rome and the Last Years—The Jewish
    Opposition to Paul, Then and Now.

Part IV
DISASTER BREAKS

11. *Josephus: Traitor? Patroit?*   151
    Family, Education, Young Priest—General—John
    of Gishchala—Jotapata—9 Ab, 70—Domestic Life
    —Historian, Apologist, Defender of His People—
    Restoring Josephus to His Own.

12. *Yohanan Ben Zakkai: Builder of the
    Portable Fatherland*   173
    Jerusalem Under Siege—Father of the Future—
    Teaching in Jerusalem—Yavneh—"Prepare a
    Throne for Hezekiah."

Contents

Part V
TALMUDIC MASTERS AND APOSTOLIC FATHERS

13. *Akiba: Fortress of the Law*   189
    Akiba and Paul—Facts and Legends—A Mighty
    Harvest—Old Testament Canon—Synagogue—
    Systematizer of the Law—Hermeneutics and Law
    —Religious Teaching—Calendar—Zealotry and
    Messianism Again—Martyrdom.

14. *Apostles and Martyrs: The Church Triumphant*   208
    From Synagogue to Church—The Blood of the
    Martyrs—Preaching the Gospel, Schisms, More
    Blood—The Keys to the Kingdom.

15. *Quo Vadis? Issues and Vision*   222
    The True Religion—Issues—Vision

APPENDIXES

I. *The Letters of Saint Paul*   233

II. *Deicide*   235
    Then and Now—Pronouncement of the Second
    Vatican Council, October 28, 1965.

III. *The Works of Josephus*   240

IV. *The Martyrdom of Rabbi Akiba: A Page from
    the Talmud*   253

Notes and Bibliography   255

Index   266

Preface

The object of this book is, by focusing on the key personalities of the time, to survey the landscape and trace the primary forces and issues that created the Great Divide between Jerusalem and Rome, the Synagogue and the Church. The aim is to bring into focus the images of the men who stood at the crossroads and directed the energies of the first centuries before and of the Common Era. Pagans and pietists, saints and sinners, the crucified and the crucifiers—sages, terrorists, mystics, ascetics, visionaries—played their roles as rabbinic Judaism and New Testament Christianity emerged and separated. Most of them were driven by forces they knew not and shaped the destinies of the new Judeo-Christian civilization to our own day. In Herod and in Hillel we see the raw power of Rome in an antagonistic embrace with the faith in the Law of the academies; in the thinking and activities of the Pharisees, Sadducees, Zealots, Essenes, apocalyptists and Messiaists we observe with fascination the desperate reach for the Messiah who would redeem and heal and unroll a new heaven over a regenerated earth. John the Baptist crying in the wilderness; Jesus transfigured and Jesus on the cross; Pilate sentencing Jesus and washing his hands of all guilt; Saul of Tarsus captivated and transfigured on the road to Damascus into Paul the Apostle to the gentiles; Josephus walking over the corpses of his comrades whom he had betrayed at Jotapata and then writing his histories, with some pangs of conscience, for a harlot's hire; Yohanan ben Zakkai turning his back on flaming Jeru-

salem and retiring to an obscure village and laying the
foundations for the portable fatherland for his people
that has withstood all the onslaughts of some two thous-
and years; Akiba at the stake; the rabbinic masters and
the Church fathers rearing their walls, to shut in and to
shut out—these personify the passions that have given
us our Judeo-Christian civilization, with all its blessings and all its woes.

The Western Wall of the Temple—the Jews' "Wailing Wall"—is on the front pages of our newspapers today, once again drawing the faithful, and once again the
object of hate. The spiritual wall it symbolizes is in the
hearts and devotions of countless millions in Jewry,
Christendom and Islam. The Ecumenical Council of
Vatican II and centuries of brilliant scholarship and
earnest aspiration in all communions aimed at tearing
down this invisible battlement in the minds of the faithful in Christendom and in Jewry are primary, unfinished
business of all men of good faith. There is no understanding the issues involved, no way of thinking and acting intelligently, for Jew or for Christian, unless we
stand in reverence before the men who personify the
issues of the first century, and try to understand.

Religions are expressed most authentically in the personalities of the faithful, not in the official creeds, not in
the sanctified rites. Hence our effort is to focus our
camera on the faithful sons and builders of Judaism and
of Christianity who labored at the crossroads like Jacob
at the river Jabbok, and struggled with their destinies.

The present book is meant for the layman who has
done little serious reading in the beginnings of Rabbinic
Judaism and New Testament Christianity. The rather
ample notes will guide him to the more detailed studies;
they also point to the differing, often conflicting, interpretations of the primary issues separating mother and
daughter faiths. These studies are readily available.

The author's attempt in the present volume is to view the landscape and observe the men who created the Great Divide. In his heart is a prayer voiced by the prophet Isaiah more than twenty-six hundred years ago.

There shall be a highway and a way,
And it shall be called the way of holiness.

Beryl D. Cohon

Men at the Crossroads

Rome and Jerusalem

HEROD AND HILLEL
Two Men—Two Worlds

*No two men ever were as different as were Herod and Hillel:
"Herod the Great," as he is sometimes designated in history, a
ferocious evil genius of whom an ancient historian wrote that
"he stole along to the throne like a fox, he ruled like a tiger,
and he died like a dog," raving mad; and Hillel, cherished in
the sacred tradition of his people as gentle, humble and beloved
teacher of lovingkindness, peace, patience, faithful expounder of
the word of God. These two men lived at the same time, in the
same land, controlling the two worlds of the little land of Judea:
one, the political, military, economic—this world; the other, the
world of Torah—all that was sacred to the faithful Judeans.
By recalling their personalities—the values they cherished, the
ambitions that lured them, the methods they followed, the powers
they controlled—we may gain insight into the worlds of Rome
and Jerusalem, the world of pagan political power and the world
of Torah. This insight we must have if we are to understand the
teachings of the Talmudic masters and the Judaism they shaped;
this insight we must have, further, if we are to understand emerging Christianity. The roots of both, Rabbinic Judaism and Christianity, are deep in the blood, tears and prayers of this period.*

1

Herod—Idumean King of the Jews

Herod Is Proclaimed King

In the year 40 B.C.E. the Roman Senate, on the authority of the Roman rulers of the time,* decreed Herod King of Judea. It was a brazen decree; for its authority it had nothing more than the iron fist of Rome. The Jewish people were in no way consulted. Herod was a member of a hated race; at most he was only partly Jewish, and was not a Jew at all to the pious masses and their religious leaders. Still more, he was replacing the Maccabean dynasty. As if to climax this arrogance with an added flourish of impudence, Herod, escorted by his Roman sponsors, marched up the Temple of Jupiter and there offered a sacrifice to the pagan god for having been made king of the Jews.[1]

How did Rome acquire the power to appoint the King of Judea, and why Herod?

How Judea Became A Roman Province

Twenty-four years earlier—in the year 63 B.C.E.—the Roman General Pompey was invited by warring Jewish factions to come into Judea and establish peace in their country. Pompey had been carrying on a difficult war

---

*Antony and Octavius, who later became the Emperor Augustus.

19

with Arabs in Damascus, in the neighborhood of Judea, for the control of that part of the world. Judea was in the throes of civil war. The descendants of the Maccabees were a disgrace to the heroic founders of their dynasty. All the grandeur and glory of the sons of Mattathias who had fought for freedom of faith, routed the Syrian tyrant, cleansed the sanctuary and restored their national independence a century earlier—as celebrated in the festival of Hanukkah to this day—had turned into a series of bloody intrigues. Pagan politicians and greedy ecclesiastics corrupted the life of the nation. The High Priesthood, officially the most sacred office in the land, went to the highest bidder or to the most slippery politician. The grandsons of the Maccabees who had fought against the paganism of the Syrian Greeks turned Judea into a pagan state very much like all other pagan states. In the manner of the time, they carried on wars of conquest on the neighboring peoples and imposed their Judean cult on them with the sword. This resulted in a bitter harvest, as we shall see, in the person of Herod. It was the most degrading period in all Jewish history.

In the year 67 B.C.E. war had broken out between the two brothers, Hyrcanus II and Aristobulus II. They were the last survivors of the Maccabean dynasty. Their mother, Queen Salome Alexandra, had willed the throne to Hyrcanus, the older of the two. This included the High Priesthood. But Hyrcanus was a weakling, "of a slow and slothful temperament."[2] His brother Aristobulus was keen and reckless, and ambitious for the throne of Judea. A series of intrigues and messy conflicts followed, abetted by a foreign adventurer, Herod's father Antipater.[3] Once again Jerusalem wept in blood and ashes with none to comfort her. In the ensuing thirty years, historians estimate some thirty thousand Jews were killed in civil warfare. That was the end of the

Maccabean dynasty and the beginning of Judea as a Roman Province, or as a Roman *Tributary State*.

Both brothers turned to Pompey—the Roman general then warring in Damascus—seeking to bring that part of the world under Roman rule. He had coveted Judea when the warring brothers appealed to him for help and invited him to come into their country and impose peace. Each sought the Roman's favor for his own purposes. Each came with an army and a following, bearing gifts. Hyrcanus had more of the pious people and Pharisees on his side; Aristobulus had more of the Temple aristocrats, the Sadducees, on his side.

A third group joined in seeking the Roman's favor and inviting him to come in. They were mainly devout people who were disgusted with the two brothers and all they represented.

It was an incredible situation: two descendants of the once glorious Maccabees, involving the throne and the High Priesthood of Judea, the aristocrats and the common people, and a third group ("a thousand Jews of highest rank," reports Josephus), each group hated the others, and each for its own purpose turned to the same foreign general begging—even bribing—him to bring the Roman legions into their country and keep the peace. It was precisely this Roman who had been looking enviously at Judea for his own reasons. He must have smacked his lips when the delegations came to him. The most pious wanted him to take their government over altogether; all they wanted was to be left alone in the administration of their cult. Pompey, of course, jumped at the invitation. Soon the cat taken into the home to drive the mice away turned into a tiger and devoured its host.

Thus, in June of 63 B.C.E., Pompey's soldiers stormed Jerusalem and broke into the Temple, the sacred shrine of the nation. The masses offered suicidal resistance, but refrained from fighting back on the Sabbath. Some twelve thousand Jews are believed to have perished on that one Sabbath day. The devout and their leaders soon changed their minds about not fighting on the Sabbath.

Pompey and his guard entered the Holy of Holies, where the High Priest alone, once a year on the Day of Atonement, was permitted to enter. Josephus credits the pagan with sparing the sacred treasures of the Temple: "the golden table, the sacred candlestick, the pouring vessels, a great quantity of spices; and among the treasures, two thousand talents of sacred money."[4] Two years later, in Rome, Aristobulus, scion of the legendary Maccabees, in chains, led Pompey's triumphal procession in abject defeat before the debauched howling Roman mobs.

How Herod Established Himself in Power

A series of bloody revolts followed, born of the bitter despair of the Judean masses. All of them ended in tragic futility. For a time the weak-minded Hyrcanus strutted as King and High Priest. But he had been appointed by Rome, and was only a front for Rome and its shrewd and evil agent, Antipater, whose sole concern was to acquire power for himself and his sons. He placed Jerusalem under the control of his oldest son, and to his second son, Herod, he assigned the government of Judea. His ferocious reign held the country in terror. Sheer despair drove the Judean leaders to an attempt to bring him to justice, and Hyrcanus was finally induced to cooperate in summoning him to a supposed trial before the feeble Sanhedrin.

That was a tragic spectacle. Herod came not as an accused standing trial, but was instead dressed in purple, the symbol of his Roman authority—insolent, defiant, with a military escort by his side. The Sanhedrin was cowed into silence and inaction. All but one of the rabbinic masters, who condemned the cowardice of his colleagues and predicted that "this very man, whom you are going to absolve and dismiss, for the sake of Hyrcanus (who had been ordered by Rome to see to it that Herod was cleared) will one day punish both you and your king himself also."[5] The evil day came when this prophecy was fulfilled; Herod slaughtered the supposed King and the men of the Sanhedrin.

Herod lost no time in establishing himself on the throne of Judea. For the Roman Senate to proclaim him King and for the Judean masses and their religious leaders to accept him as their ruler were two different matters. Herod waded through pools of blood before grasping the throne. In the year 37 B.C.E., three years after the Roman Senate had proclaimed him King, he besieged the Holy City with an army of thirty thousand pagan mercenaries, reinforced by a Roman general with a vast army. For fifty-five days the battering rams stormed the agonized, terror-torn city before they could reach the inner court of the Temple. At last Jerusalem collapsed; the last Maccabean King and High Priest was taken in chains to the Roman headquarters and was beheaded.

Judea was now a *Tributary State*. The walls of Jerusalem were razed to the ground. Heavy taxation was levied on the people. Judean seaports were restricted to Roman traffic. The Sanhedrin—the supreme Judean tribunal—was stripped of all power but the ritualistic; civil and political matters, as well as police power, were vested in the Roman armies. This fact is important to an understanding of the crucifixion of Jesus. Josephus (who wrote this account, and who aimed to please the Romans —himself a supposed descendant of the Maccabees) concludes the tragic chapter:

And thus did the government of the Hasmonean* dynasty cease, a hundred and twenty-six years after it was set up. This family was a splendid and illustrious one, both on account of the nobility of their stock, and of the dignity of the high-priesthood, as also for the glorious actions their ancestors had performed for our nation: but these men lost the government by their mutual dissentions with one another, and it came to Herod, the son of Antipater, who was no more than of a vulgar family, and of no eminent extraction, but one that was subject to other kings.[6]

Herod's Character and Idumean Origin

Herod was thirty-six years old when he grasped the throne of Judea in the year 37 B.C.E. and reigned to the year 4 B.C.E.—a period of almost thirty-four years of appalling intrigues and insane murders, but a period also of great national achievement, as we shall note.

Tall, handsome, powerful in physique, Herod was an expert horseman, expert hunter, expert pugilist—equal to anything and reckless in everything. Josephus, and the later historians to our own day, testify that he was "a born leader," keen in his judgment, supremely able, energetic, cold, calculating, cruel; with it all, he was a shrewd diplomat and a great administrator and builder. No law of God or man inhibited him in his insane ambitions. Insane he was; by modern psychiatric insights he may be pronounced a paranoiac killer.

One historian, who has studied the personality of Herod closely and shrewdly, testifies: "From his boyhood Herod had been habituated to treachery, to sedition, conspiracy and rebellion, to battle, murder and sudden death. Family affection was born strong in him. He could be quixotically faithful and loyal to a relation or a friend. And yet he could murder his own kith and

---

*Another name for the Maccabean

kin. It was a strange and frightening mixture, a psychological tangle which became more involved as he grew older. It had its origin in his early youth, when the traditional family piety of the Arabs—it is one of their strongest traits—came into conflict with the stark competition for power and survival which alone governed the Roman world during his boyhood, and for some years after it."[7] His own sponsor, the Emperor Augustus, is quoted as saying in the last days of Herod's life that "I had sooner be Herod's swine than his son."

He was an Idumean, which gave him endless trouble to his dying hour. The pious sneered at him as "the Idumean slave."

The Idumeans (Arabs, biblical Edom) were the descendants of Esau, the rival twin brother of Jacob. Of these siblings the Bible affirms that they represented two peoples in eternal conflict:

Rebekah (Isaac's wife) conceived. And the children struggled within her . . . And she went and inquired of the Lord. And the Lord said unto her:

Two nations are in thy womb,
And two peoples shall be separated from thy bowels;
And the one people shall be stronger than the other people;
And the elder shall serve the younger.[8]

There was bitter hatred between the descendants of Esau and Jacob, the Edomite Arabs and the Israelites. This hatred grew with the centuries. When the Israelites, under Moses, sought passage through Edom on the way from Egypt to the Promised Land, the Edomites refused them passage. An Edomite might not enter "into the assembly of the Lord." The descendant of an Edomite and Israelite marriage might be admitted to the Temple and its worship only after three generations.[9] Continuous strife marked the relationship of the two peoples. King David subjugated the Edomites in his day; but in time they gained the upper hand and plundered Jerusalem. Judah Maccabeus conquered them, and his descendants, a century before Herod, compelled them to accept Jewish law and practices. They were Jews by forced conversion—a common procedure of the time among most peoples, but one that was abhorrent to the rabbinic leaders of Jewry. This plagued Herod and the Judean state.

To overcome the hatred levelled against him because of his Idumean ancestry, Herod faked a genealogy, pretending to be a descendant of Babylonian Jewry—an honored Jewry in his day, whence came distinguished scholars, as, for example, Hillel. This did not assuage the resentment of his stiff-necked subjects. His next effort was a much more daring one: he married Mariamne II (Hebrew, *Miriam*), a descendant of the Maccabees and granddaughter of the last King and High Priest, John Hyrcanus II, one of the two brothers whose civil warfare had delivered Judea to the Romans to begin with. This gave Herod status officially, in part; now he was in the Maccabean family. This alliance tortured him all his life. His children by the Maccabean Princess were potential rivals to the throne; Herod was fearful and insanely jealous of his wife—whom he dearly loved— and his sons by her. She responded with hostile schemes for avenging his spoliation of her royal Maccabean family. In this she was brilliantly abetted by her ruthless mother, former Queen Alexandra.

How Herod Removed Opposition

Herod came to the throne of Judea by treachery and bloodshed; treachery and bloodshed—sparing neither age nor sex—branded his reign.

On assuming power, fearing possible opposition, he purged the aristocratic descendants of the Maccabees. The ghosts of the national heroes haunted him. He summarily ordered the execution of forty-five members of the Sanhedrin—the very men who had lost their nerve when Herod was before them on trial. The prophecy of the lone rabbinic master who had the courage to speak up came true. Ironically, *his* life Herod did spare. Now the supreme court of Judea was impotent. The office of the High Priest presented a crucial problem. Herod himself could not assume the office for two reasons: He was an Idumaean; therefore, according to Bible law, he was not permitted in the sanctuary any more than would be a dog. Further, the office of High Priest belonged to the Maccabean family. Even Herod could not defy the feelings of the masses on these points. He sought to solve his problem by bestowing the High Priesthood on a convenient flunky, a Jewish priest from Babylon. To assuage the feelings of the masses he enticed the aged former King and the High Priest, Hyrcanus II—who had been mutilated and banished—to return to Jerusalem, and showered attention on him. His stiff-necked subjects refused to be impressed. His wife and her mother—proud and scheming Queen and Princess of the Maccabean dynasty—kept pressing him to appoint young Aristobulus—son and brother—High Priest. He was the legitimate heir to this sacred office. Herod finally yielded.

The handsome seventeen-year-old Priest was enormously popular, child of the Maccabees that he was. On the Festival of Sukkot the crowds at the Temple cheered the teenage High Priest, resplendent in his robes. Herod heard the cheers and sensed insurrection. Violent jealousy possessed him. After the service Aristobulus was invited by Herod's men to join them in the royal pool for a swim; he drowned. The young High Priest received a magnificent funeral. Fearing that the senile Hyrcanus II—a Maccabee—might become the center of an active opposition, he too was put to death. Insanely suspicious of his wife, Mariamne, whom he loved passionately, and who responded by scorning him, he had her executed. Josephus reports: "Mindful of her status and the nobility of her birth, she groaned when he embraced her and clearly showed that she grieved rather than rejoiced at his success . . . . Because he loved her, her attitude both angered and upset him . . . . Alternating between hatred and love, he suffered greatly. A conflict raged within him: he often wished to punish her for her contempt of him; at the same time, being in love with her, he had not the heart to destroy this woman . . . . So died Mariamne, a superior woman both in chastity and greatness of her soul. However, she lacked moderation and was overly contentious. In beauty of body and majesty of bearing she surpassed all women of her day."[10]

Herod went completely mad. He was a man possessed and haunted. "And now that she was dead that love [for her] affected him in so peculiar a manner that it seemed like divine vengeance for taking away her life. He continually called for her and unceasingly lamented her passing in a most unseemly manner . . . "[11] He ordered his servants to continue calling her. He went raving mad.

Fearful of the influence his aged mother-in-law, Queen Alexandra, might have, Herod had her executed. She was a proud, strong, resourceful and daring woman who had carried on in the spirit of her royal ancestors. Suspicious of his own three sons by Mariamne—descendants of the Maccabees as they were, and hence potential rivals to the throne—he had them tried on a trumped-up charge of intrigue and disloyalty. They were not permitted to be present at their own trial, for Herod knew that their mere appearance would have excited universal compassion. Their own father prosecuted them, demanding their death. Josephus reports: " . . . . all Syria and Judea was in great expectation, and waited for the last act of this tragedy; yet did nobody suppose that Herod would be so barbarous as to murder his children."[12] But he did. Two of his sons were strangled and the third was drowned.

An intolerable hatred fell upon him, Josephus reports further. He was feared, hated and cursed by the entire nation, though he had now an indisputable title to the succession. However, there were still some descendants of the Maccabees in the land, and his sons by his other wives also roused his jealousy. The fear within him grew like a poison tree. One of them—a man of intrigue and violence, like his father—he had executed. Deranged, inconsolate, raving, Herod roamed about his palace totally insane, calling for some of those he had slain, especially his Mariamne, whose ghost tortured him.*

Herod married ten women, "polygamy being permitted by Jewish law, and the king delighted in this privilege."[13] He was consistently unfortunate in all his marriages. Not one of his wives brought wisdom, or stability, or restraint into his life. His children—fifteen of them—brought him no comfort. He was incapable of arousing loving or comforting. His last years brought him physical and mental torture.

The country was seething with rebellion. In the year 7 B.C.E., six thousand Pharisees refused to take an oath

---

*In the Gospel according to Matthew, Herod is reported as having ordered the slaughter of "all the male children in Bethlehem and in all that region who were two years old or more." (Matthew 2.1-18) He was driven by the fear of the birth of a messiah-king who would challenge his authority. The report may be entirely legendary, in keeping with Matthew's primarily theological interest; the report however does fit Herod's personality and squares with his bloody record. It squares, further, with a number of similar reports in the lives of Heracles, Sargon I, Cyrus, Romulus and Remus, etc. Josephus makes no reference to the story in Matthew.

of allegiance to Herod. His death was anticipated eagerly by the populace, the Pharisaic masters and their disciples, especially the young. The King's imminent death was a propitious moment to strike. Some forty young men, inspired by their rabbinic masters, hacked off the golden eagle Herod had erected over the Temple gate, hated pagan symbol of Rome that it was. Slaughter of the young patriots followed. "He burned alive the chief perpetrators and the learned men; the rest of the seized men he delivered to the officers for execution."[14] That was on the 13th day of March in the year 4 B.C.E.

A loathsome disease racked his body and his mind. Josephus gives us a clinical description. "Herod's disease spread over his entire body, and he was racked with complex pains. He suffered from continuous fever, though in a mitigated form, intolerable itching of his entire body, constant pain in his intestines, dropsylike tumors in his feet, inflammation of his abdomen, and an ulceration of his genitals which bred maggots. In addition he had difficulty in breathing, and convulsive spasms in all his limbs. The diviners pronounced his maladies a judgment for his treatment of the learned men."[15] At least once he attempted suicide.

He brooded over the joy his death would bring to his country. Seeking to prevent his funeral from turning into an occasion of national rejoicing, Herod ordered some of the revered personalities of the nation imprisoned in the public arena at Jericho and left strict orders that upon his own death they be butchered by his bodyguard. The nation would then mourn on the day of his death. The order fortunately was not carried out, and these respected leaders of the people returned to their homes. While Herod's body was carried in pagan pomp —the last day or two in March, 4 B.C.E.—the nation joyfully celebrated.

Herod's son Archelaus, who inherited the lion's share

of Herod's kingdom, including the title of King, arranged a spectacular funeral. Josephus reports it in vivid details: "The bier was solid gold, studded with precious stones, and the bed was of varigated purple. On it lay the body, also covered with purple. A diadem was on Herod's head, and over it a crown of gold. At his right-hand side lay a scepter. Herod's sons and various kin surrounded the bier. Next came the guards, the Thracian bands, the Germans and the Gauls, all of them equipped as for war. The rest of the army, preceded by its commanders and subordinates, marched in front, armed and in order. They were followed by five hundred of Herod's servants and freedmen, bearing sweet spices. The body was conveyed to Herodium, a distance of two hundred furlongs, Herod having left orders to be buried there. So ends the history of Herod."[16]

Herod As Administrator

Despite his jealousies, fears, intrigues, murders, Herod was a great administrator and builder. "For sheer ability," a historian affirms, "he ranks perhaps second to none in all Jewish history, and his reign was memorable, for more reasons than one, in the annals of his people."[17]

Enjoying absolute power, as long as he did not offend the Roman masters, he achieved many successes. He suppressed brigandage, which had plagued the nation, and established order. He revised the laws governing the country, modelling them largely after the Roman pattern. In doing this he stripped the Sanhedrin of all power, reducing it to a purely academic body in charge of the religious practices of the Jewish community. The civil, the criminal, the military he gathered into his own hands. After his death this power was taken over by the Roman rulers: that is why Jesus was tried before the Roman governor and executed by the Roman army.

He enlarged the kingdom of Judea, reclaiming lost territories. He fortified the frontiers and imposed peace. (Herod's peace, that is—peace by the sword, but peace nevertheless.)

He was a great builder. "With the possible exception of the Emperor Hadrian, Herod the Great was the most passionate builder of antiquity."[18] He erected not only magnificent buildings but established cities and seaports. He built and developed the Mediterranean sea coasts and thus established communications and commerce with foreign nations. Caesarea was probably the most important city he had reared. He named it after Caesar Augustus, his Roman master. Herod knew how and whom to flatter. By the sea, some seventy-five miles east of Jerusalem, it became one of the great ports of the nation. Pious Jews, however, hated the city, for it was a symbol of Roman paganism. He sought to exploit the copper mines of Cyprus and to bring needed metals into Judea.

He promoted an enormous building program. This included a magnificent palace in Jerusalem, with ample room for hosts of foreign emissaries and guests; an enormous gymnasium in the Holy City with a nearby amphitheater where were held wrestling matches, charioting races, even gladiatorial and wild beast contests. (This outraged the rabbinic masters and the pious Jews.) He erected temples to the Greek gods, an especially beautiful one to Apollo, to please the Greek, Syrian and Roman elements of the population of Judea. His fortress Masada, a complex of fort, palace and executive quarters, recently excavated, was an astonishing achievement, breathtaking in conception and marvelous in construction.[19] His most resplendent building was the Temple at Jerusalem, replacing the Temple Solomon had built, and which had been destroyed by the Babylonians in 586 B.C.E. and which the Jews returning from Babylon tried to rebuild in their time, under the leadership of Zerabbabel. Herod's Temple and the fortress Masada were two of the wonders of the Mediterranean world.

On the Passover in the year 20 B.C.E., Herod announced his plan to the vast throng assembled for the Passover sacrifices. At first the Judean masses distrusted him; gradually, however, they cooperated with him. Ten thousand skilled craftsmen and one thousand priests were put to work; one thousand wagons were used to haul material from all parts of the country. It was some ten years in the building. Work on this Temple went on even after his death. The Temple was the central fortress of the country, as well as its capitol, as well as its central shrine. Josephus describes the building in much detail and adds:

> When the morning sun burst upon the white marble of the Temple, Mount Moriah glittered like a hill of snow, and when its rays struck the golden roof of the sacred edifice, the whole mount gleamed and sparkled as if it were in flames.[20]

The Romans, under Titus, destroyed this Temple in the year 70 C.E. Only the Western Wall stands today. Israeli armies recaptured it from Jordan in June 1967.

In the years 25-24 B.C.E. famine came upon the land; suffering and death were everywhere. Herod opened his treasures and shared vast stores of food with the masses. More, he imported supplies from Egypt. He even stripped his palace of its precious appointments and converted them into cash to purchase supplies for the famished Judeans. It is estimated that he sent as much as 1.2 million bushels of corn to his famished subjects. Some fifty thousand persons were maintained at his own expense. Never had there been such a vast, imaginative program of relief in Judean history.

All this required vast sums of money. Much he drew from his own resources. Most of it, no doubt, he derived from heavy taxation. The people were taxed mercilessly, not only to finance the building program but to supply Herod with the funds he needed to satisfy the Roman overlords. Huge sums went to Rome regularly. A statue of him, in appreciation of his enormous gifts, was erected in the Acropolis of Athens. The Judean masses paid a frightful price under the pressure of tax collectors. The rabbinic masters of the time had ample warrant to advise their people to "seek no intimacy with the ruling powers."[21]

Before dropping the curtain of compassion on Herod, let us observe that the mainspring of his tragedy was that he did not understand Jews nor Judaism; he did not appreciate what was sacred to the Jewish masses and their religious teachers. Pagan Arab that he was, raised in the spirit and environment of brigandage, Roman heathen lewdness, explosive and violent by nature, quick with the sword, surrounded by thousands of pagan mercenaries, how could he possibly understand Hillel, and the other rabbinic masters, with their emphasis on Torah, learning, piety, life under the Law—justice, compassion, humility?

Herod's Will: Judea Dismembered

Herod left several daughters and six sons. Some of them, who had not been murdered, he ignored in his will altogether. To three sons, by two wives, he apportioned parts of Judea and its government. The oldest of these, Archelaus, he appointed King. Another son he appointed *Tetrarch* of Galilee and a portion of Judea east of the Jordan River. To a third son he willed the northeastern district of Palestine. Thus the country was carved up among his sons, none of whom had the capacity to rule wisely. Furious opposition to Archelaus came from the Judean masses. Some 3,000 were slaughtered on the Passover in the year 4 B.C.E. The Governor of Syria intervened on behalf of Herod's son with an army of 20,000. In Roman fashion, Archelaus was accepted after an untold number of towns and villages were exterminated, an estimated 20,000 rebels crucified, and 30,000 Jews sold into slavery.

Judea now became a Roman possession, administered by Governors appointed by Rome, and who are known in Jewish history as *Procurators*. These men were greedy scoundrels, caring not at all for the land or the people they governed. Their chief concern was to extract as much booty as possible. They taxed and plundered with none to restrain them. The fifth of these, and the most notorious, was Pilate. It was under his administration that John the Baptist was executed and Jesus was crucified, as we shall note.

Hillel and Shammai: Pharisaic Sages

While Herod held the political and economic life of Judea in his cruel hands and ruled ruthlessly, hated and cursed by the Jewish masses, Hillel taught in the academy, generously interpreted the sacred traditions of his people, beloved and revered by all.

The religious traditions of the Jewish people, preserved and fostered as their most precious heritage, transmitted to them by lawgivers, prophets, sages, from the days of Moses on Mount Sinai, were in the possession of the academies. "Moses received the Torah on Mount Sinai, and transmitted it to Joshua, Joshua to the elders, the elders to the prophets, the prophets transmitted it to the Men of the Great Synagogue."[1] That was their primary creed. To Herod it meant only a constant source of rebellion; to the Jewish masses and their teachers it meant their life and the length of their days. By it they lived; for it they died.

It was here—in the Torah as interpreted and reinterpreted by the masters in the academies—that Jewry realized itself as a people dedicated to the Holy One. Not by the pagan pomp and power of Herod and his Roman heroes, not by murderous soldiers, certainly not by circuses and gladiatorial combats did Jewry live, but by "all that proceeds from the mouth of the Lord." The true heroes of the people, therefore, were the faithful scholars in the academies; the security of the nation was with the children in the academies studying God's word.

Herod and Hillel, and all they represented, were worlds apart, and they were crowded into one little land. At best there was an unwritten truce between the domains they represented: at times there was bitter polemic and bloody rebellion.

A Babylonian In the Jerusalem Academy

We know very little of the basic facts of Hillel's life. All we have are scraps of traditions, stories—some true, some fanciful—a number of sayings, some legal decisions, mainly in the realm of ritual, notes of his expositions of the Torah made by his students, inferences drawn by scholars.

We do know that he was a Babylonian by birth and that he came to Jerusalem as a comparatively young man, or perhaps in early middle age, in the middle of the first century B.C.E. His dates are believed to have been 70 (some scholars say 60) B.C.E.-10 C.E. Thus he lived through the brutal times of Herod.

The academies of the Holy City and their distinguished masters lured him. He needed further study of Torah, he felt. To earn his daily bread he engaged in manual labor. This was in keeping with rabbinic teaching and practice. Hillel probably carried water and chopped wood to maintain himself as a student.* A brother had offered him partnership in a paying business, but he refused, preferring a life of scholarship, even if it meant poverty. In this too he became the model of his people. The rabbinic preachers say: When a man appears before the Holy One in the World-to-Come, he is asked, "Did you study the Torah?" If his answer is, "I was a poor man and could not afford the leisure for

---

*It has been calculated that his daily income was about fourteen cents in American money.

study," he is rebuked with the statement: "Were you poorer than Hillel?"[2]

He studied under the revered masters Shemayah and Abtalion. He seems to have taken their advice and sought "no intimacy with the ruling powers."

Was that a point of strength or a point of weakness? Was the beloved, gentle scholar an unconscious pacifier in the brutal hands of Herod? Before many years had passed the stranger won a high reputation as a keen and broad interpreter of the Torah; before many more years had passed he grew into a legend of kindliness, patience, a deep and profound expositor of God's word. Religious Jews, generation after generation, to our own day, revere his memory. "Be of the disciples of Aaron," he taught, and his successors pointed to him as the exemplar of this ideal, "loving peace and pursuing peace, loving mankind and bringing them close to the Torah."[3]

In time he succeeded his famous masters. Just what title he held is not clear. A loving posterity refers to him as *Nasi*, Prince. Were he of royal descent he might have been head of the Sanhedrin at the time of Herod. But this office he could not hold; it could be filled only by a High Priest and a Sadducee. Hillel was a commoner and a Pharisee. The title may have been an unofficial appelation of esteem by the masses. According to apocryphal tradition, further, he was believed to have been a descendant of King David on his mother's side.

We do not know anything about his children, excepting that one of his grandsons was Gamaliel, a leading master of the time. In the New Testament he is reported as defending the right of Peter and the apostles to preach their doctrine, despite the angry tumult of the people and the injunction of the Sanhedrin. In the Acts of the Apostles (5.34 ff.) we read: "But a Pharisee in the Sanhedrin called Gamaliel, a doctor of the new law who was highly respected by all the people, got up and ordered the apostles to be removed for a few moments. Then he said: 'Men of Israel, take care what you do about these men . . . I advise you to leave these men to themselves. Let them alone. If this project or enterprise springs from men (only), it will collapse; whereas, if it really springs from God, you will be unable to put them down. You may even find yourselves fighting God.' "

In this broad view and generous attitude toward an opponent Gamaliel followed his grandfather. Gamaliel, it is believed, was one of the teachers of Saul of Tarsus, who became Saint Paul.

Folklore

Tradition has woven a garland of legends about Hillel, extolling his gentleness, patience, magnanimity, his passion for learning—the romanticized endearing ideal of the academies. These stories and anecodotes may or may not be taken literally. Some, no doubt, may be factually true; but literally true or not they reveal a lovable, magnanimous teacher who welcomed converts when his impetuous colleagues scorned them, who reduced all of Judaism to the Golden Rule in the negative version. "What is hateful unto you don't do to another," addressing it to an obtuse and arrogant pagan bloke, with the shrewd, pointed suggestion: "The rest is commentary; go home and study."[4] Stories of his passion for learning, of his magnanimity, forbearance, humility are cherished legends in rabbinic lore; they have delighted Jewish children for the past two thousand years.

Aphorisms

Some of Hillel's sayings are still current. Their popularity in Hillel's own time is attested to by the fact that they circulated among the masses as well as among the scholars. We find them in Hebrew, the language of the academies, and in Aramaic and Babylonian, the languages of the masses.

> If I am not for myself, who will be for me?
> If I am for myself only, what am I?
> If not now, when?[5]

His version of the Golden Rule is penetrating and challenging. Half a century later we hear Jesus offering it in positive form as the root principle of his teaching: "Whatsoever you wish that men would do to you, do so to them; for this is the Law and the Prophets."[6] Perhaps both derived it from a third source. Teachers in Jewry and in Christendom have long debated which is the wiser version for men to follow.

Further aphorisms:

"Judge not your neighbor till you are in his place." Again we hear Jesus propounding the same lesson: "Judge not that ye be not judged."[7]

> Separate not yourself from the community (or congregation.)

> Say not, "When I have time I will study;"
> You may never have the time.

> The more flesh, the more maggots;
> the more possessions, the more care;
> the more women, the more witchcraft;
> the more bondwomen, the more lewdness;*
> the more bondmen, the more thieving;
>
> the more study, the more life;
> the more schooling, the more wisdom;

---

*Hillel may have had in mind female slaves.

the more counsel, the more understanding;
the more righteousness, the more peace.

An ignorant man can not be pious . . .
A timid man can not learn;
A passionate man can not teach.
He who is preoccupied with business can not be wise.
In the place where there is no man, you be a man.[8]

A consistent personality is revealed in these stories
and aphorisms: a patient, broadly-gauged, devoted
teacher, dedicated to God and His Torah for His people
Israel. Later disciples spoke of him with admiration:
"Let a man always be humble and patient like Hillel,
and not passionate like Shammai."[9]

Scholar and Jurist

As an original scholar and jurist, Hillel is famous for
two contributions.

First, he emphasized the spirit of the Torah beyond
the literal text. He sought the long-range view. *Second,*
he sought to establish specific rules for Bible interpretation.

In interpreting the law, Hillel's chief concern was to
make the Torah a living force, controlling every area
of life, personal and social—an emphasis that became
the central characteristic of Pharisaic teaching. He took
most seriously the rabbinic principle, "turn [the Torah]
over and over again, for everything is in it."[10] Moses
had commanded, "Ye shall live by them"—the statutes
and ordinances that he taught the children of Israel. To
establish this principle in exact scholarship he formulated seven rules of Bible exposition, basing himself on
earlier attempts at Bible interpretation by earlier masters. They mark an epoch in Jewish scholarship.

It is significant that no miracles are associated with Hillel's memory, no heavenly voices dictating decisions.

Hillel and Shammai

Hillel is paired with Shammai in rabbinic tradition. The two represent a basic difference in temperament and social outlook, which impelled two schools of thought. They are known as *Bet Hillel* and *Bet Shammai*. In our time we would consider the School of Hillel as the "liberal," the "progressive" the "advanced;" the School of Shammai we would designate as the "conservative," the "traditionalist," the "fundamentalist."

Shammai presents a contrast to Hillel in every way. While Hillel was a Babylonian, Shammai was a Palestinian. By temperament Shammai was irascible, explosive, strict in interpretation and in religious discipline. In a famous story we are told that when an impudent pagan came to Shammai and asked to be converted to Judaism while he, the pagan, balanced himself on one foot, Shammai ordered him from the house; Hillel accepted him and gave him the shortest—and most famous—presentation of Judaism, as we have already noted: the Golden Rule. The rest was commentary which one must study. Conflict between the two scholars was inevitable: the progressive, generous, liberal vs. the conservative, restrictive, literalistic. Some 316 controversies are reported in the Talmud as obtaining between the two schools. About a sixth of these were accepted by the schoolmen according to Shammai; the rest followed the Hillel school. Grounded in the same Torah, the two schools diverged, as jurists do in every age in all democratic traditions. Most of the cases in dispute were concerned with ritual, domestic affairs, education, scholarship. They had little to do with Herod and Roman hegemony.

As the war with Rome advanced, the divergence between the two schools widened. In time—after the
Temple and State had fallen in the year 70—the scholars
closed the gap with a compromise. Both opposing systems
of interpretation represented the words of the living God;
however, where Bet Shammai is opposed to Bet Hillel,
the opinion of Bet Shammai is considered as if not embodied in the Mishnah at all.[11]

"Prosbul"

A famous decision made by Hillel illustrates the spirit
of the man: interpret the Torah to cover every con-
tingency in the everyday life of the individual and the
community, and aim at "a better order of society." It
is known by a Greek word *prosbul,* "before the council."

The Bible decrees a Sabbatical year: "At the end of
every seven years thou shalt make a release. This is the
manner of the release: every creditor shall release that
which he hath lent unto his neighbour; he shall not exact
it of his neighbour and his brother; because the Lord's
release hath been proclaimed." (Deut. 15.1-2)

This Bible legislation was meant to bring relief to
the small farmer who was compelled to seek credit It
sought to protect society from the vicious tendency of
the rich growing richer and the poor growing poorer.
In practice, however, it made the life of the people it
sought to benefit all the harder. By the time of Hillel
urbanization was advancing; credit liberalization was
urgent. But credit was frozen, since all loans were can-
celled on the Sabbatical year. A number of bad harvests
added to the strain. The situation grew desperate. The
rabbinic authorities had to act. Shammai pointed to the
Bible text and maintained the established interpretation.
The law was divine and no man might take liberties with

it. Hillel advanced the needed relief, borrowing the
scheme from Hellenistic law: What the individual might
not do the courts might. He proposed that the certificates
of indebtedness be transferred to the courts, which in
turn, would satisfy the creditors. Bible laws specified
persons, not courts. This broke the barrier to the freer
flow of credit; the law stretched to cover life's circumstance.[12] Hillel brought the same emphasis to bear on
every area of life, personal and social: worship, phi-
lanthropy, marriage and divorce, receiving proselytes
and integrating them in the community of Israel, scholarship, tithing. The law did not fetter the individual and
his community; the law was dynamic, releasing and
guiding the individual and his society. Thus the rabbinic
masters affirmed: "When law came into the world, freedom came into the world."[13]

Hillel, Shammai, Herod

Herod, it is believed, appointed Hillel to his post in
the academies and thus as propounder of the law. While
most of the law dealt with ritual it concerned itself also
with tithing, as in the case of the *prosbul* decision, and
affected the civil life. Peace-loving and accommodating
by nature, did not Hillel in effect, perhaps unconsciously,
strike a bargain with Herod? To Caesar belong the
things that are Caesar's, to God the things that are
God's. The very same formula we hear enunciated half
a century later by Jesus.[14] Ultimately it meant surrendering this world to Caesar and pacifying the masses with
the promises of the Kingdom of Heaven. Was Hillel,
unconsciously, moving in this direction?

In the year 6 the Roman Procurator decreed a tax on
the Jews and ordered a strict census. Both Hillel and
Shammai protested. "Tax Collector" and "Customs Col-

lector" became abhorrent terms. These Jewish agents of Rome might not give testimony in court. The two schools seem to have acted in agreement in opposing the census and the tax. But it was the intransigent Shammaites who forged the more determined resistance to Rome. The Hillelites accommodated themselves to the circumstance. The militant Zealots drew their numbers from the disciples of the fundamentalist Shammai, not from the ranks of the liberal Hillel. The Shammaites it was who joined the zealots in the battle cry of the Maccabees of an earlier day: "Be ye zealous for the Law and give your lives for the covenant of your fathers."[15] The Hillelites learned to live with Caesar.

In this particular crisis the Shammaites carried the day in resisting Rome; the Hillelites shrank into the background. Since the surrounding people had surrendered to Rome, the Shammaites joined the Zealots and interdicted communication between Jews and gentiles, aiming at an economic boycott. The Hillelites opposed this drastic move.

The question may be raised: Did not Hillel—the gentle, peace-loving Hillel—unconsciously, by accommodating himself to Rome, surrender this world to Caesar? And did not Shammai—the fundamentalist, intransigent Shammai—by his very intransigence, stand up to Caesar and all his works?

PART II

Birthpangs of the Messiah

THE ONCOMING CRISIS

Both Jewish and Christian sources speak of "the pangs of the Messiah." The Kingdom of God was in the heavens and its messenger was on the way, if not already on earth; but the coming of the Kingdom would be preceded by woes, pain, upheavals. Nation would rise against nation and kingdom against kingdom; the very earth would rock with convulsions, famine would sweep the land. An apocalyptic passage in the Gospel according to Mark catches the fury of the impending doom: "The sun shall be darkened and the moon shall not give forth its light, the stars shall fall from their courses, and the hosts of heaven shall totter. . . . Brother shall betray brother to death, and the father his son, and children shall rise against their parents. . . ."[1] Jesus spoke of "the days of the Messiah;" the Pharisaic masters in their academies heard "the footsteps of the Messiah." Popular preachers amplified the excitement in every little synagogue throughout the land. Ultimately, however, beyond all the upheavals and woes was a new day, a reborn earth, a redeemed humanity. The star of Bethlehem was beckoning.

We pause before the map of Judea, the threatre of the cataclysmic drama, and observe its major formation: the social-political-religious formations and the passions and warfare of the age.

The central group and by far the largest, was the Pharisees, *the masters in the academies, their disciples, the masses. The* Sadducees *were the priveleged aristocracy, comprising perhaps no more than five percent of the population. The* Essenes *were the pacifists and ascetics who constituted a segregated, monastic community. The* Zealots *were the terrorists of the day, the "dagger men." Roaming the land as itinerant preachers were the* apocalyptists *and* messianists *proclaiming the imminent cataclysmic*

*end of the world and the coming of the Kingdom of Heaven.
Basically the last three were Pharisees. Numerically insignificant,
their influence in stirring the imaginations and fears of the people
was enormous. They expounded ancient texts in every little synagogue throughout the land.*

> How beautiful upon the mountains
> Are the feet of the messenger of good tidings
> That announceth peace, the harbinger of good tidings
> That announceth salvation;
> That saith unto Zion:
> "Thy God reigneth!"[2]

3

Sadducees and Pharisees

Two Classes: Their Positions in Society

The Sadducees and the Pharisees constituted the two dominant portions of Judean society. They differed basically in their socio-economic positions and in their religio-political beliefs.[3]

The Sadducees represented the aristocracy, the vested Temple interests, from the High Priest down: priests, Levites, functionaries of every grade; also the royalty, the nobility, the wealthy landowners. The Temple hierarchy claimed descent from Zadock, the High Priest of the first Temple, built by Solomon almost a thousand years earlier. Thus the Sadducees were invested with hereditary sanctity transmitted down through the many generations. They were an inbred aristocracy. They held their offices and enjoyed their prerogatives by the right of inheritance, and owed no accounting to any one outside their own well-established ranks. Only rivalry among themselves, or rebellion, or threats of rebellion among the masses, checked their power and privileges. They had little influence on the population intellectually or spiritually. The center of their interests—and authority—was the ritual and the administration of the central shrine of the nation, the Temple.

The Pharisees were the common people, and they were the overwhelming majority: the artisans, the merchants, the civil servants, the peasants, the fishermen.

They looked to the rabbinic masters in the academies for their spiritual guidance. Their meeting places were the humble folk synagogues, which they built for themselves and administered as they saw fit. They did accept the aristocratic Temple, with all its pomp and ceremony (and its vested bureaucracy), as the central shrine of the nation; thus it was decreed in the Torah. They paid their tithes, made their pilgrimages, offered their sacrifices. But their lives in every detail were Torah-centered; every aspect of life was under the law, and they brooked no interference from Caesar in things that belonged to God. Hence there were constant tension and frequent clashes with the state officials and their Sadducean collaborators. Their affections were in the lowly synagogues; there they spoke their prayers and heard the sacred texts expounded by scholars and preachers; there they met their fellows as one covenanted community. So large a segment of the population, with emphasis on the individual conscience, naturally led to divisions; the Essenes for a time, and the Zealots. Jesus preached in these synagogues and there he found his earliest followers; Paul too preached in these synagogues as another Pharisee, and there found his earliest disciples.

Tension, intellectual strain, rivalry for power between the Sadducees and the Pharisees, in and out of the Sanhedrin, was inevitable and constant. They differed sharply in their worldly interests and in their religious beliefs. They clashed repeatedly in their interpretations of the law and consequent theologies and ritual. At times, depending largely on the political situations of the day, the Pharisees gained a measure of power. As we have seen, Herod appointed Hillel—the leading Pharisee—to the Sanhedrin, which was, and had been, dominated by the Sadducees.

The Sanhedrin, with its civil and political power, its direct dealings with the Roman Procurator, was in the hands of the Sadducees; from the Sadducean ranks came the collaborators with Rome. They had more at stake in worldly affairs. The academies, the synagogues, the schools were in the hands of the Pharisees. From the ranks of the Pharisees came the scholars, the teachers, the interpreters of the Torah, the popular preachers. Upon the Pharisees rested more heavily the burdens of the state: taxation, forced labor. From the ranks of the Pharisees, too, came the patriots, the leaders in every attempt for freedom, the innumerable martyrs of the nation.

The urbanization of the age, which had advanced constantly, and the new demands for reform in socio-economic conditions, which had come from the spread of Hellenism since the days of Alexander the Great, prodded the Pharisaic masters in the academies to seek new interpretations of the laws of Moses and to make the Torah a more fitting instrument in the daily life of the masses. Growing urbanization and the steady penetration of Hellenism became persistent dynamics in the interpretations and reinterpretations of the divine texts. Unconsciously the Pharisees created a veritable revolution in the Judaism of their day. Hillel's efforts to release the credit system of the day, which had been strangled by an inflexible interpretation of the Bible, may be seen as an example of the radical changes the Pharisees achieved with their method of interpreting and reinterpreting the Bible.[4]

From the Pharisees came the synagogue, a folk institution aimed at meeting the religious, social and educational needs of the Judean masses. Local synagogues functioned in the shadow of the Temple and all through the country, in every town of the land—they represented a place for worship, for study, for social service and communal responsibilities. The Temple was aristocratic, devoted to the national cult with its animal sacrifice and hereditary priesthood; the synagogues were informal, humble, folkish, where every man was a priest in his own right. Sanction for these activities was found in Bible texts, often by ingenious interpretations. When the Temple fell to the Roman legions in the year 70, the Sadducean hierarchy was relegated to the limbo of history. The Synagogue replaced the Temple and the rabbinate replaced the priesthood. Now every man was a priest, even as the laws of Moses commanded: "Ye shall be unto me a nation of priests and a holy people."[5]

With the emergence of the Synagogue to the dominant position in the life of the Judean masses came a new impulse in education. If the Torah was meant for every soul in Israel, every Israelite had to be learned in the Law. Hence the first start in universal education came from the Pharisees in their synagogues; the beginnings of a public school system was made in the year 66 B.C.E. With the Temple only a bitter memory, prayer—which included study—and *mitzvot* replaced the animal sacrifices.

Written and Oral Torah

The instrument with which the Pharisaic masters shaped a universal religion out of a national cult was the concept of an Oral Law. The concept created a deep gulf between the Pharisees and the Sadducees.

The Sadducees accepted the Torah literally. They were the true fundamentalists of the time. From God Himself, through Moses on Mount Sinai, they received the Torah, written with God's own fingers. This was the Written Torah, reduced to ink on parchment, cherished and studied in the academies and synagogues. Every word of it was true and binding for all times. Israel had taken a pledge at the foot of smouldering Mount Sinai;

for themselves and for the ages still in the womb of time they pledged, "All that the Lord hath spoken we shall do and we shall hearken."[6] Israel is thus a covenanted people under an eternal Law. Not a letter of the Torah may be changed or ignored. Jesus spoke as a characteristic Pharisee when he declared: "For truly, I say to you, till heaven and earth pass away, not an iota, not a dot will pass from the law until all is accomplished."[7]

The Pharisees were at one with the Sadducees in this major premise: the immutability of a divinely revealed Torah. But they added one deeply significant modification. This modification meant a revolution in Judaism. With the Written Torah God gave Moses also an Oral Torah. The Oral Torah was just as divine, just as binding as the Written. The Written cannot be understood without the Oral interpretations. More, the Torah was meant for all time, for all the people, and for every soul in Israel. "You shall live by them (the words of the Torah)."[8] *You* meant every man. In a growing society with new challenges the persistent problem always was how to stretch the old laws to cover the new developments. The individual must find his peace and his freedom *within* the Law, under God.

For the Sadducees, if circumstances developed that were not covered by the Written Law, the people simply met these new situations as they saw fit, no longer obligated to the Torah. Hence Torah no longer applied to all of life. The cultus never changed. The gap between religion and life widened and deepened.

"Moses received the Torah on Mount Sinai, and transmitted it to Joshua; Joshua to the elder; the elders to the prophets; and the prophets to the men of the Great Synagogue." That was the Pharisaic premise.[9] But Torah meant two Torahs: Written and Oral. The masters in the academies were the representative of "the men of the Great Synagogue."

The Oral Torah became the instrument for change and revision, and for bringing religion into harmony with the daily life of the individual and his community. The Pharisaic masters were profoundly convinced that they were only applying, not changing, the laws and commandments. In reality they were investing the old laws with new interpretations and reinterpretations. They developed, therefore, an elaborate system of Bible exegesis and thus found biblical warrant to meet every religious, social or political problem that presented itself under the pressure of the times. In time this learning and the application of the Law to everyday life developed into the Talmud. "Turn [the Torah] and turn it over again, for everything is in it; contemplate it, wax gray and old over it, stir not from it, for you can not find a better rule than this."[10] When new economic circumstances created a barrier to the free flow of credit in the days of Herod, for example, Hillel broke through the barrier by resorting to Bible exegesis. "Blessed be the glory of God from His place," affirmed the prophet Ezekiel.[11] The prophet was in Babylon and by "His place" he meant the restored Temple on Zion, which was the great hope of that age. The Pharisaic expositors of Bible text interpreted "His place" to mean everywhere in the world, in Babylon as in Palestine, as in Rome and in every land in the ages yet unborn, for God *is* everywhere.

Thus the Pharisees with their Oral Law formula and their emphasis on making religion the controlling force in the life of every Jew and every Jewish community, transformed Judaism from a static creed based on a rigid text, administered by a hereditary priesthood, into a living ethical religion, taught by scholars and sages of a covenanted people.*

---

* See chapters on Hillel, Johanan ben Zakkai and Akiba in present volume.

4

The Essenes

The Essenes were a small group, numbering perhaps not much over four thousand. Their headquarters was at Engedi, an ancient village on the Western shore of the Dead Sea. Their settlements were scattered throughout that harsh area. In 1947, the world was startled by the discovery of very ancient scrolls, commonly designated as the *Dead Sea Scrolls*. These supplement the information given us by Josephus, who had lived among the Essenes in their desert settlements for some three years, and the information given us by Philo, the Jewish philosopher and historian of Alexandria, Egypt, of the first century. The several non-Jewish historians do not add much to the data given us by these two.

The Dead Sea Scrolls describe the life of a group of ascetics who lived in a series of encampments in the western part of the Dead Sea country. Their headquarters was at Qumran, where some two hundred persons lived. The large majority of experts agree that the men of Qumran and their associates lived between the years 125 B.C.E. and 68 C.E., when the Roman legions overwhelmed them. The beginnings of the Essenes are believed to date from the days of the Maccabbees, or a little earlier. That the men of Qumran were a branch of the Essenes has been accepted by most scholars. If they were not identical in their beliefs, they were strikingly similar.[1]

Their name, *Essenes,* has been variously translated

as *pious, puritans, to be silent,* or *mysterious, retired, holy.* Some twenty such translations have been suggested. Something of each of the qualities intimated in the translations are to be found in their philosophy.

Their primary aim was to attain holiness by living up to every detail of the Torah, as they understood it— every detail of ritual and morality. They considered themselves, personally and physically, as the temples of the Holy Spirit.

The human instincts—for pleasure, gain, enjoyment, sex, ambition, personal achievement—they suspected as evil; they therefore sought to attain purity by suppressing these basic human instincts. This, they believed, would give them the power to perform miracles and thus hasten the coming of the Messiah.

They sought "the kingdom that was not of this world." Everyday life was too gross; there was too much trafficking with sin. They, therefore, turned their backs upon the world and its barbarism and competition, and sought peace of mind and composure of soul by settling in desert country far removed from the din and clatter of cities.

They renounced, for themselves, marriage and family life, though in the early days of their movement a small group of them did marry. They felt that marriage would distract them in their search for purity and holiness. Women they considered a defiling influence. To perpetuate their fellowship they adopted boys and trained them in the Essenic ways and thought. It has been suggested by scholars that the celibate priesthood of the Church, as well as Christian monasticism, are derived from the Essenes. A number of scholars argue that Jesus too was an Essene. This, however, is challenged by other scholars.

They owned no property. Before one might join their order he was required to sell all his wordly possessions and contribute the proceeds to the common treasury. Every man was allotted, from this common stock, as much as he needed. In this sense they were religious communists. There were no rich and no poor among them, no masters and no servants.

Their meals were taken in common and constituted a religious rite. The dinner table was their altar. A strong religious discipline controlled the order of the meal and the conduct at the table. Silence, meditation, were absolute requirements. They never ate meat, which would have necessitated the killing of a living creature. Some scholars see in the common meal and the Essene's conduct at table the beginning of the Holy Communion of the Church.

They always dressed in white, and placed great emphasis on cleanliness. Daily baths were part of the official discipline. Perhaps baptism, as it came into Christian practice, is foreshadowed here.

Candidates for membership were carefully screened and rigorously tested over a three-year period of probation. Each man was required to prove himself worthy, through self-abnegation and self-mastery, of achieving what the sect considered purity. Blasphemous speech was punished; repeated violation meant expulsion. The "Manual of the Discipline," one of the Dead Sea Scrolls, describes in detail the discipline, the structure of their organization, the authority of the priests and their subordinates. It was a rigidly regimented, authoritarian community. Differences of opinion were sternly outlawed as "stubbornness of heart."

They were hard working. The day began at sunrise. Some labored in the fields, some prepared food for the community, some the clothing they needed; others healed the sick, or taught the young. A number devoted themselves to the meditation of the mysteries of life and death, and God. The Sabbath they observed rigidly.

They lived in the expectation that God, in His own good time, would raise up a prophet to lead and redeem them, as is promised in the book of Deuteronomy: "I will raise them up a prophet from among their brethren, like unto thee [Moses]; and I will put my words in his mouth, and he shall speak unto them [the people] all that I shall command him."[2] They lived in the expectation that this Teacher of Righteousness would arrive and save the world. The sooner they attained holiness the sooner the Teacher would come.

They were pacificists, though there is some evidence that they joined in the revolt against Rome. They abhorred violence. They would not own slaves and would not resort to slave labor, although that was a legitimate institution in their time, even according to Bible law. They would not accept any gain from the making of war implements, though that—then as now—was a legitimate enterprise. Josephus testifies, on the basis of his personal association with the Essenes: "Although they were tortured and racked, burnt and torn to pieces, and went through every torment to force them either to blaspheme their legislator, or to eat what was forbidden them, yet could they not be made to do either of them; no, nor once to flatter their tormentors, or to shed a tear. But they smiled in their very pains, and laughed those to scorn who tortured them, and gave up their souls in great cheerfulness, as expecting to receive them again."[3]

They considered themselves the true Israel. The Zealots were horribly violent. The Sadducees and the Pharisees were only a compromise with the evil world, they believed. They rejected the world and all its evils and all its vanities, and concentrated on the inner life— prayer, religious rites, self-abnegation—in a holy fellowship, expecting the Teacher of Righteousness to bring about God's Kingdom. Philo testifies: "Among all men, they alone are without money and without possessions, but are nevertheless the richest of all, because to have a few wants and to live frugally they regard as riches. Among them is no maker of any weapons of war . . . nor do they follow any occupation that leads to covetousness."[4]

Removed from the storms of life, its temptations and its duties, its sorrows and its burdens, they turned their backs on their people, their country and their shrine. They cherished peace of mind, or tranquility of soul. One of the psalms discovered at Qumran gives moving expression to this piety:

> I thank Thee, Lord, because Thou hast saved my soul
>   from the pit and from the Sheol of Abaddon,
> And Thou hast caused me to climb to the eternal heights.
> I walk in the way with a quiet mind.
> I know there is hope for those created from dust because
>   of the nearness of the eternal.

What finally happened to these devout men? They had retired not only from the world but from history. They never became part of Judaism. For all their heroic idealism and self-sacrifice, and for all their piety, they had separated themselves from the living community. When the Roman legions overwhelmed Judea, the Essenes were swept into oblivion. Perhaps Hillel had the Essenes in mind when he urged, "separate not yourself from the community."

5

Zealots

The opposites of the ascetic Essenes were the Zealots —relentless "dagger men" who took the law into their own hands. They were the underground terrorists; every man would carry a concealed dagger,* in order to strike down any one deemed a traitor, or a collaborator of Rome. What percentage of the population they comprised is not known. They were not an organized group as were the Essenes. Some of their leaders had as many as ten thousand warriors in their armies at crucial times. When in 70 C.E. Jerusalem was under Roman siege, in its last gasp, some 20,000 Idumeans joined the Zealots.

They have been characterized as brigands, terrorists. That they were: but they were also more than that. They were defending their faith and their country, all that was holy to them, to the last drop of blood—*their* blood, and the blood of everyone in their way.

They were warriors and religionists, patriots and martyrs, pious and murderous. They were Pharisees in their religious beliefs and observances, and relentless terrorists against pagan Rome.

Like Mattathias, father of the Maccabees, back in the year 168 B.C.E., they struck down the idolators and the weak-kneed, and cried, "Whosoever is zealous of the law and the Covenant, let him follow me!" Many did. They fled into the mountains, even as the Maccabees had done in their time, and carried on guerrilla warfare.

Sica, short Roman dagger; hence *dagger men, assassins.*

They fought with fury, and at times, with genius. Their stand at Masada is an amazing epic. Recent excavations have established that these Zealots, for three years under siege in their rock fortress, treasured their sacred scrolls, paid their tithes, cherished their synagogue, and observed the rituals of their Pharisaic Judaism.

The primary source of our knowledge is the writings of Josephus, who from their standpoint was a traitor. There was violent hatred between the Zealot leaders and the priestly aristocrat, who—while leading a Judean army against Rome—was militarily an incompetent meddler, and worse, a traitor. His writings are the reports of a collaborationist passing judgment on the underground.

There was fierce hatred between Josephus and the Zealot leaders, particularly the three who held out against Rome in Jerusalem and the very Temple environs in legendary heroism: John of Gischala, Simon bar Giora, Eleazar bar Simon, as we shall note in the chapter on Josephus.

John of Gischala* was the leader of one extremist group. A man of tremendous energy and military ability, he gathered about himself some five thousand zealots, financed them out of his own private resources (which he had acquired in shrewd business dealings), rebuilt the walls of his native Gischala, which had been destroyed by the Romans, with funds he realized by confiscating a Roman supply of grain. This he had seized against the orders of his military superior, Josephus. At one time he sought to assassinate Josephus, whose half-hearted military leadership he considered traitorous. The wily Josephus escaped the army of pious assassins. John, driven by hunger, surrendered only after the Temple was in complete rubble.

---

*A city in Galilee, which held out longest against the Romans, and which was razed by them.

Simon bar Giora—probably a proselyte—was the leader of another extremist group, which considered John too moderate. Simon, it is believed by some historians, had at one time as many as ten thousand men in his ranks. Finding the High Priest of the day barring his way—or suspecting him of collaboration with the enemy—Simon put him to death. For awhile he considered himself the Lord of the embattled Holy City. At last he was taken by the Romans and, after having been dragged in chains before the Emperor in the triumphal procession, he was hurled from the Tarpeian Rock, a peak of the Capitoline hills used by the Romans to execute condemned prisoners.

A third Zealot leader competed for the leadership in the last agonizing days of Jerusalem and the Temple. He was Eleazar, son of Simon. For a time he was in possession of the inner Temple court.

The mettle of the Zealots stands immortalized in the mountain fortress of Masada, overlooking the Dead Sea. It was the last stronghold to yield to the Roman battering rams and flaming torches. When at last the Romans finally did take the fort in April 73, the stillness of death met them. Under their leader Elazar Ben Jair the entire encampment was at peace in death; by a sacred compact every man put to death his own loved ones with his own hands, and finally the men killed each other. Of a population of 960, only two women and five children survived to report the gory story. The supreme tragedy is that this fantastic self-sacrifice was futile.[1]

Josephus, years later, living as an aristocratic refugee, and a recipient of the favors of Titus, wrote his version of the siege and took vengeance on his Zealot opponents. He daubs them for posterity as bloodthirsty, covetous, ready liars, greedy for glory.

6

Apocalyptists and Messiahs

Visions and "The End of Days"

Fairy tales, it has been observed, are made of the dreams of the poor. They are escapes from cruel reality into a wonderous dream world. The realities in the lives of the Judean masses were horrible: Herod and his murderous exploitations, taxation, violation of what people cherished as sacred; the kingdom divided and misruled by Herod's sons; hated Procurators exploiting without conscience for some forty years; rebellions and raids by Zealot bands and countless crucifixions in Roman retaliation; forced labor; pillage, carnage, brigandage, bloodshed without end. Generations were born and generations died in this pitiless state. To add to it all, an earthquake rocked the bleeding little land. Waves of insanity must have swept the population. Wandering preachers roamed the countryside proclaiming the end of the world, and summoning men to repentance. The wrath of God was upon them!

Men saw visions of the "end of days," and proclaimed the Kingdom of Heaven* where there would be no tyrants, no cruelties; when death itself would be van-

---

*Apocalypse, to uncover, revelation of the ultimate secrets, including the life after death. God would surely intervene in his own miraculous way and bring salvation to His people. The Messiahs were the deliverers, sent by God. We speak of them as "false Messiahs," as if there were true Messiahs.

quished "and sighing would be no more." They were
the apocalyptists; some suffered deep messianic hallu-
cinations; some were ecstatics who identified themselves
with ancient characters, and in their names spoke in
divine seizures or trances, as a present-day medium
identifies himself with some departed person and speaks
in his name. A fantastic literature developed.[1] The
rabbinic masters rejected most of this literature and
warned against trafficking with the supernatural. They
closed the Old Testament canon at this time. One factor
that spurred them on to complete and seal the Bible in
its final edition was probably their conscious intent of
saving the authentic Scriptures from a corruption with
the apocalyptic. They were building "a fence around the
Torah."

Earthquake and famine added to the misery and
incited further the minds of the already unbalanced.
Apocalyptic literature flowered like a poison tree.

Ancient visions of liberation and redemption broke
upon the masses with enthralling ecstasy. The prophecies
of Isaiah, Jeremiah, Zechariah of earlier centuries, obscure verses in the Psalms, acquired new brilliance and
contagion. The monstrous figures of the book of Daniel
of the more recent past haunted the people in deadly
literalness and comforted them, as the book of Daniel
was meant to do in an earlier age. The Messiah was
coming; he would soon crush the evil nations and ride
into Jerusalem on his white ass in glorious splender,
even as Zechariah had promised.

The Messiah was the ideal King, divinely predestined.
In the course of the centuries the messianic legend acquired fantastic characteristics. He was the scion of the
House of David, a righteous prince, just and mighty,
or he might be a heavenly Redeemer, who would crush
the oppressor, not by the sword but by "the rod of his
mouth would he slay the wicked."[2] Like Daniel and his

companions, Israel under Herod—and the Procurators before and after him—was in the fiery furnace. The just God who delivered the faithful in Daniel's day would deliver them too. "The Guardian of Israel sleepeth not nor slumbereth;" He would not "allow the faithful ones to see destruction." He would wipe away all tears "and sorrow and sighing would be no more."[3] Even the dead would arise from their graves and return to Zion.

The writing was on the wall: God had numbered the days of the arrogant kingdom and found it finished. In the mind of God its doom was sealed. Emotional preachers roamed the land exhorting the pious in the synagogues. The advent of the heaven-sent Messiah became part of the daily prayers. Old Zechariah's promise was coming true: the Messiah was at the gates of Jerusalem, meek and humble, but in divine glory.

These messianic expectations had a fantastic appeal to the suffering masses. The worldly and the heavenly messiahs became confused in the minds of the people, and perhaps in the minds of the messiahs themselves. Certainly the Procurators did not stop to distinguish the political disturber of the peace from the ecstatic. It was at this time that the belief in heaven and hell developed, which soon became primary beliefs in both Judaism and emerging Christianity.

In the offing was John the Baptist, crying in the wilderness, proclaiming the Day of the Lord and doom, summoning the people to repentance, redemption and baptism. In the offing, too, was Jesus of Nazareth, according to Luke, John's cousin, whom John had baptized. His baptism transfixed him with a vision of a new heaven and a new earth and shifted the course of civilization.

The Judean masses were in the throes of "the pangs of the Messiah."

7

Procurators: Pontius Pilate

By Herod's will Judea was dismembered and apportioned among three of his sons, who ruled under the watchful eye of Rome. Their rules were notorious for misrule and rapacity. Subsequently the unhappy land was placed under a series of Roman imperial agents known in history as Procurators. "The best of them," historians testify, "had no understanding of Jewish peculiarities, and the worst, by their rapacity and inexorable severity, drove the people to rebellion."[1]

As a Roman possession under these Procurators and their agents Judea was seething with rebellion, famished and desperate after decades of war and merciless taxation. Each festival, when devout pilgrims crowded into the Holy City to make their sacrifices and keep their sacred vows, was an occasion for riots. Taxation was in the merciless hands of private tax collectors, scorned in the New Testament as evil "publicans." The Procurator had his own army. His soldiers, with all their arrogance and brutality, were everywhere. On the Passover of the crucifixion, for instance, Pilate was in Jerusalem with an army of three thousand armed men. Their orders were to put to death anyone suspected of disloyalty to Rome. The High Priest—supposedly a descendant of Aaron, brother of Moses—was a hired flunky of the Roman overlord. He might minister at the altar on the festivals, or the Day of Atonement; but only if the Procurator gave permission. The sanctuary of the Holy

One of Israel was under imperial protection. Checks on power were largely theoretic; Rome was far away; communications, from our vantage, were fantastically bad, and who was there to say to Rome, "What doest thou?" The office of High Priest was bartered to the highest bidder; invariably it went to the most servile character.

Rome could enforce its authority quite simply in dealing with these ecclesiastics. The robes of office, without which they could not function at the altar, were in the custody of the Procurators. It was a simple matter for the Romans to withhold the High Priest's sacred pants! The Great Sanhedrin, which met at Jerusalem with its seventy elders, did retain a measure of authority; however, it was limited to innocuous matters of ritual and theology, and even that depended upon the members' good behavior. In matters of state, particularly in matters of taxation and capital punishment cases, power was in the hands of the Procurator. It was only prudent for the practical Roman rulers to watch for the boiling point and possible explosion. Explosions did take place repeatedly; the army was on hand.

The Procurators, we read, "were mostly incompetents and scoundrels. Felix . . . 'governed Judea,' says Tacitus, 'with the power of a king and the soul of a slave.' Festus ruled more justly, but died in the attempt. Albinus, if we may believe Josephus, plundered and taxed assiduously, and made a fortune by releasing criminals from jail for a consideration. Nobody remained in jail but those who gave him nothing. Florus, says the same friend and admirer of the Romans, behaved like 'an executioner rather than governor,' despoiled whole cities, and not only stole on his own account, but connived at other robberies if allowed to share the loot. These reports retain some odor of war propaganda; doubtless procurators complained that the Jews were very troublesome people to oppress."[2]

Pontius Pilate

The most infamous of the Procurators was Pontius Pilate, the fifth in the series. He ruled for ten fateful years: 26-36 C.E. The fact that he maintained himself in office for a decade testifies to his ability to serve himself. He had greater authority than most of his predecessors. It is important to remember that he had supreme judicial power. It was during his reign that John the Baptist was beheaded and Jesus was crucified.

We know nothing of his family background. His name may have been derived from *pileus,* the Latin for the cap of a freed slave. His official residence was in Caesarea, administrative capital of Roman Judea, and when in Jerusalem at Herod's palace. He had a force of some three thousand men, whose primary duty was to keep Judea subjugated. This was particularly crucial at the time of the feasts. Thus Pilate was in the Holy City with his army on the Passover when Jesus was tried and crucified, surely the most crucial rendezvous in history. His name will thus ever be a symbol of infamy.

Brutally obstinate, Pilate nevertheless knew how to bend before the storm. When he set up standards in Jerusalem on the Passover, flaunting the image of the Emperor and flouting the feelings of the pious populace, thus rousing riots, he pulled back. When Tiberius gave orders that he remove certain shields he had erected because they were considered idolatrous and hence were sparking uprisings, he yielded. He had no hesitation in deploying Temple funds to his building projects; his army kept the Roman peace. He had no compunction against ordering the slaughter of a group of Galileans while they were offering their sacrifices on the sheer suspicion that they were plotting some mischief. He committed similar wanton slaughter on a group of Samaritans gathered on Mount Gerizim for what was an archeologic venture. Rumor had spread that Moses had hidden some vessels on the mountain; pilgrims came to retrieve them. Pilate suspected an insurrectionist plot. Many were slaughtered. Complaint reached the Legate in Syria and Pilate was summoned to Rome to explain his action. The Emperor died before Pilate could appear before him.

His part in the trial and crucifixion of Jesus has been rehearsed endlessly since that fatal day. We shall return to this scene.

Legends about him spun by subsequent ages reveal the contempt in which his memory was held. This is only natural in view of the villainous part he played in such an intensely emotional situation as the crucifixion. However, it must be remembered that the tendency, clearly evident in the New Testament, to heap all the blame on the Pharisees and the Jewish priests, lifted some of the blame from Pilate.[3] Extraordinary pressure, the Gospel writers report, was applied upon Pilate by the Jewish elders; the Procurator supposedly was driven to act as he did despite himself.

The Abyssinian Church sainted him. Popular legend was not so forgiving. According to one tradition he was banished from his post; later he committed suicide. His body was thrown into the Tiber River; the river resented his corpse and flooded its banks. Committed to the Rhone River, the waters spewed him out in disgust. Finally he was taken to a point in the highest Alps and dumped into the deepest tarn near Lucerne. The mountain peak is still known as Pilatus.

We shall return to Pilate and view him more closely when we recall the trial and crucifixion of Jesus.

PART III

The Birth of Christianity

8

John the Baptist: A Voice Crying
in the Wilderness

The person of John the Baptist is concealed deep in the mists of legend. Scholars find it extraordinarily difficult to separate the fanciful from the factual and to bring forward the image into some sort of intelligible focus. The diversity of interpretation among historians is wide. Some doubt his very existence. That is not at all surprising to the student of the Bible. The same tangled legendry—supernaturalism, dream-stuff, repetition and contradiction of reports and pious propaganda—obtains in the lives of other heroes of the Bible: the Patriarchs, for instance; Moses, Elijah, Jesus, and many others. The student, as best he can, must sternly put aside all inherited personal prejudice and fanciful childhood conditioning, however endearing, and examine the material as objectively as it is possible for him to do.

Legends

The legends from which the basic "facts" in the life of John are deduced are reported in the Gospels.[1] Josephus gives us a brief passage, which has been debated by scholars.[2] John was beheaded in the year 29 C.E. The material we have in the Gospels is believed to have been written some half century after the reported events had taken place. These already corrupted reports were copied and edited further by pious disciples who were more devoted to faith than to fact. What is more, the men who wrote the reports were not interested in writing objective history; they were interested in overcoming their opponents and winning disciples. We must remember, further, that those were years of violent religious hatred; the evangelists dipped their pens in the wells poisoned by a holy war. We cannot read this material too cautiously. The Josephus passage is questioned by eminent historians. In addition, Josephus was careful not to arouse the ire of Rome; therefore he toned down the messianic character of John's activities, which had been interpreted by Rome as potential political rebellion.

Elijah Reborn

John was born in the last few years of Herod's reign, which closed in the year 4 B.C.E. That, possibly, is the year when Jesus was born. John's father was a priest, by the name of Zehariah; his ancestry, according to tradition, went back all the way to Aaron, brother of Moses. On his mother's side, Luke reports, he was a cousin of Jesus. The legendry of a later age is obvious. His birth was announced to his father by the angel Gabriel. He was to be dedicated to the service of the Lord from birth. These reports remind one of the stories of Isaac and Samson, whose births too were heralded by angels. Like the prophet Elijah, John was to be "the messenger of the Lord." He was predestined to summon men to repentance, prepare them for the coming of the Lord, and bring peace, salvation and forgiveness of sins. The angel assures his father:

> and he shall drink no wine or strong drink,
> . . . he will be great before the Lord,

and he will be filled with the Holy Spirit,
even from his mother's womb.
And he will turn many of the sons of Israel to the Lord
their God,
and he will go before him in the spirit and power of Elijah,
to turn the hearts of the fathers to the children,
and the disobedient to the wisdom of the just,
and make ready for the Lord a people prepared.[3]

These words are practically a literal repetition of the report in the book of Malachi announcing the coming of Elijah. Like Elijah, John's mission was to proclaim the coming of the Messiah: "Behold, I will send you Elijah the prophet before the coming of the great and terrible day of the Lord."[4]

In the Desert

The Judean people, desperate under the brutal exploitations of Herod's descendants and the Roman masters, were praying for a deliverer—someone sent by God to come and lift the burdens of sorrow from their hearts, and the sins that had brought on these sorrows. Thus John came as the Elijah who would summon men to repentance, achieve the remission of sins, proclaim salvation, and prepare the way for the Messiah, the annointed of the Lord. He was given the name John as a symbol and a promise: "John" means "Yahweh gives grace." Even his physical dress is described after the manner of Elijah's: "Now John was clothed with camel's hair and had a leather girdle around his waist, and ate locusts and wild honey."[5]

John left his parents, and went into the desert, in the area of the Jordan River and the Dead Sea. Identifying himself with Elijah, he entered the same desert area into which Elijah had fled. Here the Essenes had their encampments (and where the Dead Sea Scrolls were found in 1947, at Qumran). Why he had given up his priestly tradition and the Sadducean privileges we are not told. We can only infer. The boy was under the spell of a call, dominated by a religious vision.

The desert has had a strange fascination for certain types of religious people. Moses fled into the desert in his hour of crisis; in the desert he heard the voice of God; in the desert he saw the burning bush; from a desert mountain he transmitted the Law. Elijah roamed the desert for forty days and nights, haunted by the voice of God; in the desert he received comfort offered him by angels. Prophets and Psalmists often speak of the desert as the abode of God, and also as the dwelling place of the broods of evil spirits. The Essenes settled in a desert. Jesus, as we shall see, went to the desert to silence the voices within him. The haunting silence, the endless tracts, the pitiless elemental forces and furies play in the desert and incite visions, and rouse awe. Thus the desert is the fierce background to much in Judaism and Christianity in biblical times.

John was influenced by the Essenes and their concentration on becoming personal vehicles for the Holy Spirit, seeking escape from the sins of the world by taking refuge in the wilderness. He took Isaiah's words literally, as a personal mandate:

> Hark! one calleth:
> "Clear ye in the wilderness the way of the Lord,
> Make plain in the desert a highway for our God."[6]

Isaiah was a popular prophet with the Essenes. John may have come under this Essenic influence. The baptism he administered later was like the baptism administered by the Essenes. Like the Essenes, further—and like the desert-dwelling Rachabites centuries earlier and the Nazarites—he touched neither wine nor strong drink.

It is possible that he had lived with the Essenes in their desert encampments for some time and then dissented from them, before taking the final vows. Driven by the spirit—as Jesus was—into the desert, he lived for a time the life of a hermit, emerging only to preach the message: repentance, return to God, salvation, and the coming of the true Messiah and the Kingdom of Heaven.

People were attracted to this colorful ascetic.

Baptism

Baptism was a common Jewish practice, established in Bible and rabbinic teaching. Ceremonial bathing, or washing, was practiced in practically all the Semitic religions. It was the means of atonement for certain sins; it brought one closer to God. Later it became the required ritual for conversion. God Himself will in time pour waters of purification upon His people of Israel and establish His Kingdom. The Essenes made it a dogma in their faith, and invested it with magic power. John gave it a new emphasis: the one that would come after him, Jesus, would not baptize with water but with the Holy Ghost. "Behold, the lamb of God, who takes away the sin of the world."[7]

Among the throngs—all Jews—who came to hear John preach and to be baptized by him in the river Jordan was Jesus. John recognized him as the one he had been expecting and whose coming he had been proclaiming. John accepted him humbly. Jesus was baptized and with this baptism came a crucial transformation in his life.*

---

*This is the traditional Christian view. It is questioned by critical scholars. Some deny that John and Jesus had ever met. On the basis of the "critical sifting of the gospel account and of the testimony of

Martyrdom

John's preaching brought him into conflict with the
royal court. He attacked bitterly the Tetrarch of Galilee, Herod Antipas, the son of Herod the Great. He
was placed under arrest. His oratory was fanning revolution. More, the Tetrarch and his wife had ample reason for fearing and hating him. Herod Antipas had
seduced his brother's wife. John had lashed out against
them, even as Elijah had lashed out against Ahab and
Jezebel and as Nathan had lashed out against David.
John was clearly, in his own mind and in the minds of
the Gospel writers, the reincarnation of Elijah. He was
committed to the notorious fortress of Machaerus, in
Galilee, which had been built by Herod the Great, and
was subsequently decapitated.

The beheading of John the Baptist, his head delivered
on a platter to the stripling great granddaughter of
Herod the Great, dancing nude before the drunken
court on the demand of a whoring queen, is as famous
as it is disgusting. This gory scene became one of the
great themes in Western literature, music, painting,
theatre:

> . . . an opportunity came when Herod on his birthday gave a
> banquet for his courtiers and officers and the leading men of

Josephus there would seem to be little support for the modern conjecture that Jesus was started on his career through contact with the
Baptist, and that he repeated the latter's message even after John's
tragic death had sundered the bond of teacher and pupil. It would,
accordingly, appear more probable that the paths of Jesus and John
did not cross at all and that our gospel accounts preserve little or
nothing of the actual history of this enigmatic man. As the years
rolled by, John, although originally quite distinct from Jesus, was
gradually brought into the Christian picture, if not into the Christian
fold."

Morton Scott Enslin, *Christian Beginnings,* Harper & Brothers, N.Y.
1938, p. 151

Galilee. For when Herodias' daughter came in and danced, she pleased Herod and his guests; and the king said to the girl, "Ask me for whatever you wish, and I will grant it." And he vowed to her, "Whatever you ask me, I will give you, even half of my kingdom." And she went out, and said to her mother, "What shall I ask?" And she said, "The head of John the baptizer." And she came in immediately with haste to the king, and asked, saying, "I want you to give me at once the head of John the Baptist on a platter." And the king was exceedingly sorry; but because of his oaths and his guests he did not want to break his word to her. And immediately the king sent a soldier of the guard and gave orders to bring his head. He went and beheaded him in the prison, and brought his head on a platter and gave it to the girl; and the girl gave it to her mother . . .[8]

Thus ended the life of John the Baptist, the New Testament version of Elijah the Tishbite. But his spirit has been marching on in the long centuries of the Church and world history, for he was the herald of the Messiah, the Christ.

9

Jesus of Nazareth: Palestinian Rabbi
or the Resurrected Christ?

Jesus as another Palestinian rabbi or Jesus as the unique, resurrected Christ?

Here is the Great Divide between Jewry and Christendom, between Synagogue and Church; here is where the waters of faith divided originally. As the ages advanced this divide deepened and broadened. Here is where the Great Divide is today; here is where it shall be in the ages ahead. Ultimately, the issue was, always has been, is today, and will remain to the end of days: Jesus as another Palestinian preacher or Jesus as the heavenly Messiah?

I

JESUS THE PALESTINIAN RABBI

A Word on the Sources

Before proceeding with any delineation of the personality and significance of Jesus as the source of the Great Divide in Judeo-Christian history we must recall, as succinctly as possible, the problems confronting the student who strives for the facts in the case and for integrity of reason.

First, we must appreciate fully the inadequacy of the literary sources and the hazardous bases for making any judgment on the life and teaching of Jesus.

The non-biblical sources do not help us. The brief, highly dubious passage in Josephus only rouses more debate.[1] Whatever kernel of fact there may be in this passage is of late origin, written under circumstances that would not permit Josephus—recipient of Rome's favor—to dwell on the political revolts against his royal patrons. The cloudy paragraph does not add anything to the information we deduce from the Gospels. The fragments in Roman histories give us only oblique, fleeting references, adding nothing special. Along with the disputed reference in Josephus they buttress one point: they add a bit more testimony to the historicity of Jesus, making the denial of his very existence all the more difficult.

The earliest Christian sources are the letters of Paul; they are nearest to the time of Jesus. However, from the standpoint of factual material they are, unfortunately, of no value. Paul saw Jesus only in a trance; he never knew him in the flesh. Paul is therefore a trustworthy witness only to the historicity of Jesus; he has not a single detail to give us from personal contact with him. Paul's preoccupation is with the heavenly Messiah.

The primary literary sources for the "facts" in the life and teachings of Jesus are the four Gospels. These bristle with difficulties, known to all students of the New Testament.

Not one of the four Gospels was written from first-hand knowledge; they are second, third and fourth hand reports, based on rumors and legends circulated by adoring worshippers in an age rocked with alarms: apocryphal frenzy, total illiteracy, obession with demonology and other-worldly messianism. Wars and alarms of war, mass insanity, unimaginable misery, abetted by earthquakes, made accuracy of oral reports from generation to generation an impossibility. The first three, the Synoptic Gospels ("synoptic," *common viewpoint*) are the more reliable; but they contradict each other at vital points; and, again, each is removed in time from the life of Jesus and from the scenes of his activity. Jesus was crucified in the year 30 (or 29.) The earliest of the Gospels, Mark, was composed shortly before the fall of the Temple in the year 70; Mark makes no clear reference to the destruction. Thus, scholars reason, he is about half a century removed from the crucifixion. This Gospel underwent revision at the hands of later editors before it attained the form in which we have it. The Gospels according to Matthew and Luke are usually dated between the years 80 and 100. These too underwent revision by later editors. The fourth Gospel, John, is placed after the turn of the century, some seventy-five years after the crucifixion, by which time Christian belief had transmuted the spiritual life of Judea. It is the least reliable from the standpoint of external data. Its preoccupation is with the divine origin and nature of Jesus, summoning all men to accept Jesus as "the Christ, the Son of God." A respected scholar summarizes the tangled material: "The books were written in Greek for non-Jewish circles outside Judea; they are therefore removed at some distance both in time and place from the native environment of Christianity. They reflect changes in ideas and circumstances, the growth of ecclesiastic organization, and altered attitude toward the Jewish people, a Christology more appealing to Gentiles."* The first three Gospels, it is

---

*"But having in the Synoptics three kindred versions of the story of Jesus the reader is in a position to see, even without scholarly equipment, that these witnesses agree in substance in what they have to tell, and that their variations, often explicable, confirm rather than contradict the reliability of what has been transmitted through changes of language and at second, third, or fourth hand." Hugh J. Schonfield,

believed, are based on an earlier document lost to us. This presumably was written originally in Aramaic and translated into Greek. The translation, no doubt, introduced further variations.

The Acts of the Apostles is a secondary source, forming a sequel to Luke. It is concerned mainly with the growth of the Church, more particularly with the work of Paul; it therefore has nothing special to offer us on the earthly life of Jesus.

Second, the Gospel authors and editors were not interested in history—at least, not in the way in which we understand this discipline. Their preoccupation was with broadcasting the "good news" of the heavenly Messiah and winning converts. They were not historians; they were preachers. And each had his particular holy bias. Their passion was to convert all men and bring them to salvation through Jesus the Christ. They validated their good news by pointing to the promises in the Old Testament. Where specific prophecies were not fulfilled in the life of Jesus they invented incidents and improvised texts. They did this in the utmost sincerity. The Gospel writers "were artists, not photographers, and into their portraits they painted, as all artists do, far more than their physical eyes had seen."[2] Further, they were overwhelmingly concerned with the death and resurrection of the Redeemer, not with the itinerant Galilean preacher. Christianity begins with the resurrection from the tomb.

Third, The Gospels present an extremely tangled skein of technical problems: conflicting testimony on basic matters; authentic versus edited and re-edited, translated and retranslated texts; differences of theologic emphases; obscurity of historic backgrounds to specific events or pronouncements attributed to Jesus. Jesus

A History of Biblical Literature. P. 171. (A Mentor Book, The New American Library, 1962)

spoke largely in the apocalyptic terms of Palestinian
Jewry of two thousand years ago. A vast gulf separates
the methods of his reasoning and the contents of his
thinking from ours of the twentieth century. His meta-
phors need analysis and exposition by specially trained
experts in Bible study. New Testament scholarship is
slippery ground for the seasoned scholar; for the lay
reader it is treacherous terrain. The enormous scholarship by modern critical scholars, from the seventeenth
century to the present, only creates an insurmountable
wall for the lay reader. The prodigious labors of devoted
and brilliant men—mainly Protestants—only cancel out.
Albert Schweitzer, himself a distinguished figure in this
field of scholarship, testifies: "There is nothing more
negative than the result of critical study of the life of
Jesus," and shies away from the net effect of this study
on the Christian believer.[3]

Fourth—the most hazardous of all—is the emotional
conditioning, positive or negative, we bring to our confrontation with the image of Jesus.

For centuries have we—Jews and Christians alike—
been conditioned by partisan, pious biases. We can not
strip off these layers of sanctified stereotypes at will, as if
we were removing our coats; they have become part of
the very flesh and bone and tissue of our spiritual lives.

The Christian (most assuredly the devoted Christian,
and only to a lesser degree the indifferent or the devoted
scholarly Christian who seeks historical integrity) is
conditioned from childhood by the image and words of
Jesus the Redeemer. He is nursed on Jesus much more
than he realizes: not only in childhood and not only at
Church and holy seasons, but in every area of his cultural and social life—at weddings and funerals; at political assemblies; at concert halls and in the art galleries,
theatres and forums; in novels and poems—he meets

the image of Jesus, a vision of all that is sacred and lovely.

The Jew, too, meets with a vision of Jesus in the Western world despite himself, but invariably it has a contrary impact. To the Jew familiar with his peoples' history Jesus is an image of persecution: Crusades, Inquisition, pogroms, Nazis. The image rouses fear, or at least rescentment. To the scholarly minded Jew he represents, for the most part, the personification of the irrational.

The problem for Christian and Jew, believer or atheist, in every camp, is to disenthrall himself of his inherited stereotype; he must engage in serious soul-searching and expose his mind and his soul to a fresh and severely honest view of Jesus, and advance gently, but firmly, facing the light as God gives him the power to glimpse it.

We invoke the personality of Jesus the Palestinian rabbi, following the researches of the critical scholars, Jewish and non-Jewish alike. We shall return to the same aspects and stages of his life when we seek to recall Jesus as the resurrected Christ, basing ourselves on the testimonies of devout Christian scholars. Always, of course, the Bible text is primary.

Childhood and Youth

A mountain of learned reports has been produced by astute researchers in New Testament scholarship the world over on the personality, career and teachings of Jesus. But hardly a statement can be made without arousing debate. We submit the following "facts" in the life of Jesus fully aware of the hazards involved. Most of them are conjectures, based on the sources, by

scholars of ability and integrity; some are only educated
guesses. The reader should check these assertions in the
basic studies of Jesus; he should read the New Testament with a good commentary. And he should not hesitate to replace many a period with a question mark. No
layman can read the Bible—Old or New Testaments—
without a reliable commentary.[4]

Jesus was born in Nazareth, in Galilee, sometime
between the years 2 and 6 B.C.E.*

Nazareth is described as "the flower of Galilee,"
surrounded by mountains, forests, flowering fields, or-
chards, palm trees, fig trees, pomegranates. Jesus refers
to these flowers and their gorgeous colors and sees in
them enchanting parables of religious truths. He was a
sensitive, esthetic, brooding child with a fervid imagination.

His father was Joseph, a carpenter by occupation; his
mother was Mary. He followed his father's craft. It
was good Jewish practice of the time for a father to
teach his son a trade. It is conjectured that his father
died while Jesus was a lad. As the oldest son it was his
obligation to take his father's place as the head and
provider of the family.

Jesus had four brothers: James, Jose, Judah and

---

*"The Bethlehem stories, regardless of their homiletic beauty, ap-
parently rest on no historical foundation, but must be regarded as pure
legend. A critical examination of the two accounts—the one assuming
the fixed residence of the parents in Bethlehem, the homage of Magi
guided from the East by a miraculous star, the edict of the cruel king
(strangely akin to that told of the infant Moses), the flight into Egypt,
and subsequent return to Palestine, but to Nazareth, not Bethlehem;
the other telling of a most unusual journey from Nazareth to Bethlehem,
undertaken by the expectant mother in compliance with the requirement
of a supposed census, the inability to find lodgings, the resultant birth
in a stable, the vision of angels granted to shepherds, and their visit
to the manger—reveals that they are mutually exclusive, contradicting
each other at every point. Their value is real; nonetheless, this value
does not lie in the realm of history."

Charles Scott Enslin, *Beginnings of Christianity* p. 154-155

Simeon, and probably two sisters. James is identified in the Gospels as "brother of Jesus," "James the righteous." He was slow in following Jesus in his messanic role; he adhered steadfastly to the ceremonies and everyday practices of Judaism, resisting Paul's persistent efforts to break away from the traditional Judaism of the time. He may be termed orthodox. He died a martyr's death in defense of the Judaism he cherished.

We may safely assume that Jesus received the usual education the Pharisees provided for their sons. His vernacular was Aramaic; he must have been reasonably familiar with the Hebrew of the synagogues. That he came of the Pharisaic segment of the populace there is no reasonable doubt. In time a gulf developed between him and the Pharisaic masters. The Pharisees represented the large majority of the population.

There were differences of emphasis among them. Whether he attended an organized school we do not know. A school for boys was functioning in Jerusalem when Jesus was a boy; by the year 66 a system of public education was in effect throughout the country. The commandment, "You shall teach them [the words of the Torah] diligently to your children" was taken most earnestly. If not in a school, in the synagogues assuredly, his imagination was deeply stirred by the itinerant preachers who roamed the land, going from synagogue to synagogue. They propounded the Law and the Prophets in every humble village on every Sabbath and festival. Some of these expositions were no doubt academic and innocuous, but others fanned the flames of apocalyptic messianism. The impressionable boy heard and was shaken by these prophecies and oracles.

Jesus heard the wrath of the prophets damning the sins of the privileged, the arrogant, the sinning rulers, corrupt priests, rapacious tax collectors, Temple and royal aristocracy, and the heedless masses no less; he heard and was shaken by the proclamations of doom about to burst over the sinning nation; he saw the fantastic visions of Daniel as elaborated by the apocalyptic messianists; he heard, too, the tender voices of the psalmists announcing salvation and redemption. Roman oppression, cruel taxation, pagan idolatry, pitiless suffering all about him gave a sharp edge to the rumblings of doom. "Scarcely a year went by during this century," reports Joseph Klausner, "without wars or other disturbances: wars, rebellions, outbreaks and riots, and all of them with their concomitant of incessant bloodshed; and this state of things prevailed in the land of Israel throughout the whole epoch which preceded Jesus and prevailed also during his lifetime . . . Were we to count up one by one those who fell in the wars and rebellions and those murdered by Herod and the Procurators during this dreadful century, we should reach a total of not less than two hundred thousand men—an appalling number for such a comparatively small country . . . "[5]

The heavens were pregnant with doom; Judea was in the throes of the birth pangs of the Messiah. But salvation was on the way. Israel was not widowed, he heard the prophet affirm. The Guardian of Israel will not abandon His people, the psalmist consoled. God's anointed was on the way; redemption was nigh. Jesus heard the glad news announced with certainty by the preachers; he heard and was captivated. In time Jesus joined these itinerant preachers and distinguished himself as a master of parable, which every man, however humble his learning or lowly his station, could understand and cherish as a personal message of a divinely endowed preacher of God's word.

> There shall come forth a shoot
> from the stump of Jesse,

and a branch shall grow out of his roots
And the Spirit of the Lord shall
   rest upon him,
the spirit of wisdom and understanding,
the spirit of counsel and might,
the spirit of knowledge and the
   fear of the Lord.

He shall not judge by what his eyes see,
   or decide by what his ears hear;
but with righteousness he shall
   judge the poor,
and decide with equity for the
   meek of the earth;
and he shall smite the earth with the
   rod of his mouth
and with the breath of his lips he
   shall slay the wicked.
Righteousness shall be the girdle of
   his waist,
and faithfulness the girdle of his loins.

The wolf shall dwell with the lamb,
   and the leopard shall lie down
     with the kid,
and the calf and the lion and the
   fatling together
and a little child shall lead them.[6]

The people who walked in darkness
have seen a great light. . . .
For to us a child is born,
to us a son is given;
and the government shall be upon his shoulder,
and his name will be called
Wonderful Counselor, Mighty God,
Everlasting Father, Prince of Peace.[7]

I will tell of the decree of the Lord:
He said to me, "You are my son,
today I have begotten you."[8]

Baptism

Jesus heard these promises, drawn from the eschatologic portions of the prophets and the Psalms; he heard
with wide-eyed wonder the messianists expound the
monstrous figures of the book of Daniel and the visions
of the Book of Enoch. A new heaven was about to break
over the suffering nation; a new earth would shelter all
in her generous lap. God's intervention was imminent.
He was possessed by these visions and promises. He
identified himself with their fulfillment. "The spirit of
the Lord God is upon *me* . . . He hath anointed *me* . . ."[9]
My son, I have begotten *you.*" All the while John was
crying in the wilderness: "Prepare ye the way of the
Lord . . . repent . . . after me comes he who is mightier
than I."[10] Jesus was enthralled.

Crowds were streaming from everywhere in the land
and from every segment of society toward the Jordan
River when the austere, ascetic John, attired in camel's
hair and leather girdle, was summoning men to repentance and baptism. Especially were the Essenes, the apocalyptists, the messianists drawn to this herald of the
Messiah. Among these was Jesus.

The Gospel according to Mark reports the supreme
revelation and its transforming impact on Jesus:

> In those days Jesus came from Nazareth of Galilee and was
> baptized by John in the Jordan. And when he came up out
> of the water, immediately he saw the heavens opened and the
> Spirit descending upon him like a dove; and a voice came from
> heaven, "Thou art my beloved Son; with thee I am well
> pleased."*

Jesus was on the road to Golgotha to fulfill himself
as the heavenly Messiah. The specific words may be

* But see Chapter 8.

legendary and come from the pen of a later evangelist; the event they report is crucial in the career of Jesus.

Profoundly shaken by this experience, he retired to the desert, as had Moses and Elijah before him. He was in the grip of doubt and self-searching. The Gospels describe his spiritual turmoil as "tempted by Satan."

"And Jesus himself when he began to preach was about thirty years of age," Luke reports.*

Jesus the Pharisee:
Social and Religious Conditioning and Teaching

Jesus was saturated from infancy with Pharisaic Judaism. That was the central force in his preparation for his destiny. Pharisaic Judaism it was that gave him the morning star as Messiah. In the crucial hours of his life it was Pharisaic Judaism that gave him the strength and the comfort he needed. In the overwhelming revelation that came to him when he emerged from the baptismal water administered by John it was a verse from the Psalmist, according to the Gospels, that caught the awesome vision: "You are my son; today I have begotten you."[12] In the hour of his extreme agony of body and soul another verse from the Psalms it was that voiced his pain: "My God, my God, why hast Thou foresaken me?"[13] These he absorbed in the synagogues

---

* 3.23. It is intriguing to note that despite the powerful impact the act of baptism had on him, Jesus does not stress the importance of the rite, nor do the Gospel writers. Some scholars support the thesis that baptism and its protagonist, John, were originally alien to Christianity. ". . . it appears not unlikely that the incorporation of John into the Christian picture was a deliberate and studied attempt by early Christians to vanquish an embarrassing rival. The religions of antiquity provide numerous examples of a new god gradually supplanting an old and eventually being regarded as his son. The most effective way of getting rid of a rival is to align him with one's own cause." Morton Scott Enslin, Christian Beginnings, Harper & Brothers, N.Y., 1938, p. 152.

of the Pharisees. The theology, the rituals, the emotions of the Synagogue permeated his personality. "Think not that I have come to abolish the law and the prophets; I have come not to abolish them but to fulfill them. For, truly, I say to you, till heaven and earth pass away, not an iota, not a dot, will pass from the law until all is accomplished. Whoever then relaxes one of the least of these commandments and teaches men so, shall be called least in the kingdom of heaven; but he who does them and teaches them shall be called great in the Kingdom of heaven . . . it is easier for heaven and earth to pass away, than for one dot of the law to become void."[14] "This is rabbinism with a vengeance."[15]

"In the various quick glimpses of the clashes of Jesus with the Pharisees with which the gospels provide us, one thing is certain: never do they charge him with what today would be styled heresy. In all respects he was a seemingly devout and orthodox Jew, with complete and unquestioned acceptance of and devotion to an all-wise and all-powerful God."[16]

All his ministrations he devoted to his fellow Jews exclusively, speaking in their vernacular Aramaic in their little synagogues. He instructed his disciples not to "give dogs what is holy; and do not throw your pearls before swine. . . ."[17] Dogs and swine refer to the non-Jews. Only once, and reluctantly, did he minister to a non-Jewish woman, exorcising an evil spirit from her little daughter. He kept the Sabbaths, observed the festivals, made his pilgrimages to Jerusalem in keeping with the laws of Moses, held *seder,* himself paid the tithes to the Temple and encouraged others to do it. All his life he prayed to the God of his fathers.

Jesus validated the entire ceremonial law.

In his beliefs as in his practices he was a faithful son of the Synagogue. Asked, "Which commandment is the first of all?" Jesus replied "The first is, 'Hear, O Israel:

The Lord our God, the Lord is one; and you shall love
the Lord your God with all your heart, and with all your
soul, and with all your mind, and with all your strength.'
The second is this, 'You shall love your neighbor as
yourself.' There is no other commandment greater than
these."[18]

The first is the primary affirmation of Pharisaic Judaism; Jewish martyrs without number, during the lifetime of Jesus and before and after him, went to their
deaths reciting these words and sanctified His Name;
the second was affirmed and reaffirmed by the rabbinic
masters.

Ethics, Social Action, Prayer

Significantly, Jesus does not answer his Pharisaic in-
terrogator with prophetic teaching, such as Micah's.
"He has showed you, O man, what is good and what the
Lord requires of you: to do justly, love mercy and walk
humbly with your God;"[19] nor with Isaiah's "Wash yourselves, make yourselves clean; remove the evil of your
doings from before my eyes; cease to do evil, learn to
do good; seek justice, correct oppression; defend the
fatherless, plead for the widow."[20] He prefers the Law
of Moses and its theologic authority. Jesus was no social
reformer; he had no interest in social reform. Social
activists in synagogue and church in our time are hard
put to validate their activism on the basis of the teachings or example of Jesus. His clearing the money-changers
out of the Temple was a concern with Temple propriety,
or to put himself in line (or an evangelist put him in
line) with Jeremiah's Temple Sermon.[21]

Jesus could not be a social reformer for the reason
that he was enthralled by the conviction that the world
was coming to an end. A new Kingdom was imminent.

The change would be brought about by God, not by social engineers.* In this new world there would be no eating, no drinking, no hunger to be assuaged, no pain to be relieved—no social evils, that is, that needed reform. Neither wealth nor poverty would have any meaning. In fact, wealth is an evil in itself; poverty is a positive good. The rich man would go to Gehenna for no other reason than that he was rich, not because he oppressed his neighbor or "sold the poor man for a pair of shoes;" the poor man would go straight to "Father Abraham's bosom" for no other reason than that he was poor, not because he loved his neighbor as himself, did justly, loved mercy and walked humbly with his God. In the Sermon on the Mount**, we hear no echoes of the flaming words of social protest, such as Isaiah 58, for instance: liberating the poor, feeding the hungry, clothing the naked, opening the eyes of the blind, concern for the disinherited; or Isaiah's attack on the "wild grapes" of Judah: corrupt courts, an exploiting landowning aristocracy, dispossessing the poor peasant, avaricious priests, drunkenness.[22] The Sermon includes superbly noble beatitudes: "Blessed are these who hunger for

---

*We have a striking example of this thinking in our time. The *Naturai Karta,* the extremist Orthodox Jewish community in Jerusalem, will not recognize the State of Israel for the reason that it was established by humans—Hertzl, Weitzmann, Ben Gurion—not by God Himself through His Messiah.

**The Sermon is considered by most critical scholars as a collection of sayings spoken by Jesus at various times under varying circumstances; some believe these sayings to have been attributed to him by later editors.

"Attempts to see in Jesus the champion of a social gospel, shared wealth, and other pleasing qualities and attitudes so dear today in the eyes of the socially concerned, are doomed to failure. He refuses to don our clothes or share our ideas, for he lived in the first, not the twentieth century. His concern was not to better the world which was long to last; instead it was to cause men to await a cataclysm in which the present world and all its concerns—mostly due to man's strange neglect of God's providence—would vanish, and a new utopia emerge." (N.S. Enslin, *Prophet of Nazareth,* p. 135.)

righteousness sake . . . Blessed are the merciful . . .;
Blessed are the pure in heart . . .; Blessed are the peace-
makers. . . ."[23] But the social activist will not find in it
the flag he needs. He must turn elsewhere for Scriptural
inspiration and authority.

Jesus's ethics and social outlook were other-wordly.
Slum clearance, overcrowding, unemployment, strikes,
lockouts, racism, even war, were of no social concern to
him. These were not the problems of his day. His fixa-
tion was on the Kingdom of Heaven. Perhaps that explains—or helps explain—his extremism: "If your right
eye causes you to sin, pluck it out and throw it away. . . .
If your right hand causes you to sin, cut it off and throw
it away. . . . If any would take away your coat let him
have your cloak also. . . . Love your enemies and pray
for them that persecute you. . . ."[24] Scholars have con-
tented that "Jesus scarcely introduced any ethical teaching which was fundamentally foreign to Judaism."[25]
However, he carried these teachings to extremes and
thereby invested them with altered significance—his own
brand of wine in the old Pharisaic bottles.*

In the matter of prayer, Jesus follows the rabbinic
masters of the day. "The Lord's Prayer" is a restatement of the rabbinic affirmations of the *Kaddish*. In the
more practical matter of divorce Jesus took the orthodox
position of his day. His Golden Rule is another version
of the rule as advanced by Hillel.[26]

In practice, however, Jesus did deviate from the func-
tional Judaism about him. To moderns these deviations
seem trivial. As his ministry advanced the deviations,
probably, became more frequent. He was a bit less scru-
pulous, for instance—or grew less, and his disciples even

---

* It should be remembered that some critical students disagree strongly
on the authenticity of the extreme teachings we are citing. Perhaps
these pronouncements were attributed to him by the later evangelists.
The question, however, remains: What did Jesus teach?

more so—in some observances. He was charged with being "a glutton and a wine bibber" instead of engaging in ascetic practices as did John and *his* disciples in their efforts to hasten the coming of the Messiah. He consorted with "sinners and publicans." He permitted his followers to take minor liberties with Sabbath regulations. He engaged at least once in open polemics against the dietary laws. Perhaps his most serious offense against public feeling was his presumed arrogation of authority for himself: "You have heard that it was said of old . . . but I say unto you."[27] In the eyes of some rabbinic authorities—it is likely—he set himself above the laws of Moses.

Such differences of belief may be traced among the leading masters of the time. No authoritarian unanimity of belief was imposed by the rabbinic sages. Differences of opinion and divergencies of interpretation were normal and accepted—even approved—procedures among them, as for instance, between Shammai and Hillel. All their differences and disputations were *within* the Torah, revealed to Moses on Mount Sinai, of which they were the authoritative custodians.

It was Paul who lifted these differences from their setting *within* the Law and set them *against* the Law. "Jesus remained steadfast to old *Torah;* till his dying day he continued to observe the ceremonial laws like a true Pharisaic Jew."[28]

The bitter tirade against the Pharisees put into the mouth of Jesus, as reported in Matthew 23, issues from the heat of a holy war. It may malign Jesus as much as the Pharisees. Men in bitter frustration, particularly in religious matters, speak words they regret in calmer hours. Perhaps Jesus did speak some of these cruel sentences; perhaps they were only attributed to him by later zealots. We drop the curtain of charity on the author or editor, whoever he was. Ample refutations have been made by scholars in Christendom as in Jewry. These are easily accessible to the student.[29]

Miracles

Jesus performed miracles and won his following largely as a miracle-worker. From the standpoint of the Pharisaic masters he was involved in this practice excessively. "He is possessed by Beelzebub, and by the prince of demons he cast out the demons."[30]

Performing miracles was an accepted practice. The more miracles a man performed the holier a man he was; the holier he was the more miracles he performed. Later ages, extolling the greatness of their holy men, elaborated on this legendry and thus proved the superiority of *their* holy men. Even so sober a personality as Yohanan ben Zakkai is reported to have practiced the art. Some rabbinic personalities of the age were outright miracle workers, such as Honi, or Simeon ben Yohai. Most of them heard heavenly voices. The masters in the academies, however, looked askance at the practice. They sensed sorcery or witchcraft and sought to discourage it. They would not accept testimony in court, nor make judicial decisions in the academies, on the basis of miracles or heavenly voices. The Torah "is not in heaven," they reasoned.[31] It has been entrusted to man on earth, by which he must live. Therefore scholars must interpret it in keeping with their needs and their best judgments, not rely on heavenly voices and supernatural manifestations. In the corpus of rabbinic law, the *Mishnah,* which at the time of Jesus was in its early stages of development, no reference is made to angels. Most of the masters in the academies, no doubt, believed that miracles did have validity. Did not God speak to Moses through a burning bush? Was not the giving of the Law to Moses on Mount Sinai an overwhelming miracle embracing the entire Torah? And did not God reveal himself to Elijah and Elisha and enable them to raise the dead? And did He not speak to Isaiah, Jeremiah, Ezekiel in supernatural ways? They could not outlaw miracles and cherish the Torah at the same time. However, their practical common sense impelled them to frown at the art and suspect it as possible sorcery.

Jesus was in line with the accepted traditions and practices of Judaism as a worker of miracles. The sick, the blind, the lame, the demented, the epileptic, the paralytic flocked to him in despair; he raised the dead and drove the demons from the possessed. No doubt this legendry luxuriated in his name with the passing of the years. Whole chapters of fantastic apocalyptic writings—and pagan legends as well—are behind these reports. However, the sages had their personal doubts and private fears. He was trafficking too much with sorcery.

A word on miracles from the standpoint of the critical student must be spoken.

We must bear in mind the fact that the ancients—Biblical and rabbinic alike—had no awareness of secondary causes in the processes of nature. There was one—and only one—cause: God and His righteous will. What to the sophisticated moderns is a natural change in a universe regulated by natural laws, to the Biblical folk was a direct and purposeful intervention on the part of God. We assume, for instance, that Nebuchadnezzar's army besieging Jerusalem in the days of Isaiah was swept by a bubonic plague; to the biblical author and his pious readers it was God's direct intervention on behalf of His people. Thus at least some of the miracles Jesus is presumed to have performed are explainable on natural grounds. Others may be explained on psychiatric bases, or on the basis of hypnosis and agitated personal-

ities, or illusion, or hallucination, or fervid imagination
of unbalanced disciples or worshippers. Some may be
explained on the basis of the passion of the New Testament writers to "prove" that Jesus was the true Messiah
and was fulfilling the prophecies of the Old Testament.
Some are based on pagan precedents—the Mithra cult,
etc. Galilee especially was filled with mentally deranged
people in the wake of Herodian and Roman cruelties.
To the present-day sophisticates such reports as the
Israelites crossing the Red Sea, or Moses turning his
rod into a serpent and then back into a rod, or Elijah
bringing down the fire of Yahweh on the Baalim, are
only folklore and legendry told and retold by highly
imaginative story tellers. The critical reading of the
Bible—Old and New Testaments—is liberating; the historic-critical approach removes much which is an affront
to the intelligence. Jesus and the Pharisaic masters could
not take such an easy way out of the dilemma. To them
—children of their time as they were—miracles were
direct manifestations of God; they proved that the man
who performed them was in special favor with God.

"Good Tidings to the Afflicted"

In the wilderness, to which he had retired to quiet
the turmoil within him, Jesus battled with himself for
a time. The Gospels report he was involved in this intense struggle with himself for forty days. The number
is suspect. The flood which inundated the virgin earth
in Noah's day lasted forty days; Moses brooded on
Mount Sinai for forty days, receiving the Law at the
hands of God; Elijah roamed the wilderness in conflict
with himself and the powers of the time for forty days.
In the Bible forty is often a round figure.

Grave doubts assailed Jesus and tore at his soul. "The

Satan tempted him," the Gospel writers report. It was natural enough. Possessed by the sense of his messianic destiny, he recoiled, as Moses had done long before him when *he* heard the Voice from the burning bush, as Jeremiah had done when the Voice summoned him to be "a prophet unto the nations." Like Moses and like Jeremiah—and the many, many men of destiny in history—Jesus obeyed the Voice despite himself. He seems to have been fully aware of the suffering that awaited him. He would be persecuted by the crowds and their leaders and rejected. Perhaps the fate of John the Baptist roused fear. The Romans dealt decisively with messiahs. The "pangs of the Messiah" foretold by the prophet haunted him, and created for a time an imbalance in his soul.

His ministry was short: perhaps only one year, or even less—29-30 of the Common Era, as the Synoptic Gospels report; perhaps three years, as John reports. Most scholars accept the one year report as the more likely. The radical nature of his message which sparked political disturbance, gives added weight to the probability of the shorter term.

Jesus preached mainly in the synagogues along the northwestern shore of the Sea of Galilee, beginning in Capernaum; he also performed miracles. Capernaum, Peter's home town, was a flourishing fishing center. Huge crowds were attracted to Jesus. Galilee was politically a deeply disturbed area. It was giving the Romans no end of trouble; seething rebellion was indigenous to it. Crowds were therefore easy to come by.

His first disciples were two sets of brothers who had engaged in fishing. They responded to his call to be "fishers of men." The strongest character among them was Simon "called Peter," the rock upon which, according to subsequent Christian legendry, the Church of Rome was founded. He was anything but a rock; he was

a weak, vacillating man, as we shall see. Jesus stayed
in Simon-Peter's home in Capernaum and operated from
there—for a short time, presumably.

The burden of his preaching was the imminent advent
of the Kingdom of God. "And after John was arrested,
Jesus came into Galilee, preaching the gospel of God,
and saying, 'The time is fulfilled, and the kingdom of
God is at hand; repent, and believe in the gospel.' "[32] A
new heaven and a new earth were about to replace the
world as men knew the world. Pain, sorrow oppression,
death itself would be swallowed up forever; personal
redemption, salvation for every soul, however humble,
was on the wing. Jesus picked up where John had left
off. "But he went out and began to talk freely about it
and to spread the news, so that Jesus could no longer
openly enter a town, but was in the country; and people
came to him from every quarter."[33] That he himself
was the preordained heavenly Messiah he had withheld
from the crowds, even from his chosen disciples for a
time; at last his own feeling and the emotions of the
crowds overwhelmed him.

He was a supremely gifted preacher. Unlike most of
the Pharisaic expounders of the Torah Jesus preached
in the form of parables. These he drew from nature and
from the everyday life about him. He kept proclaiming
the sensational news of the coming of "kingdom not of
this world," but "a new heaven and a new earth."

His reputation as a miracle-worker and his sensational
proclamation of the impending cataclysmic end of the
world, we may assume, created the excitement and drew
the crowds. He may have—as scholars of repute affirm—
feared to push his reputation as miracle-worker; his
reputation, however, swept him headlong into this ad-
venture. He healed the sick, made the blind see, the
deaf hear; he fed thousands with fish normally sufficient
for very few, walked on water, exorcised demons, raised

the dead to new life. Adoring disciples and Gospel
writers amplified this supernatural reputation. What
was reported of Elijah and Elisha of an earlier day,
Jesus could do and do better. Such is the stuff of which
garlands of legends are woven.

In Capernaum he met the local customs official, who,
it is believed, may have been Matthew in whose name
the Gospel came down in Church history. Perhaps this
tax collector collated the sayings and wonder-working
tales that later writers retold and enlarged.

As tax collector for Rome, Matthew was hated—at
least suspected—by the local populace. Also, he was lax
in his ceremonial observances. Still more, he was a
Roman collaborationist. Association with him did not
enhance the popularity of Jesus among the Jewish masses
and their rabbinic leaders. Even Jesus's own mother
and brothers turned against him—in an effort, no doubt,
to save him from the dangerous embroilments in which
he was involving himself:

> And his mother and his brothers came; and standing out-
> side they sent to him and called him. And a crowd was sitting
> about him, and they said to him, "Your mother and your
> brothers are outside, asking for you." And he replied, "Who
> are my mother and my brothers?" And looking around on
> those who sat about him, he said, "Here are my mother and
> my brothers! Whoever does the will of God, is my brother,
> and sister and mother."[34]

In his native Nazareth on a Sabbath he preached in
the local synagogue, taking his text from Isaiah 61:

> The spirit of the Lord God is upon me, because the Lord
> has anointed me to bring good tidings to the afflicted; he
> has sent me to bind up the brokenhearted, to proclaim liberty
> to the captives, and the opening of the prison to those who are
> bound; to proclaim the year of the Lord's favor, and the day
> of vengeance of our God; to comfort all who mourn; to

grant to those who mourn in Zion—to give them a garland instead of ashes. . . .

The reaction was natural. Some of the fellow townsmen were astonished: Was this the young man they had known? Was he another Galilean rebel plunging them into a new blood bath?

Where did this man get all this? What is the wisdom given to him. . . . ? Is not this the carpenter, the son of Mary and brother of James and Joses and Judas and Simon, and are not his sisters here with us?[35]

Jesus was on the road to Golgotha.

We must bear in mind, constantly, and at the present stage in the career of Jesus particularly, the all-embracing fact: messianism was the frenzy of the age. And the messiah had two faces: the earthly political liberator of Davidic stock foretold by the prophets, and the heavenly Redeemer—visionary, mystic, miracle-worker, who came down "with the clouds of heaven" from the "the throne of glory." The two were one, depending upon the enthusiasm of the hour and the individual, expressed in the title attributed to Jesus at this time: *King-Messiah*. We may surmise that it blended in Jesus's own mind, lured as he was by the messianic vision, and transformed by it.

Passover in Jerusalem

Faithful Pharisee that he was, Jesus joined the pilgrim throngs for Jerusalem on the occasion of the Passover (in the year 30, perhaps 29). Was that his first visit to the Holy City? We do not know. Mosaic law commanded, "Three times a year all your males shall appear before the Lord your God at the place which he

will choose; at the feast of unleavened bread. . . ."[36] The
place He had chosen was Jerusalem. Those were colorful and, in the days of Jesus, explosive occasions. Passover was *the* occasion. The city was a rumbling volcano.
That was the time when the Procurator—this time,
Pilate—moved to Jerusalem with his enormous legions,
which were armed and on the alert. Every pilgrim was
a suspect rebel. From Galilee especially came the zealot
pilgrim rebels. Jesus was a Galilean, and he was followed by his special retinue: the twelve apostles he had
chosen and, quite likely, by chance stragglers who were
cheering him as King-Messiah.

In the neighborhood of Caesarea Phillipi he tacitly
accepted his disciples' recognition of him as the heavenly
messiah. He begged them to keep the information to
themselves. He felt himself on the verge of a precipice
and was fearful.

With his little band he pushed on towards Jerusalem.
On the outskirts of the city he at last disclosed himself
as the Messiah. Next to his baptism this was the most
decisive step in his career. He finally had made peace
with himself. Two of his disciples procured an ass colt
somewhere in the neighborhood. Jesus mounted the
young beast. A crowd gathered; garments were spread
before him as before a king. Some cut branches of palm
trees and cheered.

> They brought the colt to Jesus, and threw their garments on
> it; and he sat upon it. And many spread their garments on
> the road, and others spread leafy branches which they had cut
> from the field. And those who went before and those who fol-
> lowed cried out, "Hosanna! Blessed is he who comes in the
> name of the Lord! Blessed is the kingdom of our father David
> that is coming. Hosanna in the highest!"[37]

This report may be the result of the persistent effort
of the Gospel writers, or of later editors, to equate

every episode in the life and activities of Jesus with the fulfillment of divine prophecy, or it may be a report of what actually happened. In the book of Zechariah it is written:

> Rejoice greatly, O daughter of Zion!
> Shout aloud, O daughter of Jerusalem!
> Lo, your king comes to you;
> triumphant and victorious is he,
> humble and riding on an ass,
> on a colt the foal of an ass.[38]

If this is a report of an actual performance, Jesus was wilfully—or naively—courting his crown of thorns.

Jesus is now the King-Messiah. Both faces of the messiah are clearly revealed. The pious Jews were no doubt shaken with religious frenzy: God's awesome promise, voiced in Scripture, was fulfilling itself before their very eyes. Pilate and his legionnaires, and the Sadducean politicians, were no doubt suspicious of another Galilean rebel and fanatic.

That was on Monday before the Passover. The festival fell that year on the Sabbath.

Jesus and his retinue went directly to the Temple, in keeping with established convention. For the next several days he visited the Temple daily, expounding his belief of the impending Kingdom of God to any one who would listen to him; every night he would return to his lodging in Bethany. His host was a most lowly person, Simon the Leper. (Perhaps the text should read *Simon the Lowly,* or *Simon the Essene.* The Aramaic lends itself to such minor change.) On the third day, two days before the arrest, he enacted in public a most exciting incident. Outraged by the trafficking in pigeons and money changing in the outer court of the Temple—in connection with the sacrificial cult—he furiously turned on the traders and "drove the money changers out of the Temple."[39] Was he consciously imitating Jeremiah's attack made in the prophet's Temple sermon: "Had this house, which is called by my name, become a den of robbers in your eyes?"[40] Perhaps. Perhaps, too, here is another instance of the Gospel writers improvising and attributing to Jesus an incident to match Bible prophecy. Mark reports:

> And he taught, and said to them, Is it not written, "My house shall be called a house of prayer for all the nations?" but you have made it a den of robbers.[41]

Basically, Jesus was only enforcing rabbinic law; but who gave *him* the authority to do it? Temple officials were outraged. The next day they challenged him: by what right was he taking the law into his own hands? Jesus replied with a hazy parable, hinting that he was acting by divine commission. Was he the Messiah? Was he advocating rebellion to Rome? Pressed for an explanation he fenced adroitly. He asked for a Roman coin. Pointing to it he called attention to the image of Caesar and retorted: "Render to Caesar the things that are Caesar's, and to God the things that are God's."[42]

How could the Temple authorities deal with him without sparking a riot on the one hand or Roman retaliation on the other? Clearly, he had an explosive following; just as surely, he was exposing the community to Roman vengeance. They decided to arrest him after the holiday. The crowds would have scattered by then and the excitement abated.

But something unforeseen happened.

One of the Twelve, Judas Iscariot, tipped off the Sadducean authorities, practical politicians and collaborators with Rome, where and when Jesus was resting after holding *seder* on the eve of the Passover: in the upper chamber of a humble Jerusalem water carrier's quarters.

He might be disposed of without public notice. The
fatal arrest took place in the Garden of Gethsemene on
the Mount of Olives.[43]

In the crucial hour his disciples failed him shamefully.
They were asleep. Roused once, and roused again, and
roused a third time, their eyes were too heavy with wine
and their minds stupefied. As described in Mark 14 this
scene in the life of Jesus is enormously pathetic. Jesus
sensed supreme danger; he was frightened. The hour
had come.

> And they went to a place which was called Gethsemene; and
> he said to his disciples, "Sit here while I pray." And he took
> with him Peter and James and John, and began to be greatly
> distressed and troubled. And he said to them, "My soul is
> very sorrowful, even to death; remain here and watch. [Or,
> "keep awake."] And going a little further, he fell on the ground
> and prayed that, if it were possible, the hour might pass from
> him. And he said, "Abba, Father, all things are possible to
> thee; remove this cup from me; yet not what I will, but what
> Thou wilt."
> And he came and found them sleeping, and he said to Peter,
> "Simon, are you asleep? Could you not watch (or *keep awake*)
> one hour . . . ?" Again he went away and prayed, saying the
> same words. And again he came and found them sleeping . . .
> A third time, and he said to them, "Are you still sleeping
> and taking your rest? . . . "[44]

Peter—"the rock"—despite his affirmations of loyalty
unto death, at the hour of supreme crisis denied altogether knowing his Master.

We may note here that Jesus was unfortunate in the
apostles he had chosen. Not one of them had caught his
vision; not one had the stamina to stand by him in the
crucial hour of his need. Their mission was to carry the
gospel of the Kingdom through Jesus the Christ, but
their chief concern was their own personal privileges
and honors in heaven. "Behold, I send you out as sheep

in the midst of wolves; so be wise as serpents and innocent as doves," he had briefed them.[45] They may have
been innocent as doves, but wise as serpents they most
certainly were not. They were self-centered and obtuse,
and had not the capacity to see the star that guided their
Master. Peter especially was a disappointment to Jesus.
Early in their association Jesus referred to him as Satan.
Later, Paul excoriated him as a "lying brother." Judas
Iscariot has come down in history as the very personification of infamy. "Judas's kiss" is a byword for perfidy.
It may be observed that Judas never had his hour in
court. He alone left his native land to follow Jesus out
of sheer conviction. Why did he turn against Jesus?
The evangelists are too preoccupied with righteous in-
dignation in condemning Judas to give him a hearing.

Trial and Crucifixion

Scholars and preachers the world over, writing in
every language of the Western world, and moving on
various levels—from complete acceptance of every word
of the New Testament as absolute divine truth to critical
denial and including all levels in-between—have produced
a mountain of literature expounding, affirming, amending
or flatly denying the accounts of the trial and crucifixion
of Jesus as reported in the Gospels: Mark 14-16, Matthew 26-28, Luke 22-24, and John 13-21. Certain historic considerations must be borne in mind as we read
these chapters.

1) We simply do not know the facts and have no way
of finding them out, unless some hitherto unexpected
source material is discovered, after the manner of the
discovery of the Dead Sea Scrolls. The "facts" advanced
by all scholars, of whatever school, are—as we have

already noted—educated guesses embroidering a legend, at best only inferences drawn from the Gospels.

2) All four Gospels are affirmations of belief and faith, not records of facts. The writers are not interested in external data. The Gospel writers were profoundly emotional disciples, passionately devoted to Jesus as the resurrected, heavenly Messiah, though each had his particular theological slant. This compounds the perplexities for the critical scholar.

3) Each was profoundly convinced that Jesus the Christ was sent by God in fulfillment of prophecies recorded in the Old Testament. Many a detail, in the trial and crucifixion accounts especially, is enlarged—or invented altogether, in profoundest sincerity—to prove a verse in the Hebrew prophets, the Psalms or the book of Daniel. The abuse to which Jesus was subjected at the trial, for instance, is meant to fulfill pronouncements in the book of Isaiah concerning the suffering servant:

> I gave my back to the smiters,
> and my cheek to those who pulled out the beard;
> I hid not my face from shame and spitting.[46]

Jesus remained silent at his trial; that was according to Isaiah:

> As a lamb that is led to slaughter,
> And as a sheep that before the shearers is dumb,
> So he opened not his mouth.[47]

The horseplay of the barbaric Roman soldiers who did the horrid act of crucifixion was in fulfillment of verses in the Psalms:

> " . . . they divided my garments among them, and for
> my raiment they cast lots . . . They gave me poison for

food, and for my thirst they gave me vinegar to drink.[48]

4) Each of the Gospel writers heaps the entire blame for the crucifixion on the Jews. Together they create the image of the entire Jewish people as "the Christ killer" and therefore the accursed of God. Hence the burden of guilt is lifted from Pilate and concentrated on the Pharisees. Pilate, it is reported, was forced to act against his own better judgment under the pressure of the Jewish mob; even his wife pleads with him not to put to death an innocent man. He washes his hands of all guilt (a Jewish ritual performed by a pagan overlord of the Jews). Led by their Pharisaic masters the crowd would not permit Pilate to show Jesus clemency. Better that the available clemency be given to a common thief. The Jewish leaders it was who spat into his face and cried for his blood: "His blood be upon us and our children!"[49] Hence the guilt of deicide rests upon the Jews forever and ever. Here is the poisoned well in Jewish-Christian relations.*

Historians affirm that these embellishments of the trial and crucifixion record come from the end of the first century, some three quarters of a century after the crucifixion. By then the theology of the emerging church —and especially the thinking and fervor of Paul—acquired a separatist and intolerant form.

5) At the time of the trial and crucifixion the Jewish community did not have the legal authority to try capital punishment cases. They could only investigate and recommend to the Procurator. The power had been taken away from them by the Romans when they reduced Judea to a captive territory. In the Gospel according to John the Jewish leaders, pressing the case against Jesus on the reluctant Pilate, say, "It is not lawful for us to

*See Appendix—Deicide.

put any man to death."[50] Rabbinic sources give further testimony to this effect.

6) The specific facts in the trial and crucifixion are incomplete and badly tangled. The day and hour of the trial are reported variously in the Synoptic Gospels and in John: on the eve of the Passover, which was a Sabbath, or—to avoid a legal difficulty—a day earlier. How may we accept as fact a report that places a capital punishment trial at night, which is contrary to rabbinic law, and on a Sabbath? The trial has been characterized as "judicial murder" on the part of the Jewish authorities. An enormous literature has been produced analyzing, defending, denying, amending the reports.[51]

The legal complications are lifted in a measure by a theory advanced by Klausner, to the effect that the session in the house of the High Priest, before turning Jesus over to Pilate, was not a trial at all; it was only a preliminary investigation.

7) Above all, it must never be forgotten that the trial and execution as reported in the Gospels was a political one. Every detail in the accounts points to this conclusion.[52]

The first question Pilate is reported as having put to Jesus was, "Are you the King of the Jews?" Galilee was a constant source of rebellion; Pilate had ample warrant to suspect anyone whom the crowds cheered as messiah. The political face of the messiah was the only one that concerned the Roman. The trial was thus on the charge of treason. The punishment for treason was explicitly prescribed in Roman law: death by crucifixion. The Roman soldiers who actually put Jesus to death have their sport: they dress him in purple, symbol of Roman imperial rank; they jam a crown of thorns on his head; they stick a reed resembling a scepter in his right hand, and jeer, "Behold! the King of the Jews!" On the cross beam holding the broken body of Jesus they inscribe the legend: "The King of the Jews!" (or, "This is Jesus, King of the Jews!" or, "Jesus of Nazareth, King of the Jews!").[53]

The High Priest who had grilled Jesus in his palace in the dead of night and who turned him over to the Procurator was the most notorious High Priest-politician of the time, Joseph ben Caiaphas. He came of a family of priests who left an infamous reputation for terrorizing the populace with physical violence. He maintained himself in office eighteen years. He knew how to collaborate with Pilate. Each of his predecessors had lasted a year or less. He had good reason to fear any religious-political disturber of the peace. We may safely assume that legal niceties did not disturb him in dealing with Jesus. In time, it is likely, he was removed from office along with Pilate on the basis of their unwarranted cruelty, which was stirring rebellion.

Further, crucifixion was a Roman method of execution. The modes of execution prescribed in rabbinic law, invoked when capital punishment was still within the power of the Jewish courts, varied with the nature of the crime. These were: hanging, strangulation, stoning, burning; but never nailing the victim to a cross bar.

What follows after the crucifixion—the resurrection, the empty tomb, the vision of salvation and redemption, the cross on Calvary—belongs to the story of the resurrected Christ. No longer are we in touch with the Palestinian rabbi. The story now belongs to faith, not to history.

What Manner of Man?

What manner of man emerges from a critical reading of the Gospels in search of the historical Jesus? Clearly, the image is varied and contradictory, infinitely complex.

The conventional image of Jesus as "meek and mild,"
the innocent lamb led to slaughter, can not stand analysis.
He was capable of wrath, and gave way to violent impulse at times, as for example, when he drove the money
changers out of the Temple. He was capable of harsh-
ness, as, for instance, in reacting to his own mother and
brothers, or his brusqueness with the distraught non-
Jewish mother who sought his help in healing her daughter.[54] However, he orders his disciple, "let the children
come unto me, and do not hinder them; for to such belongs the kingdom of heaven."[55] His diatribe against
the Pharisees—if the words are his—was bitter. Nevertheless, he would have men turn the other cheek to the
unjust assailant and give the robber "his cloak also." He
was shrewd and evasive in reacting to opponents. That
is amply attested to in his conduct at the trial before the
rump Sanhedrin and, later, before Pilate, if there is any
historically sound data in the records. He assumed
authority boldly, challenging the Establishment of the
day: "It was said to you of old . . . but *I* say unto
you . . . "[56] He preached magnificently with inspired self-
assurance in synagogues and countrysides, winning the
hearts of his hearers. His proverbs and parables—
shrewd, sharp, captivating—are beyond compare. He
had an amazing gift for winning the reverence of men.
He was divinely selfless. Visionary *and* realist, he seems
to have radiated divine contagion. He mixed with crowds
and was even charged with being "a wine bibber" and
associating with "sinners and publicans." He was preoccupied with demons, trafficking with evil spirits. The
poor, the disinherited, the diseased, the demented felt
divine compassion in him and were healed by his touch.
He saw in all of them God's children.

Historians have sought to categorize him according
to the religious groupings of his day. Some insist he was
a Pharisee of the Pharisees, however much or little he

may have differed with them. Dissent—*within* the law—
was the hallmark of the Pharisees. Other historians
reason that he belonged to the lower social and religious
stratification of the Pharisees, the *amme haaretz,* who
were closer to the soil of the country than to the academies of Jerusalem. Some insist that he was an Essene,
sharing their mysticism, their other-worldly disposition,
yearning for the heavenly Messiah and his salvation.
Others see in him another Hebrew prophet, in direct
communion with God, fearlessly proclaiming God's word
to sinning Israel. A Zealot he could not have been. Their
emphasis on direct action—the "dagger men"—on behalf of their nationalistic religion is alien to everything
in the personality and teachings of Jesus. Total lack of
concern with the fate of his country is the great lacuna in
his preachments. Was he an apocalyptist and Messianist?
There is much to confirm this view.[57]

By his unique personality, Jesus did not fit into any
of these categories. Something of each of these is in
him, but he defies all of them. Men of such extraordinary
perception and passion in the spiritual life of mankind
as Jesus was are what "sports" are in biology. Jesus is
his own category.

That he came of Pharisaic stock—and perhaps from
the humblest level of society, the *amme haaretz*—seems
most likely. That he remained steadfast to his Judaism
as he understood it there can be no serious doubt. He
made his pilgrimage to Jerusalem and the Temple on
the Passover as the laws of Moses prescribed, paid his
tithe and advised others to do it, wore his fringes as
ritual required, held *seder* with his associates as did every
faithful Jewish householder, prayed all his life to the
God of his fathers. By Him he was enthralled; in Him
he found his consolation. With but small differences, such
as obtain among all faithful in every communion, Jesus
observed every ceremonial requirement. The soil and

landscape of Palestine is in every parable he spoke. "The life of Jesus could not have been spent, nor the teachings of Jesus given, in any other environment than that of the Jewish community. The Jewish society, and Jewish values, are presupposed in everything he said or did so completely, assumed so naturally, that no open reference to them is necessary. What he had to say about God and man would not have been understood in any other environment."[58] "Jesus remained steadfast to old Torah; till his dying day he continued to observe the ceremonial laws like a true Pharisaic Jew."[59]

II

JESUS THE RESURRECTED CHRIST

Transfiguration and Transubstantiation

The same Gospels that give us—by inference, conjecture, deduction on the part of the critical scholars—an intimation of the personality and teaching of the Palestinian rabbi, give us a full, glowing view of Jesus as the heavenly Messiah. That was the primary aim of the Gospel authors.

Many problems confront the devout student—problems in text, harmonizing conflicting data, filling in lacunae, identifying specific historic situations behind certain pronouncements and incidents on the part of Jesus; above all, making peace with the "mysteries," or with what defies reason. The heart will not adore what the mind disowns. Pious Christian scholars have given us brilliant analyses of New Testament texts and contents. Ultimately, however, it is faith—not analysis, not delving for objective facts—that leads to the glad acceptance of the testimony of the Gospels.

As the heavenly Messiah, Jesus moves on earth but is above the earth; he speaks and pleads and suffers with and for sinning humans, but is himself more heavenly than human—solitary in the midst of the crowds, unique, awesome—inexorably moving towards the fulfillment of his divine destiny: the Cross on Calvary and the salvation of Israel and mankind.

> He was in the world, and the world was made through him, yet the world knew him not. He came to his own home, and his people received him not. But to all who received him, who believed in his name, he gave power to become children of God; who were born, not of blood nor of the will of the flesh nor of the will of man, but of God.[60]

The Gospel writers transform the Palestinian "Son of Man" into the "Son of the living God." He is now the perfect fulfillment of God's promises voiced by the Hebrew prophets and psalmists. He is transfigured into an awesome vision:

> And after six days Jesus took him Peter and James and John, and led them up a high mountain apart by themselves; and he was transfigured before them, and his garments became glistening, intensely white, as no fuller on earth could bleach them. And there appeared before them Elijah with Moses; and they were talking to Jesus. And Peter said to Jesus, "Master, it is well that we are here; let us make three booths, one for you and one for Moses and one for Elijah." For he did not know what to say, for they were exceedingly afraid. And a cloud overshadowed them, and a voice came out of the cloud, "This is my beloved Son; listen to him."[61]

Henceforth, this vision has held enthralled the devout Christians.

His call is "Follow me!" The Kingdom of earth, with all its woes, is yielding to the Kingdom of Heaven. Jesus

was the divine herald. His mission was to die on the
cross and bring redemption to sinning humanity.

The Gospels recall his career and his teachings; but
their primary concern is to proclaim the good news of
the coming of the heaven-sent Messiah and his precious
gift of salvation. Repent. "Prepare ye the way of the
Lord." Thus, while they give us specific utterances and
record specific events, their chief concern is with the
divine mysteries behind what man can grasp and record.
The glow of the supernatural, therefore, predominates.
To understand fully, the critic must turn worshipper.

His life on earth is rehearsed: his conception, baptism,
temptation, preaching, suffering, dying on the cross, rising from the tomb—all in keeping with divine prediction,
so that the Scriptures may be fulfilled.[62]

> Now the birth of Jesus Christ took place in this way. When
> his mother Mary had been betrothed to Joseph, before they
> came together she found to be with child of the Holy Spirit;
> and her husband Joseph, being a just man and unwilling to
> put her to shame, resolved to divorce her quietly. But as he
> considered this, behold, an angel of the Lord appeared to him
> in a dream, saying: "Joseph, son of David, do not fear to take
> Mary your wife, for that which is conceived in her is of the
> Holy Spirit; she will bear a son, and you shall call his name
> Jesus, for he will save his people from their sins." All this
> took place to fulfill what the Lord had spoken by the prophet:
> "Behold a virgin shall conceive and bear a son, and his name
> shall be called Emanuel."[63]

His supposed Davidic ancestry is no longer emphasized; begotten of the Holy Spirit, his human father is
an embarrassment.

Each of the four Gospels, as we have observed, makes
its peculiar emphasis; their variations, however, are within one all-embracing consensus: the divinely endowed
Messiah come to redeem mankind, even as all the disputations of the Pharisees were within one all-embracing

belief: the divinely-revealed law given to Moses on Mount Sinai. Thus the Gospel according to Matthew is primarily a manual of Christian teaching, with Jesus as Israel's Messiah, He is not only transfigured but is transubstantiated. He himself made it clear to his chosen disciples:

> Now as they were eating [the Passover meal,] Jesus took bread, and blessed, and broke it, and gave it to the disciples and said, "Take, eat; this is my body." And he took a cup, and when he had given thanks he gave it to them, saying, "Drink of it, all of you; for this is my blood of the covenant, which is poured out for many for the forgiveness of sins. I tell you I shall not drink again of this fruit of the vine until that day when I drink it new with you in my Father's kingdom."[64]

Mark sketches the portrait of Jesus of Nazareth as the Son of God, the hero of supernatural works. The miracles, which are a stumbling block to the critical student, are proof of his divinity. They who have eyes to see will note, believe and adore. Luke traces the genealogy of Jesus from Adam as the divinely-ordained Savior of all men, however sinful and despised they be.

> Just so, I tell you, there will be more joy in heaven over one sinner who repents than over ninety-nine righteous persons who need no more repentance.[65]

This conviction is expressed through engaging parables: the faithful shepherd, the good Samaritan, the prodigal son, the upright judge, and a number of others. In John the climax of the Messiah-Redeemer is reached. Jesus is the Logos, the Word, the only begotten son of God.

> In the beginning was the Word, and the Word was with God, and the Word was God. He was in the beginning with God; all things were made through him, and without him was not

anything made that was made. In him was life, and the life was the light of men. The light shines in the darkness, and the darkness has not overcome it.[66]

Jesus is now "the way, and the truth, and life; no one comes to the Father but by me."[67]

Henceforth the believer in the Gospels must take his shoes off his feet, for he is standing on holy ground. Critical analysis, the handmaiden, must yield to the mistress, faith. By faith and faith alone are the true believer's perplexities resolved and intellectual peace found. The dictum of the old Hebrew prophet finds supreme fulfillment: "The righteous liveth by his faith."[68]

Jesus the Christ, the Redeemer, the Savior, not Jesus the Palestinian rabbi, has dominated the ages.

Between the presentations of the Palestinian rabbi and the resurrected Messiah are many other portraits of Jesus, created by devout but critical scholars and believers. They vary with the scholars and the intellectual climates of the ages. They are carefully documented. In his name the pure in heart, of all branches of Christendom, see God—men such as Francis of Assisi of Medieval days, Albert Schweitzer of our own time; in his name, too, tragically, fanatics burned and slaughtered fellow humans, and crucified their Master over and over again. Crusaders murdered and pillaged in his holy name as they travelled to the Holy Land to redeem holy places. Torquemada burned people at the stake in his name to save their souls. Many a drunken pogrom gangster crossed himself as he butchered his Jewish neighbor on Easter Sunday in celebration of his resurrection; many a Prince of the Church goose-steeped with the Nazis. Founders of religions are betrayed not so much by the doubters and unbelievers as by their zealous disciples.

The temper of the age and the bias of his following determined the image of Jesus in every age. In the days of the Crusades he was a militant figure inspiring—even lashing—his official followers into battle; in our time he is—for hosts of devout men—a social reformer driving the money changer—the exploiters, the racists, the bigots—out of the Temple. Practical, flat-minded men see him as a Big Business Executive. Personal piety, however unorthodox, utter devotion, superb integrity, a full measure of devotion on the part of the latter-day evangelists enter into the twentieth-century representations of Jesus, even as in ancient and Medieval days. The heterodox, varied imagery of him will continue, image dissolving into image, as the ages advance and men cherish the sacred and raise their eyes to the Star of Bethlehem.

Paul of Tarsus: Slave of Christ, Apostle to the Gentiles

Next to Jesus, Paul is the most dominant figure in the founding and history of Christianity. He is credited by historians with being the real founder of Christianity and the Church. Neither emerging nor later Christianity is thinkable without Paul. Most zealous of the apostles —volatile, extremist, relentless in his driving passion for the faith "in Christ," at once bitterly unyielding and opportunistic, visionary and builder—he became the central creative genuis of the new faith.

"For me to live is Christ."[1] He was the enthralled slave of Christ. That was the primary compulsion of his life. He was a man possessed by one passion: " . . . that at the name of Jesus every knee should bow in heaven and on earth and under the earth, and every tongue confess that Jesus Christ is Lord, to the glory of God the Father."[2] He cut the emergent faith from its Jewish moorings and projected it as a world-conquering faith in the name of the Christ. " . . . although without Paul Christianity had reached gentiles, it is Paul more than any other man who was responsible for the fact that Christianity was not a Jewish sect but an independent body with an independent life."[3] It is agreed that it was Paul who laid the foundations of Christian theology that have survived to our own day.

A picture of Paul has come down to us from a composite apocalyptic book of the second century; competent scholars credit it as trustworthy historic material:

"A man of moderate stature, with crisp (scanty) hair, crooked legs, blue eyes, large knit brows, and long nose, at times looking like a man, at times like an angel, Paul came forward and preached to the men of Iconium: 'Blessed are they who keep themselves chaste [unmarried]; for they shall be called the Temple of God. Blessed are they that mortify their bodies and souls for unto them speaketh God. Blessed be the souls and bodies of virgins; for they shall receive the reward of their chastity.'"[4]

Sources

The primary literary source for the life and teachings of Paul, and for the revelation of his personality, is his letters to his disciples and congregations in Asia Minor, Greece, Rome, and Palestine. These formidable tracts, which define Paul's teachings in an intimate, personal manner, express his hopes, his fears, his passions, his sorrows, his bitter frustrations. He stands revealed as the impassioned and embattled, often embittered, apostle of the Lord Jesus.

All his Epistles must be read with caution. They cover a period between the year 50 and 63-64. They were in the process of revision for one century. They are "extraordinarily difficult to interpret,"[5] one scholar testifies, and many concur. Students have difficulty establishing their exact dates and the specific circumstances that prompted them. The "facts" are inferred, for the most part. It must be borne in mind that these letters are occasional pieces and present only a part of the total body of Paul's work. The rest has been lost to us. It must be remembered, further, that he wrote these letters in later life. Recollections of events—and especially personal speeches and behavior—after a stormy life are bound to be out of focus, particularly in the case of so emotional and so volatile a man as Paul. "Earlier convictions passionately held and then passionately abandoned after a volcanic internal crisis, can not but present themselves in distorted shape."[6] Not all of the reputed Epistles of Paul are genuine, and there are always the problems that generally occur in transmission and translation of Bible documents. Many figures of speech are alien to us; corruptions in text are common.

Nevertheless, Paul's letters are the primary source, and they reveal an original, towering intellect—a fanatically sincere personality, consumed with a passion for his Lord Christ. He was primarily the propagandist heralding the good news of salvation in Christ. He was not the teacher, not the pastor, not the patient builder. Always, under any and all circumstances, he was the evangelist. "His calling, as he conceived it, is to plant, not to water. He not only does not wish to build on other men's foundations; he does not really enjoy building on his own."[7] He was too tempestuous a spirit for that.

The Facts of His Life—Environment and Personality

Paul was a younger contemporary of Jesus. Jesus was born about the year 2 B.C.E.; Paul, according to the best estimation, was born several years later. The year of his death is not known precisely either. It is believed that he died after the year 63, perhaps in 64, or even as late as 65, a victim of Nero's hatred of the Christians. Though contemporaries, Jesus and Paul had never met.

Paul was born in Tarsus, the Greek-speaking capital

city of Cilicia on the Mediterranean Sea, which was part of Syria. Tarsus, a cultural and business center, had a population of approximately half a million. It enjoyed a good harbor and commanded the only pass through the Tarsus mountains. The military and trade routes between East and West, across Asia Minor, passed through the city. The population was heterogeneous, and included Jews. It was a center of Hellenistic culture and also a seat of Jewish learning. A contemporary of Paul's testifies that he had "found the atmosphere of the city harsh and strange and little conducive to the philosophical life, for nowhere are men more addicted than here to luxury; jesters and full of insolence are they all; and they attend more to their fine linen than the Athenians did to wisdom."[8] All the vices of an ancient pagan port were to be found there. The luxurious ritual devoted to the worship of Baal-Tarz, the nature deity of the locality, annually cremated and annually reborn; the riotous Mithraic processions; the rampant degenerated Hellenism—imported for the most part by sailors—the practice of prostitution and unnatural vice, taken for granted by the Greek and Asiatic elements of the population—all this must have outraged a zealous and sensitive young Jew.

Paul was thus reared in the Diaspora, as a member of the Jewish minority, conditioned under the threat of a menacing and glittering pagan Hellenistic environment, for which the Jews had one contemptuous word, *idolatry!* This had a far-reaching effect in determining his religious life. Young, highly intelligent, sensitive, he was undoubtedly affected by the Greek as well as by the Jewish culture about him. Even his radical conversion, all-consuming in his personality, did not change his Hellenistic views of the Scriptures, which represented "strange fires" from the standpoint of the Pharisaic masters. The Hellenistic allegoric method seems to have fitted the natural bent of his mind.

His pious parents named him Saul. We know hardly anything specific of them. His father was evidently a reasonably well-to-do free man and Roman citizen. Paul seems to have had a sister in Jerusalem, and her son, Mark, was a comfort to him at critical points in his life. He refers to himself as a "Hebrew of the Hebrews," of the tribe of Benjamin, and a zealous Pharisee, student of the Law.[9] Later in life, while engaging in missionary work, he changed his name to Paul. It was not an uncommon practice for Jews to have gentile versions of their Hebrew names. Perhaps *Paul* is derived from "little," or "the little fellow." He was raised in strict conformity to the religious standards of his people and his faith. By nature he was a sensitive, affectionate youngster, given to questioning and argumentation.

We have no clear exposition of the Synagogue practices in Asia Minor at this time. Most of our knowledge of the Judaism of this period comes from Palestine Jewry. However, we do know, of course, that Jewish life had its center and inspiration in the Synagogue, which served as the people's house of worship, communal center and school house.

The Jewish community of Tarsus was, no doubt, as faithful as any. Saul was circumcised on the eighth day of his life, in keeping with the Biblical requirement. He received his earliest instruction in the home and in the synagogue, as did all Jewish boys. In the synagogue the Torah was read in Hebrew on the Sabbaths and holy days and freely translated into Aramaic or Greek. The prayers were in both Hebrew and Greek. The sermon, delivered by any competent member of the community or itinerant preacher, was in the vernacular and was devoted to the exposition of the oral traditions of Judaism

—the free, unofficial interpretations of Bible text: legends, snatches of biography of the authoritative masters, fanciful fables and homilies. No doubt young Saul heard expositions of the apocalyptic coming of the Messiah and of "the end of days," which were the dominant themes of the age. By nature he was susceptible to this type of preaching and belief.

We have no intimation that he ever married. Family felicity is completely missing in the records. His constant derogation of "the flesh" and his "blessed be the virgins" lead us to the belief that he was too much of an ascetic for normal family life.

He was a child of a minority culture. The Jewish-Gentile relationships seem to have been reasonably good in the Tarsus of his day. We hear of Jews eating with non-Jews. Young Saul quite likely resented this as a violation of the faith. He was undoubtedly familiar with the Mosiac laws demanding separation from the heathens and their idolatries: "Ye shall not walk in the customs of the nations . . . Ye shall not go after other gods, of the gods of the people that are round about you."[10] Such stern teachings appealed to his nature. Later in life he affirms his authenticity as a good Jew: "If any other man thinks he has reason for confidence in the flesh, I have more: circumcised on the eighth day, of the people of Israel, of the tribe of Benjamin, a Hebrew born of Hebrews; as to the law a Pharisee, as to zeal a persecutor of the church, as to righteousness under the law blameless."[11]

For a time young Saul is believed to have studied under Gamaliel I in Jerusalem, a leading scholar and jurist, and prominent member of the Sanhedrin. Gamaliel was a most attractive personality. We today would call him a "liberal." He was teaching and interpreting the Torah in the tradition of his illustrious grandfather, Hillel. In Acts Gamaliel is represented as a wise and patient man.

When a mob, under extremist leaders, attacked Peter and the apostles, Gamaliel stood up to them and pleaded for understanding and patience:

> But a Pharisee in the council named Gamaliel, a teacher of the law, held in honor by all the people, stood up and ordered the man to be put aside for a while. And he said to them, "Men of Israel, take care what you do with these men . . . keep away from these men and let them alone; for if this plan or this undertaking is of men, it will fail; but if it is of God, you will not be able to overthrow them. You might even be found opposing God.[12]

If Saul sat at the feet of this man, he undoubtedly gained specific information from him, but he did not catch the master's spirit, nor his approach to the law. Saul was too authoritarian a young zealot for that.

He spoke the Aramaic and Greek of his Jewish community. His knowledge of Hebrew was limited. His quotations from Scriptures are from the Greek versions only. He cites the *haggadah*—the non-legal, the fanciful, the mystic—in which the popular preachers engaged; he does not cite the *halacha*—the law, which was disciplined and authoritative. Scholars see reflected in his writings the Hellenistic literature, including the writings of the allegorist Philo of Alexandria, not the rabbinic of the respected academies. Always he was the fiery preacher—brilliant, excessive, violent in emphasis and speech. Recalling his student days at Jerusalem he reports: "I advanced in Judaism beyond many of my own age among my people, so extremely zealous was I for the traditions of my fathers; . . . according to the strict party of our religion I have lived as a Pharisee."[13] This involved not only ritualistic minutiae, observed in grim legalism, but the heady wine of folk mysticism: belief in angels, demons, heaven and hell, magic and miracle, apocalyptic messianism, resurrection of the dead. The prophet

Ezekiel's chariot rumbled in the heavens and roused every form of unearthly speculation. All these excited and dominated the minds of a branch of the Pharisees. Among these was young Paul. He was conditioned to become transfixed by the heavenly Messiah.

We know nothing directly of his economic status; he seems to have been financially comfortable. He shows no money worries in his travels. He was a Roman citizen, which served him in good stead at crises in his life. By trade he was a tentmaker, as was his father.

The Hellenistic environment of his youth in Tarsus enveloped and penetrated him, creating a conflict in his life. Like Rebecca he felt two worlds struggling within him, his own Torah-true Judaism and the alien, pagan Hellenism. He would be true to his own ancestral faith, but he was baited by the heathen about him.

This conflict was much more than environmental. Conflict was at the roots of his soul.

While, in his youth, he obeyed every detail of the Law he was not at peace with it. Proud of his Jewish heritage and people, in his soul nevertheless was a seething discontent.

Zealous, mystic, extremist, speculative as well as intensive activist, argumentative, even cantankerous, subject to violently shifting moods and epileptic seizures, he had a natural disposition for the other-worldly messianism that was in the air at the time. Visiting preachers in the synagogues excited his imagination constantly.

He was a split personality at war with himself. He confesses in anguish: "I do not understand my own actions. For I do not do what I want, but I do the very things I hate."[14]

He complains of "a thorn in the flesh, a messenger of Satan," and yearns for liberation from "the prison house of the body." Clearly, a psychopathic tendency dominated his personality.[15]

The Stoning of Stephen and the Road
to Damascus

In the spring of the year 35 (or 36) came the crucial transformation in the life of Paul. He was in his late twenties; Jesus, with whom Paul had never met, had been in his unknown grave for some half dozen years. Now came their first confrontation, and Paul's transformation from a zealous Pharisee to a relentless apostle to the gentiles.

A Hellenistic Jew by the name of Stephen was stoned to death in Jerusalem; Saul was involved. It was a deeply traumatic experience.

Stephen was the leader of a special group of disciples of Jesus. He had gone about the synagogues preaching the Christ Jesus, arousing acrimonius debates. He was, evidently, a brilliant and militant contraversialist. He is described in the partisan sources as "a man full of faith and of the Holy Spirit." In Acts we have a report of his stoning by an infuriated mob of zealots who had taken the law into their own hands.[16] Saul "consented."

His people were yielding to the new apostasy preached by Peter, Stephen and their associates. Saul was not a man to stand idly by. He felt the compulsion of the Law: "thou shalt surely reprove thy neighbor and not bear sin because of him."[17]

Brought before a court, Stephen outraged the presiding authorities with a long and inflammatory speech.

Then they cast him out of the city and stoned him; and the witnesses laid down their garments at the feet of a young man named Saul . . . And Saul was consenting to his death. Devout men buried Stephen, and made a great lamentation over him. But Saul laid waste the church, and entering house after house, he dragged off men and women and committed them to prison.[18]

Later in life, as an embattled apostle of Jesus the
Christ, Paul recalled the folly of his youth; it had been
a tormenting memory. Repeatedly he recalls how he
had persecuted the followers of Jesus. "For you have
heard of my former life in Judaism, how I persecuted
the church of God violently and tried to destroy it."[19]

Persecution involved physical flogging as prescribed
in the law of Moses.[20]

Horrified by the inroads the preachers of Jesus Christ
were making, Saul secured a commission from the High
Priest at Jerusalem to go to Damascus to exterminate
the rising Christian apostasy in that city. On the road
to Damascus he had the transforming experience of his
life:

> But Saul, still breathing threats and murder against the dis-
> ciples of the Lord, went to the high priest and asked him for
> letters to the synagogues at Damascus, so that if he found any
> belonging to the Way, men or women, he might bring them
> bound to Jerusalem. Now as he journeyed he approached Da-
> mascus, and suddenly a light from heaven flashed about him.
> And he fell to the ground and heard a voice saying to him,
> "Saul, Saul, why do you persecute me." And he said, "Who
> are you, Lord?" And he said, "I am Jesus, whom you are
> persecuting; but rise and enter the city, and you will be told
> what you are to do." The men who were travelling with him
> stood speechless, hearing the voice but seeing no one. Saul
> arose from the ground; and when his eyes were opened, he
> could see nothing; so they led him by the hand and brought
> him into Damascus. And for three days he was without sight,
> and neither ate nor drank.[21]

Henceforth Saul was to be the chosen instrument of
the resurrected, heavenly Christ, charged with the mission to carry the name of the Lord Jesus "before gentiles, the kings and the sons of Israel." His sight
miraculously restored by Ananias—once a loyal Jew,
now turning Christian—he was baptized as the apostle
of the religion he had been persecuting.

And all who heard him were amazed, and said, "Is not this the man who made havoc in Jerusalem of those who called on his name? And he has come here for this purpose, to bring them bound before the chief priests!" But Saul increased all the more in strength, and confounded the Jews who lived in Damascus by proving that Jesus was the Christ.[22]

Paul was now on his career as the relentless apostle of the Lord Jesus the Christ. He was now a man possessed.

The Great Divide between Paul and his people, between Judaism and Christianity, originates on the road to Damascus. Isaiah, in the hour of his vision, exclaims, "Mine eyes have seen the King, the Lord of Hosts!" Paul, referring to his hour of vision, exclaims, "Have I not seen Jesus Christ, our Lord?"[23] Henceforth the issue between Synagogue and Church is "the Lord of hosts" versus "Jesus Christ our Lord."

Missionary Journeys:
Preaching, Argumentation, Persecution, Epistles

FIRST JOURNEY

The zeal, energy, initiative and extent of Paul's missionary travels form an amazing—if not a clear—story. For some fourteen years he travelled by sea and land along the eastern, northeastern, and northern coastline of the Mediterranean Sea, enduring every conceivable privation, meeting with hostility of mobs and officials. Repeatedly he was imprisoned; five times he was flogged by synagogue authorities; three times he was beaten by Roman officers; three times he was shipwrecked, and once he was afloat for a night and a day in open sea. By deliberate choice he travelled to lands where no one had preached the gospel before. For the most part his routes took him to centers of trade and culture of the Graeco-Roman world. Practically everywhere he found the nu-

cleus of a Jewish community, and Jewish hostility to
his preaching. "It has been calculated," reports one historian, "that in his first missionary journey he travelled
about 650 miles, in the second 875, and in the third,
well over 1000, without counting other journeys before
and after."[24] In our time such distances may be unim-
pressive, but we must imagine ourselves among the
primitive conditions and the hazards of the first century.
All along Paul was working to pay his own way, and
suffering from some "bodily ailment." He pleads elo-
quently, in retrospect, and in self-righteousness, that he
had carried on "in danger from rivers, danger from robbers, danger from my own people, danger from Gentiles,
danger in the city, danger in the wilderness, danger at
sea, danger from false brethren; in toil and hardship,
through many sleepless nights, in hunger and thirst,
often without food, in cold and exposure."[25] He was
driven by a remorseless compulsion to bring the gospel
to the Gentiles. And he was in extreme haste, for he
shared the apocalyptic conviction that the world was
coming to an end; the Judgment Day was just over the
horizon.

For a brief period prior to entering on his journeys
he retired to Arabia, presumably for meditation and
stock-taking. The desert lures the disturbed soul in the
hours of crucial decision—Moses, for instance, finding
his burning bush in the desert, Elijah his cave, John the
Baptist his Way.

Teaming up with a man by the name of Barnabas, a
native of Cyprus, he started on his travels from Damascus.[26] First they journeyed to Cyprus in search of
funds for the Jerusalem congregation and preaching the
glad news of the resurrected Jesus. There they won to
their cause the Roman procounsul, Sergius Paulus, "a
man of intelligence." About this time *Saul* became *Paul*,
perhaps in honor of his new friend; perhaps more likely,

Paul had clung to him from childhood, as we have noted.

Travelling through Asia Minor he preached in synagogues of several cities, especially in Damascus and Antioch. His primary message was one: Jesus is the resurrected Messiah foretold in Scriptures.

> For I delivered to you as of first importance what I also received, that Christ died for our sins in accordance with the scriptures, that he was buried, that he was raised on the third day in accordance with the scriptures . . .[27]

The crucified Christ was ever before him.

His Jewish hearers were shocked, even outraged, especially since the preacher was the same man who had persecuted others for accepting the very same doctrine. In Damascus he was forced to flee in the stealth of night. In another city he was credited with healing a cripple. The Greeks of the community hailed him and his travelling companion as gods. The Jews, however, drove the two out of town as trouble-makers. He met with a friendlier reception in the nearby town of Erbe. From there he returned to Antioch to report to the church authorities. From Antioch the evangelization of Asia Minor began and there the first church was founded. In Antioch, too, the term "Christian" was used for the first time.

CIRCUMCISION—OF THE FLESH AND OF THE SPIRIT

The new movement was torn with dissension. The emergent religion had not yet attained coherence or authority. Further, Paul was not a man to bring calm and harmony to anything in which he was involved. His was too contentious a personality.

The issue that split the movement at this early date was the question of circumcision: Could a non-Jew become a Christian without first undergoing circumcision,

as is required by Mosaic law? The destiny of the emergent Christianity depended on the answer to this question. In the year 49 (or 50) Paul returned to Jerusalem
for a conference on this issue. The only accounts we
have of this contest comes from Paul's own testimony
and from the pro-Paul Acts.

Paul, it would seem, had done his work well and presented the conference with a *fait accompli;* he was master
of the situation. The answer, after some violent debate,
was in the affirmative, thus validating Paul's independent
decision, which he had already implemented in his missionary work. It was the Holy Spirit's pleasure, Paul
agreed, that no superfluous obstacles be placed in the way
of winning converts from among the gentiles. Circumcision was a stumbling block. Paul resorted to his classic
reasoning and the allegorical method of Bible interpretation. "Once we are in Christ, circumcision means nothing: the faith that finds its expression in love is all that
matters."[28] The allegoric method enabled Paul to reason
his way out of the ceremonial law, and out of Judaism
altogether. Thus the rising church formally took the
step that brought it to the Great Divide. Henceforth it
was a gentile movement. Peter and James, the brother
of Jesus, were saddened and embittered by this development. Paul attacked Peter violently for seeking to retain
his Jewish ties, and for being undecisive. Later, in his
letter to the wavering Galatians, he insists, "Christ has
set us free; stand fast therefore and do not submit again
to the yoke of slavery."[29]

SECOND JOURNEY

What is considered Paul's second missionary journey
took place between the years 50 and 53. A quarrel between Paul and his oldest companion, Barnabas, caused
them to separate. Accompanied by two new disciples,
Silas and Timothy, he proceeded to visit the churches

he had founded in Asia Minor; then he went on to
Greece. At Philippi the travelling missionaries were beat-
en and imprisoned for a time. The magistrate, learning
that Paul was a Roman citizen, released him and ordered
him to move on. At Thessalonica they followed their
usual practice and started their preaching in the local
synagogue, but were soon driven out of town by the
Jews, who were offended by their talk of the new Lord
Jesus. At nearby Berea they met with a friendlier reception. Leaving Silas and Timothy behind, Paul moved
on to Athens.

On the Hill of Mars, opposite the Acropolis, Paul
delivered his famous speech on the "unknown god." In
Acts (which, we must remember, is a second or third
hand source and pro-Paul) the sermon and its background is reported:

> Now while Paul was waiting for them at Athens, his spirit
> was provoked within him as he saw that the city was full of
> idols. So he argued in the synagogues with the Jews and the
> devout persons, and in the market place every day with those
> who chanced to be there. Some also of the Epicurean and
> Stoic philosophers met him. And some said, "What would this
> babbler say?" Others said, "He seems to be a preacher of
> foreign divinities"—because he preached Jesus and the resur-
> rection. And they took him and brought him to the Are-opagus,
> saying, "May we know what this new teaching is which you
> present? . . . . "

So Paul, standing in the middle of the Areopagus,
said:

> "Men of Athens, I perceive that in every way you are very
> religious. For as I passed along, and observed the objects of
> your worship, I found also an altar with this inscription, 'To
> an unknown god.' What therefore you worship as unknown,
> this I proclaim to you. For God who made the world and
> everything in it, being Lord of heaven and earth, does not live

in shrines made by man, nor is he served by human hands, as though he needed anything, since he himself gives to all men life and breath and everything. And he made from one every nation of men to live on all the face of the earth, having determined allotted periods and boundaries of their habitation, that they should seek God, in the hope that they might feel after him and find him. Yet he is not far from each one of us, for

'in him we live and move and have our being'; as even some of your poets have said, 'For we are indeed his offspring.'

Being then God's offspring, we ought not to think that the Deity is like gold, or silver, or stone, a representation by the art and imagination of man. The times of ignorance God overlooked, but now he commands all men everywhere to repent, because he has fixed a day on which he will judge the world in righteousness by a man whom he has appointed, and of this he has given assurance to all men by raising him from the dead." Now when they heard of the resurrection of the dead, some mocked; but others said, "We shall hear you again about this."[30]

The Athenians were too sophisticated for his preaching. To the "philosophers" Paul was "a babbler." Upon hearing his summons to repentance on the authority of a resurrected divinely appointed man, the Athenians turned their backs on the apostle. It was not his best effort. He left Athens with a deep sense of failure. There is no mention in the New Testament of a church in Athens.

He went on to Corinth where, for some year and a half, he preached "and argued" in synagogues on the Sabbath and whenever and wherever he found an audience, earning his livelihood by practicing his trade as tentmaker. Corinth was a city of luxury and moral laxity. Paul, the Jew turned Christian, found it shocking. It harbored a racially mixed population, including a good many Jews who, finding his preaching offensive, dragged him before the city magistrate. Here he wrote his first tract, perhaps early in the 50s, "Paul, Silvanus, and Timothy, to the Church of the Thessalonians in God the Father and the Lord Jesus Christ: Grace to you and peace."[31] Failing to win to his cause the Jews, the intellectuals, the well-placed, he turned to the obscure proletariat, the disinherited meek of the earth—the slaves, the dock workers, the small artisans—and his message was aimed at their hearts: not sophisticated philosophy, not the learned discourse, but "Christ cruci-fied." At Corinth he established one of his most effective churches.

THIRD JOURNEY

Paul's third journey took him back to some of the communities where he had founded congregations. Again at Ephesus—where stood the temple to the goddess Artemus—he stayed for three years (c. 53-56). Here he knew much suffering. Reports had reached him of quarrels and backsliding among the new Christians in the several congregations that he had organized. Two of his letters were composed here: to the Galatians and to the Corinthians.

The epistle to the Galatians is often referred to as the Magna Charta of Christian liberty. The Galatians were backsliding; they were having second thoughts about breaking completely with the Mosaic ceremonial laws. Paul writes in bitterness and in anger. The point at issue was: Must a Gentile become a Jew before he may become a Christian? Involved is the binding power of the Mosaic law and of the Mosaic covenant. Paul argues in the negative and heaps scorn upon those who disagree with him. "For freedom Christ has set us free; stand fast therefore and do not submit again to a yoke of slavery."[32] Any one who preaches a gospel contrary to his "let him be accursed."[33] He is the only true apostle; he alone was predestined and ordained of God to preach the true faith. Paul deepened still more the gulf between himself and the Jews.

His letter to the Corinthians reaffirms Paul's belief in the resurrection of the dead. It contains his loftiest affirmation of *agapé*—love, in the sense of supreme harmony of the soul, Christ's gift to his disciples. It is often designated as Love's Song of Songs. "In it Paul reaches the highest pinnacle of preacher and poet alike."[34]

If I speak in the tongues of men and of angels, but have not love, I am a noisy gong or a clanging cymbal. And if I have prophetic powers, and understand all mysteries and all knowledge, and if I have all faith, so as to remove mountains, but have not love, I am nothing. If I give away all I have, and if I deliver my body to be burned, but have not love, I gain nothing.

Love is patient and kind; love is not jealous or boastful; it is not arrogant or rude. Love does not insist on its own way; it is not irritable or resentful; it does not rejoice at wrong, but rejoices in the right. Love bears all things, believes all things, hopes all things, endures all things.

Love never ends; as for prophecies, they will pass away; as for tongues, they will cease; as for knowledge, it will pass away. For our knowledge is imperfect and our prophecy is imperfect; but when the perfect comes, the imperfect will pass away. When I was a child, I spoke like a child, I thought like a child, I reasoned like a child; when I became a man, I gave up childish ways. For now we see in a mirror dimly, but then face to face. Now I know in part; then I shall understand fully, even as I have been fully understood. So faith, hope, love abide, these three; but the greatest of these is love.[35]

But Paul signs his letter:

I, Paul, write this greeting with my own hand. If any one has no love for the Lord, let him be accursed.[36]

Riots ended his activities at Ephesus. Violent opposition came from an entirely new quarter, the silversmiths, who were engaged in a thriving business fashioning sacred trinkets: charms, amulets, altars, magical formulae, especially images of the goddess Artemis. When Paul, the rabbi turned apostle, branded these as idolatry, he was interfering with their trades and their livelihoods. Paul fled the community.

The year 56 found him travelling to Corinth again, and to Macedonia, in an effort to restore harmony among his quarreling disciples. He was dreaming of a visit to Rome. His letter to the Romans was written about this time. Scholars consider this tract to be the finest exposition of Christianity ever written. The central theme is the meaning of salvation in Christ, with particular reference to the Mosaic law and the destiny of the Jewish people. His all-consuming conviction is expressed in his oft-repeated phrase, "in Christ." "For Christ is the end of the law" [Or, *has superseded the law.*]

Again Paul widened and deepened the breach between his gospel and Judaism. In the spring of 57 (or 58) he set out for Jerusalem. His closest collaborators warned him against the move; there was too much angry opposition to him in the Holy City. Paul, however, was not a man to be intimidated.

His coming was anticipated by outraged Jewry and the local authorities. He was the harbinger of trouble. Some considered him a Messianist-Zealot. After some days in Caesarea—again despite the warnings of his most faithful followers—he pressed on to Jerusalem. He seems to have had a deep yearning for approval by the elders of the Jerusalem congregation and by James, the brother of Jesus. Also, he was bringing some funds with him for the Jerusalem congregation, which he had been collecting for some time.

JERUSALEM AGAIN

The Temple was crowded with pilgrims, come from the Diaspora as well as from Palestine, in observance of the Festival of Shabuot, which celebrates the giving of the Law to Moses on Mount Sinai. Paul was recognized by some Asiatic Jews who had come from Ephesus and who had heard his abusive talk of Jews and Judaism and his denial of the Mosaic law. He was charged by these pious pilgrims with bringing with him, in defiance of the law, an uncircumcised heathen into the Temple. This is an offense for which the Torah requires the death penalty. In addition, Paul launched into a sermon extolling Jesus the resurrected Christ to pious Jewish pilgrims in their own national sanctuary on their holy day dedicated to the law. The enraged crowd turned on him in fury, and it was only the Roman officers' quick thinking that saved him from being stoned to death.

Paul was now in serious trouble: arrest, in the teeth of an ugly mob, and charges of Messianic pretensions. He was chained and imprisoned for his own safety and transferred to "the Castle" at Caesarea for protective custody.

Prison walls only deepened and increased his zeal. He preached the resurrected Christ all the more ardently. A rare opportunity came to him when the puppet King Herod Agrippa and his sister Berenice paid a state visit to the newly appointed Procurator, Festus. Not knowing what to do with the pesty apostle the Roman agent asked the royal visitors' advice. He did not want to get involved in a squabble with Jewish fanatics. Herod Agrippa, something of a Jew himself, asked to hear Paul expound his views and present his case. Thus the embattled apostle had the rare opportunity of presenting his case before Jewish royalty and Roman authority. His self-defense is a masterly and shrewd account of his activities and beliefs.

He recalls his youth as an ardent Pharisee and battler for the faith of his fathers:

> I myself was convinced that I ought to do many things in opposing the name of Jesus of Nazareth. And I did so in Jerusalem; I not only shut up many of the saints in prison, by authority of the chief priests, but when they were put to death I cast my vote against them. And I punished them often in all the synagogues and tried to make them blaspheme; and in raging fury against them, I persecuted them even to foreign cities.

But on the road to Damascus he saw a great light and his life was transformed; henceforth he was the ordained apostle to the nations in fulfillment of the ancient prophecies:

> . . . to open their eyes, that they may turn from darkness to light and from the power of Satan to God, that they may receive forgiveness of sins and a place among those who are sanctified by faith in me . . . To this day I have had the help that comes from God, and I stand here testifying to small and great, saying nothing but what the prophets and Moses said would come to pass.[37]

His sole crime was that he was faithful to the heavenly vision and was preaching, therefore, the resurrected Christ. The Roman considered him mad. The Jewish king, apparently, dismissed him as a crank.

To the Procurator Paul was only a nuisance. He would have gladly released him, which would have meant throwing him to the mob. Presumably this too would not have worried the Roman. But Paul insisted on his right as a Roman citizen to be tried before Caesar. Was he pressing this claim because it was due him, on principle, or because he was seeking to escape the mob? Or, perhaps, because he saw a chance to go to Rome? He had dreamed of travelling to Rome for some time.

Festus solved his problem: "You have appealed to Caesar; to Caesar you shall go."[38] He was put on a boat with common criminals and sent off to Italy.

Rome and the Last Years

The journey to Rome was the most hazardous of his travelling career. Luke was aboard with him, and he gives us a detailed report of their experiences. It took nine months to reach Rome. For thirteen days the gales tossed the little ship about and drove it off course. On the fourteenth day Paul found himself on the island of Malta. For three months he waited for a new ship to take him to Italy. Eventually, in February of the year 60 (or 61), he reached Rome where he was greeted by an enthusiastic crowd. His fame had preceded him.

He stayed in Rome for some two years under house arrest awaiting trial. Evidently he was chained to a guard, in keeping with the practices of the day, but was treated kindly and was given the freedom to carry on his agitations. He invited the Jews of Rome to visit him; some did. A volatile person such as Paul could not be expected to stay inactive. Always he was driven by a divine compulsion that gave him no rest.

In Rome he wrote three of his letters: to the Philippians in Macedonia, the Colossians (perhaps) in Phrygia, and a short note to his friend Philemon.

Nothing is reported on his trial before the Emperor. Evidently it never took place. What were the charges against him from the standpoint of Roman Law? And who was there to give testimony? Rome was not in the business of enforcing Mosaic ritual laws, and his accusers, presumably, were back in Jerusalem. He may have been released without any trial. We simply do not know.

His last years are shrouded in obscurity; all we have are conjectures. Scholars recognize two traditions in the reports of the final years. According to one—given in the closing portions of Acts—he was tried and beheaded at Nero's command in the year 64. Nero hated Christians; Paul was a pestilential agitator for the Christian faith not only among the Jews of the Empire but among the non-Jews especially, and he was gaining an ever-growing following. "It is . . . wholly possible that Paul was executed as a Roman citizen on a charge of sedition against the state."[39] Peter too, it is believed, was executed at this time. According to another tradition he was freed and lived to make two more journeys, eastward to Spain and westward to Ephesus, Macedonia and Crete. Most scholars incline towards the first tradition.

The Jewish Opposition to Paul, Then and Now

Was the Jewish opposition to Paul only a matter of theology, the Holy One of Israel versus the resurrected Christ? Is theology only the Great Divide between Paul and religious Jewry today? Was it then, and is it now, a matter of "wilful blindness and hardness of heart" on the part of Jewry?[40] We must bear in mind several large, historic considerations.

First, Paul's tempestuous personality and the irrational tactic he followed made conflict inevitable. He preached violently, disputed and argued; he reviled and cursed his opponents and quarreled with his closest collaborators. "For three weeks he argued with them from Scriptures," the pro-Paul author of Acts affirms.[41] He recalls more than once how he had acted as relentless inquisitor before the vision of the Christ on the road to Damascus transformed him from a cruel zealot against

Jesus to a cruel zealot for Jesus, how he had "consented" to the stoning of Stephen; how he had dragged men and women before the authorities for punishment. He quarrelled with all his associates, including Peter and James, the brother of Jesus. The vision of the Christ did not bring compassion into his heart. It only shifted him from one camp into another and set him against his former friends. He had an insatiable hunger to dominate. His bitterness was intensified with the years. His opponents were "dogs," and that was his mildest epithet. He and he alone was the true apostle of the Lord Jesus, he insisted. He attacked devout pilgrims and zealous Jews in their own sanctuaries on their sacred days. Would we, with all our sophisticated "tolerance" and public relations, have reacted more sympathetically under such circumstances?

Second, Paul's abrogation of the ceremonial law abolished the entire law of Moses and menaced the very life of the Jewish people. Any division between the ceremonial law and the Law itself was unthinkable to the Pharisees. To the rabbinic masters the Law was freedom and life for the nation and for the individual. Paul branded the Law as a curse. "Read not *haruth* [graven] upon the tablets of the Law but *heruth* [freedom], for you can have no freeman excepting one that occupies himself with the study of the Law," affirmed the rabbinic sages.[42] "Christ redeemed us from the curse of the law," affirmed Paul.[43] They were on a collision course. By abrogating the ceremonial law Paul abrogated the entire Law, and left Jewry exposed to all the menacing forces of pagan assimilation.

And it came at a time when the Jewish nation was under the iron heel of Rome, gasping for life. "Christ had broken down the dividing wall of hostility by abolishing in his flesh the law of commandments and ordinances," Paul argued;[44] but to the Pharisees—the masters in the academies and the masses alike—this wall was their fortress, their stronghold, their ultimate refuge.

By abolishing circumcision, the Sabbath, the festivals, food regulations, Paul made conversion easy. He opened the sluices in the dyke holding back the waters of assimilation and idolatry of every sort. All that pagans had to do was pronounce the magic word *faith* and they were "in Christ," and "saved" and became "the true Israel." Thus there came pouring in all the idolatries of the pagan gods and goddesses, the mystery religions, the cults of Isis, Attis, Mithras. With all these came moral aberrations abhorrent to religious Jews. The Rabbis also admitted converts, but in a controlled, disciplined manner; within the law, not beyond, not despite the law. Paul's teaching meant dissolving Jewry from within. What the Caesars and their Procurators could not do, Paul's teaching could accomplish in one generation. "If Judaism had listened to the voice of Paul, it would have disappeared from the world both as a religion and as a nation."[45]

Third, this pagan inundation of Judaism and Jewry issued from Paul's teaching, which compromised and corrupted the idea of God.

Israel was the particular people of the universal God, living by particular beliefs and divinely ordained specific practices. Primary was the Holy One of Israel. The battle-cry of faithful Jewry, of whatever grouping, was, "Hear, O Israel, the Lord our God the Lord is One." Paul, in effect, subbordinated the Holy One to Jesus and corrupted Jewish ethical monotheism.

Paul did adhere to "one God and Father of us all, who is above all and through all and in all. But grace was given to each of us according to the measure of

Christ's gift;" . . . . "for us there is one God, the Father, from whom are all things and for whom we exist." But he goes on, "and one Lord, Jesus Christ, through whom are all things and through whom we exist."[46] God, the Holy One of Israel subordinated all things to Jesus. "Hence it comes about," declares one historian, "that Paul in one of his Epistles uses the phrase 'the God of Abraham, Isaac and Jacob' of Judaism."[47] Paul laid the basis for the Trinity. The rabbinic masters and devout masses sensed that they were at the brink of oblivion. Paul "led the Jews believing in Jesus out of Judaism, and after a time he easily induced them into a kind of compromising half-paganism, a mixture of Judaism and paganism; but he was not aware of this, he did not intend to do it, and he never imagined that this would be the outcome."[48]

Fourth, this was happening at a time when the political climate of the day was at the point of explosion. Messianic frenzy was sweeping the land; Roman soldiers were everywhere; Judgment Day was on the wing. The pious masses were in the throes of the pangs of the Messiah. Zealots were clutching their stubby daggers under their cloaks. Paul, abrogating the Torah, draining Jewry of its life-blood, was proclaiming the Lord Jesus; the Romans considered it sedition. "These men [Paul and his disciples in Christ] who have turned the world upside down have come here also, and Jason has received them; and they are all acting against the decree of Caesar, saying that there is another king, Jesus. And the people and the city authorities were disturbed when they heard this."[49] The Jewish community was exposed; it could not risk attacks on Caesar and emperor worship in their name. Paul, like Jesus before him, was considered a political disturber of the peace who menaced the security of the Jewish community, in a day when their world was about to explode.

TO THIS DAY

On the porch of the Strasbourg cathedral stand two figures, symbolizing Church and Synagogue. To the left stands the Church—a proud, vigorous woman, crown on her head, chalice in her left hand, her right hand holds in a firm grip the banner of the cross, which is firmly planted on the ground. She looks sternly at her mother, the Synagogue—an exhausted woman, about to collapse, her head downcast, her eyes veiled, her right hand holds feebly a broken staff with a blunted point. From her left hand hangs a scrap of the Law. The Church looks sternly ahead, as if to say: "The world is mine! To me is given power and dominion." At one time the crown was on the head of the Synagogue; the cup of salvation too had belonged to the Synagogue; but now, crown, salvation, power and dominion belong to the Church and the Church alone; the Synagogue is left blind. In the words of Paul: "But their minds were hardened; for to this day, when they [the Jews] read the old covenant, that same veil remains unlifted, because only through Christ is it taken away. Yes, to this day whenever Moses is read a veil lies over their minds; but when a man turns to the Lord [Christ] the veil is removed."[50]

This is the work of Paul and Paulinism. It is Paul, not Jesus, who is the impenetrable wall between Church and Synagogue. With all his panegyric on love, he injected enough venom into Christendom to make the Jew the accursed of God in Church doctrine to this day.

Paul's conception of God, of the Messiah, of the Law, of Israel, of faith, of human nature, of man's duties on earth, of family life, of the social order, of the congregation of the faithful—all these were, and are today, totally alien to Jews and Judaism. Paul's personal hatred for his people made these differences all the sharper. To Paul, Jews were "vessels of wrath made for destruction,"[51] an attitude which has nurtured the anti-Semitism of the Church to the present day. The Jewish people saw in his teachings a mixture of personal hostility, mystery religions, and sheer pagan magic.

A devout Jewish theologian, differing from Paul sharply at every point, pays him the following tribute; fair minded critics of whatever camp, rising above historic sectarianism, may join in integrity:

"Effusive and excessive alike in his love and in his hatred, in his blessing and in his cursing, he possesses a marvelous power over men; and he had unbounded confidence in himself. He speaks or writes as a man who is conscious of a great providential mission, as the servant and herald of a high and unique cause. The philosopher and the Jew will greatly differ from him with regard to every argument and view of his; but both will admit that he is a mighty battler for truth, and that his view of life, of man, and of God is a profoundly serious one. The entire conception of religion has certainly been deepened by him, because his mental grasp was wide and comprehensive, and his thinking bold, aggressive, searching, at the same time systematic. Indeed, he molded the thought and the belief of all Christendom."[52]

PART IV

Disaster Breaks

11

Josephus: Traitor? Patriot?

Traitor? Renegade? Charlatan? Or, Patriot? Defender of his people's history and honor? Man of faith or fraud?

Josephus has been called all these. He has been damned for infamy by historians, from the first century, when he lived his slippery life, to the present. The passions have subsided, cooled by the winds of some 1900 years; the basic facts remain enigmatic.

His writings, like his personality, have been dissected into shreds and hotly debated. Scholars see greatness in some spots and fraud in others. "Spurious!" say highly competent scholars, pointing to crucial passages; "genuine!" other equally competent scholars affirm; "partially true," is the calm judgment of other able men, after years of patient study. Indispensable to our understanding of the background of the New Testament and the beginnings of Christianity, we are reminded; nauseating in his piety, counter others.

The writings of this Jew—the only Jewish historian of the most fateful century in his people's history and in the history of mankind—have been preserved for us by pious Christians, for the very good reason that they give us information imperative to an understanding of emergent Christianity, and for the highly dubious reason that they refer to Jesus, a passage considered spurious by most eminent scholars. In countless churches and Chris-

tian homes the writings of Josephus have stood alongside the Bible. They have been translated, in whole or in
part, into all languages known to Christendom, ancient,
medieval and modern. One of the books of his *Jewish
War* (Book 6) was incorporated into the Syriac Old
Testament. The Jewish priest-general attained the status
of a Church Father, and his chronicle acquired semi-
canonical prestige. Bitter rivals—in letters and in war—
accuse him of treachery in the hour of crisis, and of
deliberate perversion of facts in his chronicles. The rabbinic masters let him slip into limbo. No reference is
made to Josephus in the entire sea of the Talmud. Jewish
history has ignored him; the few meager references to
him in later history are wildly legendary. Most of the
serious Jewish historians have branded him "renegade
and traitor."[1]

But an English Christian historian, writing in 1929,
testifies: "There was a time in my own country when
almost every home possessed two books, a Bible and
Josephus, in the old eighteenth century version of William Whiston."[2]

Family, Education, Young Priest

Josephus' life falls into two approximately equal divisions chronologically: The Palestinian period, from
his birth *c.* 37-38 to the year 70, a period of thirty-three
years. These were years of intimate involvement in the
religious life, political upheavals and disaster for his
people. Josephus spent them as a teenage student for the
priesthood, general and prisoner of war. The Roman
period, during which he lived the life of a favored protegé of the Roman Emperors, a man of letters, a social
favorite, hated by his fellow Jews, suspected by the Romans, the recipient of a harlot's hire at the hands of the

power that had crushed his people's shrine and state.

He gives us the story of his life in his autobiography and in scattered paragraphs in his *Jewish War*. Both sources are tricky. The portions in *Jewish War* are even more suspect than his *Life*. Scholars find him guilty of suppressing and distorting facts. "The numerous inconsistencies, of a minor or grave character, between the two accounts of his command in Galilee," testifies H. St. John Thackeray—an astute and cautious historian—"betray either gross carelessness or actual fraud, and it is to be feared that he can not be wholly exonerated from the latter charge."[3]

His autobiography is an apologia; his entire life calls for apology. In his *Life* he is defending himself against a rival historian—a fellow Jew and one-time fellow soldier in the armies against the Romans—Justus of Tiberia, whose writings, unfortunately for us and perhaps fortunately for Josephus, are lost. In his autobiography Josephus concentrates upon only six months of his life, the tragically bungled period of his military leadership in Galilee. Here he bristles with hatred for his violent opponent, John of Gishchala. Further, he strives to justify his ways as Jew and as Roman collaborationist and allows no fact to stand in his way. His autobiography, therefore, even more than his other works, must be read with caution.

Josephus was born in Jerusalem in the year 37 or 38 as Joseph ben Matthias. He dropped his Hebrew name for Vespasian's family name after he was conquered and liberated by the Roman Emperor, thus becoming Flavius Josephus. His father was a priest; his mother was a descendant of the legendary Maccabees. He is proud of his ancestry. "My life is no ignoble one," he begins his personal history. "Different races base their claim to nobility on various grounds; with us [Jews] a connection with the priesthood is the hallmark of an illustrious line." Thus Josephus wears proudly a double crown: priesthood and royalty. Nor was his father a run-of-the-mill priest. He belonged to the upper level of the priestly aristocracy of the time, "esteemed for his upright character, being among the most notable men of Jerusalem, our great city."[4]

The year of his birth was pregnant with disaster. Judea was on its way of sorrow, dragging on to its ultimate catastrophe in the year 70—the year of the fall of the state, the Temple, the final dispersion. Pontius Pilate had been recalled from Jerusalem the year before; Herod Agrippa II had just been awarded the Judean kingdom by Rome; John the Baptist crying in the wilderness, proclaiming apocalyptic doom for the sinning nation, had forfeited his head, delivered on a platter to a stripling royal whore dancing in the nude before a drunken court; Jesus had been crucified; Paul had had his vision and transfiguration on the road to Damascus. It was an ominous year. The land was seething with revolt, forced by brutal tyrants and endless slaughter; the masses were bitter with resentment; disease and insanity were sweeping the land. How did these apocalyptic winds affect the childhood and youth of Josephus and condition his spirit?

He was a precocious child, by his own admission and characteristic immodesty. Scholars of repute consulted him when he was only a lad of fourteen. "While still a mere boy," he writes, "about fourteen years old, I won universal applause for my love of letters; insomuch that the chief priests and the leading men of the city used constantly to come to me for precise information and some particular in our ordinances."[5] We have no indication of his special learning in the lore of the academies. Unfortunately, he does not identify his teachers. His native tongue was Aramaic; his expertness in Hebrew was not impressive, scholars testify. His mastery of

Greek was mediocre. He is apologetic on this score. He needed the help of Greek ghost writers to manage his grammar and polish his paragraphs.

By the age of sixteen he was immersed in the study of the three denominations of the Judaism of his day. He speaks of them as "sects"—the Pharisees, Sadducees and Essenes. Enamored of the ascetic Essenes, he lived with them in their communities for three years, becoming the devoted disciple of a hermit by the name of Bannus, "who dwelt in the wilderness, wearing only such clothing as trees provided, feeding on such things as grew of themselves, and using frequent ablutions of cold water, by day and night, for purity's sake."[6]

But Josephus was too much a man of the world, and too much of a cosmopolitan by nature, to embrace forever the isolated life of the ascetic. At nineteen he associated himself with the Pharisees, the dominant segment of the population, representing the academies, their disciples and the common people. Josephus did not, however, surrender all the priestly privileges of the aristocratic Sadducees. For a time he continued serving as priest.

At the age of twenty-six (or twenty-seven) Josephus had his first view of Rome. He was awed by its might and glamor and remained under its spell for the rest of his life. The year was 64, the year Rome was burned and Christians were accused of setting the torch to it. Josephus makes no mention of the famous fire. Perhaps he was there before the burning.

What brought him to Rome was a mission of mercy. A number of Jewish priests had been put under arrest by the infamous Procurator Felix and transported to Rome in chains, to stand trial before Nero. Josephus' ship foundered in the night. Some six hundred passengers were on board and had to swim for their lives. A ship was sighted and "I and certain others," Josephus recalls, "about eighty in all, outstripped the others and were taken on board . . . " "Through God's good providence," he adds.[7] Josephus had a genius for self-preservation, and was never at a loss for a pious word.

He landed in Puteoli, an Italian seaport. There he met an actor of Jewish origin, and through him met Nero's consort, who had a reputation as being "God-fearing," which is a technical term for being in sympathy with Judaism. With her cooperation Josephus secured the liberation of his fellow priests, whom he admired for their steadfast adherence to their religious discipline under severe conditions. Josephus could always find his way around.

On his return to Palestine in the year 65, he was sucked into the vortex of the political storm of the age.

General, Galilee

The country was seething with revolt. Senseless slaughter of the Jewish population, and equally savage retaliation, was soaking the land in blood. This was particularly true in the Hellenistic centers of Caesarea, Scypholis and Damascus. Josephus gives us sickening pictures of horror. We glance hastily into Caesarea, seat of the Roman Governor:

> . . . the inhabitants of Caesarea massacred the Jews who resided in their city; within one hour more than twenty thousand were slaughtered, and Caesarea was completely emptied of Jews, for the fugitives were arrested by orders of Florus and conducted in chains to the dockyards. The news of the disaster at Caesarea infuriated the whole nation; and parties of Jews sacked the Syrian villages and the neighboring cities . . . . The whole of Syria was a scene of frightful disorder; every city was divided into two camps, and the safety of one party lay in their anticipating the other. They passed their days in blood, their nights yet more dreadful, in terror . . . . One saw cities

choked with unburied corpses, dead bodies of old men and
infants exposed side by side, poor women stripped of the last
covering of modesty, the whole province full of indescribable
horrors; and even worse than the tale of atrocities committed
was the suspense caused by the menace of evils in store.[8]

Josephus gives page after page of such scenes of horror throughout Galilee.

Florus' pillaging of the Temple added fuel to flames
already out of control. Zealots seized the Northwest
corner of the Temple enclave, Antonia, expelled King
Agrippa, and murdered the High Priest. The priests
withdrew from their daily functions out of fear; the
population discontinued the daily sacrifices offered in
the name of the Emperor.

Cestium Gallus, Roman Governor of Syria, invaded
the environs of Jerusalem in the teeth of furious resistance by Zealots. Encamped on Mount Scopus, overlooking the Holy City, with several thousand men and
cavalry, he might have taken Jerusalem. It was all but
in his hands. Josephus looked to him to take the city;
quite likely the war would have been over. The enormous
tragedy of the year 70 might have come to a speedy
end. But something inexplicable happened. He retreated,
for reasons unknown.[9] Was he bribed by the thoroughly
debased Florus, for his own reasons? Zealot bands
turned the retreat into a rout. The peace party in Jerusalem all but melted away; the Zealots were triumphant.
Beth-horon, where Gallus' mighty army collapsed in
humiliating retreat, had held tremendous inspiration to
the Jewish patriots. Had not the Maccabees, some two
centuries earlier, routed the Syrians at the same spot?
And had not Judah the Maccabee marched into Jerusalem from these passes of Beth-horon at the head of
his pious warriors, flaunting the head and arm of the
uncircumcised Nicanor? The hand of the Lord is not too
short to bring salvation to his people now as He did

then. The chants of the Psalmist must have roused re-
newal of faith and zeal. "The Lord is for me, I shall
not fear; what can man do unto me?" We must remember that these Zealots were basically religious patriots
in the tradition of the Maccabees. Josephus' constant
references to them as "brigands," "robbers" only betrays
his bias.[10]

Josephus was under the spell of Rome. Resistance, he
was convinced, was suicide, wanton madness.

> I accordingly endeavored to repress these promoters of sedition
> and to bring them over to another frame of mind. I urged
> them to picture to themselves the nation on which they were
> about to make war, and to remember that they were inferior
> to the Romans, not only in military skill, but in good fortune;
> and I warned them not recklessly and with such utter madness
> to expose their country, their families and themselves to direct
> perils . . . . But my efforts were unavailing; the madness of
> these desperate men was far too strong for me.

Nevertheless, in spite of his strong convictions, at the
age of twenty-nine, with no military training and no
experience, in the eye of the storm, Josephus accepted
command over the most inflamed and most strategic part
of the country. The conciliatory elders in Jerusalem who
commissioned him placed at his side two priests, presumably as advisors. Or, were they there to spy on him,
suspicious of his loyalty?

It was a fantastic appointment. What motivated the
Jerusalem leaders to make it? And what motivated
Josephus to accept it? Was it to defend the country
against Rome, or was it to pacify the populace as a
Roman collaborationist? Always we have the feeling that
Josephus is managing history and his own part in it.[12]

He set about organizing the country and its defenses.
He organized a Sanhedrin of seventy leading citizens;
appointed a series of judicial units of seven men each in
the leading cities of Galilee—Sepphoris, Samaria, Ti-

beria, Tarichea—and fortified them, reinforced a number of natural fortresses, including Jotapata, where he was to enact his most brazen act of treachery. He raised and equipped, as best he could, 60,000 footmen, about 4500 mercenaries, and a considerable cavalry, and drilled them according to Roman military procedure, which was fatal in a terrain that called for guerrilla tactics, one which had yielded such spectacular success to Judah Maccabee two centuries earlier. He became involved in a series of inner intrigues in the larger cities, thus deepening the violent cleavages among the various groupings from the extreme right of the Romanizers to the far-left Zealots. He gave himself a personal body guard of six hundred men, and he needed every man.

> I was now about thirty years old, at a time of life when, even if one restrains his lawless passions, it is hard, especially in a position of high authority, to escape the calumnies of envy. Yet I preserved every woman's honor; I scorned all presents offered to me as having no use for them; I even declined to accept from those that brought them the tithes which were due me as a priest. On the other hand, I did take a portion of the spoils after defeating the Syrian inhabitants of the surrounding cities, and admit to having sent these to my kinsfolk in Jerusalem. And though I took Sepphoris twice by storm, Tiberias four times, and Gabara once; and though I had John many times at my mercy when he plotted against me, I punished neither him nor any of the communities I have named . . . . To this cause I attribute my deliverance out of their hands by God—for His eye is upon those who do their duty . . . .[13]

John of Gishchala

By the year 67 the internal situation of Judea was in a three-fold pattern characteristic of societies in crisis. We in our time speak of the Right, Left, Center.

First was the party of the "respectable people," as Josephus refers to them, the people of property, vested interests, social prominence—the Sadducean priests, the Herodian family, the Hellenists or Romanizers. They sought to maintain the *status quo* by holding the populace loyal to Rome.

"The *second* faction composed of the most insignificant persons were bent on war."[14] In reality they were the patriots, the Zealots and the most extreme terrorists, the *Sicarii,* literally "daggermen." Basically Pharisees, they were not content to wait for Heaven to deliver them; they carried their daggers under their cloaks and took direct action.[15] Josephus brands them and their leaders as "assassins," "brigands," "robbers," "agitators." Desperate patriots, they held in contempt Rome and all its works.

Third was a large middle group, uncommitted to one side or the other, sliding towards the Left as the crisis deepened. Political adventurers inevitably arise. Josephus speaks of them as "clever demagogues," with a gift for leadership and oratory, fanning local chauvinism and exploiting the general misery of the day. Each of these groups found its leaders; rivalry among these leaders inevitably followed—because of differences in personal temperaments, ambitions, judgments, strategy.

The strongest of these competing leaders of the outraged masses was John of Gishchala, a leader of intense earnestness, great military skill, and resourceful leadership—an indefatigable warrior. He was Josephus' opposite and relentless enemy.

John was a native of a small mountainous town in northern Galilee, where he engaged in olive growing. He is described as being sickly as a youth, not at all inclined to violence. He counselled his towns people against engaging in war with Rome; but Roman rapacity turned a peaceful man into an implacable warrior.

All the reports we have of him and his leadership come from his enemy, Josephus, who is violently vituperative.

. . . . There appeared upon the scene an intriguer, a native of Gishchala, named John, son of Levi, the most unscrupulous and crafty of all who have ever gained notoriety by such infamous means. Poor at the opening of his career, his penury had for long thwarted his malicious designs; a ready liar and clever in obtaining credit for his lies, he made a merit of deceit, and practiced it upon his most intimate friends; while affecting humanity, the prospect of lucre made him the most sanguinary of men; always full of high ambitions, his hopes were fed on the basest of knaveries. For he was a brigand . . .[16]

Josephus does not tire of heaping abuse on John. "He was a man of extreme cunning who carried in his breast a dire passion for despotic power and had long been plotting against the State."[17]

But even out of Josephus' outrageously prejudiced report emerges the image of a superb leader, ardent patriot, whose devotion to his country is reminiscent of Judah the Maccabee. As a man of character he towers over Josephus like a colossus.

John organized his townsfolk into an army, equipped them out of his own resources, and liberated his beloved city. Some five thousand men, mainly the young, rallied around him by Josephus' own admission. He raised large sums of money from the sale of his olive oil and paid the men under his command. Needing food for his army, he petitioned Josephus, then Governor of the province, for permission to draw on grain stored by the imperial authorities. Josephus refused. He was saving it for the Emperor—against whom he was preparing the populace —and for himself. John took direct action and helped himself. He built fortifications around Gishchala so effectively that the town held out after the province had fallen to Rome.

A large portion of Galilee sided with John. Violent enmity flared between the two rivals. John considered Josephus a traitor; as a general he was slack and incompent. At least twice John plotted to assassinate him; each time the plot fizzled. John carried the agitation to Jerusalem. He dispatched a delegation, including his own brother, with a hundred men, demanding Josephus' dismissal from command. The leadership at Jerusalem was divided, the High Priest sided with John, some leading Pharisees aligned themselves with Josephus. Again Josephus escaped a trap set for him in Jerusalem. It cost John most of his army.

John escaped to his native Gishchala and wisely shifted his energies and meager resources from fighting Josephus to fighting Rome. Trapped in his home-town fortress by Titus and his powerful army, John managed to trick the Roman into a day's truce, on the pretext of observing the Sabbath, and escaped to Jerusalem. Quickly he recruited a following. More than two thousand men from Tiberias joined his resistance force, augumented by a large force of semi-savage Idumeans who only added to the carnage and plunder. John made himself dictator, operating from the northern confines of the Temple complex.

Two other leaders came to the fore, rivaling John; each had a sizeable following. Eleazar ben Simon seceded from John's forces, taking a large unit of men with him, and Simon bar Giora, who drew around himself the Idumeans from John's forces; he took away some two thousand of them. For a brief period he headed the peace party—or what was left of the peace party—in Jerusalem. These outraged Zealots went mad with internecine warfare. They inflicted horrible massacres on each other and burned each other's food supplies.

Jotapata

We return to Josephus in Galilee preparing to meet the impending Roman onslaught.

As Vespasian's army advanced on Jerusalem, Josephus' army fell apart. Most of the volunteers deserted. Josephus immediately took refuge in Jotapata, a mountainous town in northern Galilee. It was a natural fortress. "The town of Jotapata was entirely built on precipitous cliffs, being surrounded on three sides by ravines so deep that sight fails in the attempt to fathom the abyss."[18] His intention was to escape. He was abandoning his country, deserting his army, surrendering the fortifications he had built. The local populace, however, forced him to remain and face the enemy with them. We may safely discount Josephus' account of the feeling of security his presence gave them.

The besieged patriots offered spectacular resistance, but early in July 67 Jotapata fell in a night attack. About forty thousand men, women and children were slaughtered in the siege and capture of this legendary fortress; twelve hundred mothers and babies were taken into exile. While the Romans were butchering the population, Josephus, "aided by some divine providence," took refuge in a cave. There he found forty "persons of distinction." For two days he lay hidden while Vespasian was searching for him; at night he vainly probed "for some loophole of escape." On the third day he was spotted, on information given the Romans by a woman (a stratagem devised by our hero himself?) and was ordered to surrender. He had the privilege of asking for mercy, and the Romans would be merciful to Josephus! His forty companions, however, stood true. Surrender would belie everything he had urged upon them as a general. Infuriated, they offered him the choice of committing suicide or dying by their hands. Josephus, who was never at a loss for words, harangued them on the sin of taking one's own life. God Himself had revealed to him the inevitable triumph of the Romans. Wisdom and piety lay in submitting to God's will. "But desperation stopped their ears."

. . . They were, therefore, infuriated at him, and ran at him from this side and that, sword in hand, upbraiding him as a coward, each one seeming on the point of striking him. But he, addressing one by name, fixing his general's eye of command upon another, clasping the hand of a third, shaming a fourth by entreaty, and torn by all manner of emotions at this critical moment, succeeded to ward off from his throat the blades of all, turning like a wild beast surrounded by the hunters to face his successive assailants. Even in his extremity, they still held their general in reverence; their hands were powerless, their swords glanced aside, and many, in the act of thrusting at him, spontaneously dropped their weapons.[19]

Josephus, "trusting in God," urged a desperate stratagem; let each man submit to the sword by the hand of a comrade, the order to be determined by lot. Josephus devised and managed the gory procedure. He and one other were last. He then convinced the lone survivor besides himself that it would be more acceptable to God if they lived and carried on as best they could. He ascribes his deliverance to Providence and not a trace of guilt or shame may be found in his report.

Brought in chains before Vespasian, he caught the general's fancy. He dazzled the Roman with his vaunted prophetic power; he predicted the conqueror's impending coronation as Caesar. In rabbinic literature this prediction is attributed to Johanan ben Zakkai. In July 69, the prediction came true. A freed man, Joseph ben Matthias became Flavius Josephus.

Vespasian, now Emperor, took his protegé with him to Alexandria on imperial business. Perhaps Josephus served as his interpreter or aide. From Egypt Josephus returned with Titus to smoldering Jerusalem—and a new wife, his third, a Jewish captive from Caesarea. (Josephus had deserted his first wife in Jerusalem under siege.) The Temple was still under siege; Jerusalem was in the throes of supreme agony; John and Simon were still fighting with crazed heroism amidst enormous carnage. Josephus' duty it was "to go round the walls and counsel submission."

9 Ab, 70

Titus brought up a fresh army of eighty thousand men, at a time when Jerusalem and the Temple were choked with pilgrims. These had come from all parts of the country to celebrate the Passover (in the year 70) as commanded in the Law. Simon is believed to have had eleven thousand men in his sector of the Temple compound; John had thirty thousand. It is estimated that about two and a half million people were in the city and Temple enclave. Making full allowance for Josephus' persistent proclivity to exaggerate figures, the congestion (and remembering the primitive sanitation under the burden of years of warfare) was horrible. Eleazar opened the Temple gates to the enormous hordes. Soon 8500 human corpses were decomposing in the sun in one corner of the Temple enclave.

John inflicted severe punishment on Titus' army. The trap he set at the very gates of the Temple was brilliant camouflage. Titus demanded surrender. The man who voiced the demand was Josephus. The erstwhile Jewish general, turned Roman propagandist, was urging the defenders to lay down their arms. God was now in Rome. He had abandoned his people and gone over to the side of the Romans, the erstwhile priest and commander was saying. At least one rock struck Josephus and felled him. This demoralizing propaganda, he carefully reports, he was compelled to do at the cost of his life.

Titus believed John was helplessly trapped and once more demanded his surrender. John asked for safe retreat with his arms. Again John made his escape. Finally, forced by hunger, he surrendered. Was he taken to Rome in chains for triumphal procession? The record is not clear. But Simon, Josephus reports, was dragged by a noose to the Forum in triumphal procession, to the wild cheers and jeers of the Romans keeping holiday, to be thrown to the lions in the Coliseum. Josephus describes the procession with awed admiration. Did he, perhaps, see John in chains? Did he catch Simon's eye? What were his thoughts?

On the ninth day of the month of Ab, in the year 70, the Temple finally fell. Josephus writes at great length seeking to exonerate the "gentle Titus" not only for the burning of the Temple but for the entire siege of Jerusalem. Ultimate blame for the catastrophe, he argues, rests with John, Simon, Eleazar and the fanatic Zealots —the thousands upon thousands of them who would not heed his counsel of surrender. Josephus refers to them as "the dregs of society and the bastard scum of the nation."[20]

One fortress held out for three years longer. Masada, west of the Dead Sea, was a huge rock and formed a natural fort, "abruptly terminating on every side by deep ravines," and inaccessible to the foot of any living creature." The *Sicarii* captured it and exterminated the Roman garrison. There the Zealots, under the command of Eleazar, held out till April 73. When the Romans finally entered the smouldering fort they found alive only two old women. All the rest had committed suicide. Josephus puts a speech into the mouth of Eleazar (following the literary style of the Greek authors) which is one of the most stirring passages in his voluminous writings. Talking to his trapped colleagues and their families the commander delivers an impassioned oration:

. . . . Long since, my brave men, we determined neither to serve the Romans nor any other save God, for He alone is man's true and righteous Lord; and now the time is come which bids us verify that resolution by actions. At this crisis let us not disgrace ourselves . . . . Let our wives thus die undishonored, our children unacquainted with slavery; and when they are gone, let us render a generous service to each other, preserving our liberty and a noble winding-sheet . . . . We prefer death to slavery.[21]

Towards the end of his autobiography, written in his old age, Josephus reports for the record his last "magnanimous" act in Jerusalem. Was he haunted by conscience?

Again, when at last Jerusalem was on the point of being carried by assault, Titus Caesar repeatedly urged me to take whatever I could from the wreck of my country, stating that I had his permission. And I, now that my native place had fallen, having nothing more precious to take and preserve as a solace for my personal misfortunes, made request to Titus for the freedom of some of my countrymen; I also received by his gracious favor a gift of sacred books. Not long after I made petition for my brother and fifty friends, and my request was granted. Again, by permission of Titus, I entered the Temple, where a great multitude of captive women and children had been imprisoned, and liberated all the friends and acquaintances whom I recognized, in number about a hundred and ninety; I took no ransom for their release and restored them to their former fortunes. Once more, when I was sent by Titus Caesar with Corealius and a thousand horses to a village called Tekoa, to prospect whether it was a suitable place for an entrenched camp, and on my return saw many prisoners who had been crucified, and recognized three of my acquaintances among them, I was cut to the heart and came and told Titus with tears what I had seen. He gave orders immediately that they should be taken down and receive the most careful treatment. Two of them died in the physician's hands; the third survived.[22]

In Rome today stands the Arch of Titus, which commemorates the victory over Judah and Jerusalem. The spoils of the Temple are represented on it in gloating triumph. Titus stands crowned by victory in a car driven by four horses led by a powerful female form personifying invincible Rome. Roman soldiers, crowned with laurel, carry the holy vessels taken from the vanquished sanctuary. Devout Jews have refused to walk under it to this day.

Domestic Life

Of his domestic life Josephus informs us that he married four times. His first wife remained in Jerusalem among the besieged. Vespasian gave him a captive woman for wife; he married her, in defiance of Biblical injunction. A priest might not marry a woman taken in war. She deserted him. He took a third wife in Alexandria, who bore him three children. He divorced her and married a Jewish woman of a distinguished family of Crete. She bore him two sons. He writes of her with respect. How much affection he had for his family we do not know. In the tearful scene we have just cited, standing amidst the smouldering wreckage of Jerusalem he congratulates himself upon his liberality in rescuing his brother, friends and three crucified Jews. He accepted no ransom money. But he betrays no concern for his father, mother, wife.

We do not know the year of his death. The story of his life comes to an end in his own writings, and these do not go beyond the death of the Emperor Domitian in the year 97. He died, probably, at the turn of the second century.

Historian, Apologist, Defender of His People

Josephus fared well under imperial favor. Vespasian and his two sons who succeeded him, Titus and Domitian, granted him considerable land, exemption from taxes, and an annual allowance.

From the first part of his life in Palestine to the second half in Rome was an enormous transition, and must have been a profoundly disturbing adjustment.

What memories worried him as he wrote the history of the war in which he was so intimately and so treacherously involved? A precocious youngster, a brilliant young intellectual enjoying the privileges and status of a highly favored priest, he must have absorbed memories, impressions; he must have known adulation and love, and, later, violent hatred. He waded through blood and carnage in the ruins of the Holy City and the Temple to which he had dedicated himself in his youth. He was despised by his own people as he was relishing a harlot's hire. Did these memories haunt him in the nights? How did they affect the integrity of his pen? He was a *liberatus*, a freedman, yes; but as liege of the Emperor the former Jewish priest owed his pagan master allegiance. His recollections, his judgments—were they of his own honest mind, or were they reported with an eye to his master's favor? Was he haunted by remorse? Did he, as historian, recall Jeremiah's spurning the favor of *his* conqueror, choosing the life of exile to the lush life he might have had in Babylon? Did the face of John of Gishchala emerge out of the fog of memories to haunt him?

Josephus is famous as the classic national historian of his people and the defender of their faith. But for his enormous work as historian this most crucial of centuries would have remained largely a blank. He did not defend his faith by living it, after the manner of the martyrs, or of the teachers like Johnan ben Zakkai; but he did defend it brilliantly with his pen, as an intellectual and man of letters, while enjoying the life of the non-Jew.

He is the author of four works: *The Jewish War,
Jewish Antiquities, Life* and the treatise *Against Apion*.*

Restoring Josephus to His Own

The time has come—indeed it is long overdue—for
Jewry to reclaim Josephus and restore him to its national-religious album as son and builder.

Standing amidst the smouldering rubble of shrine and
nation, Josephus might have lifted whatever he wished
as a token of remembrance, and a bit of solace. He was
so urged by Titus, the victorious general. He had served
the Roman well and the pagan warrior was generous to
the priestly collaborationist. Josephus, with tears streaming down his cheeks, he recalls, chose some sacred books,
and asked that his brother and friends be spared; he
asked further that three crucified Jews be lifted from the
crosses. As we have noted, two of them died; the third
survived.

Here is a pointed allegory. Josephus salvaged from
the ruins of his nation the sacred book of remembrance;
of the crucified nation a small remnant survived.

He came down in history as the classical historian of
the Jewish people. No other in Jewish annals carried the
book of Jewish remembrance down the ages as he did.

His history leaves much to be desired, as we have
observed. He did slant, omit and add; but with it all,
he has salvaged from the ruins the history of his people
and has illumined a century which, but for his writings,
would have remained largely a blank, black page. Further, as has been noted, we must allow for time and the
standards of the age. Did not most historians, among
all people, take similar liberties? Do we not find the
same slanting, omissions, additions, in the pages of the

---

*See Appendix III—The Works of Josephus

Bible itself—the Gospel writers, for instance, who twisted history to bolster their theology, or the Deuteronomist, rewriting and radically altering the statutes and ordinances of the Mosaic tradition?

As a literary man Josephus was no mere hack. He gives us deeply moving passages—vivid, dramatic, pulsating with the agony of an epic. Did he resort to assistants, and hired talent? Again, that was the standard of his age and of all the ages, including our own. The ghost writers have ever been with us.

As a man he was egotistic, opportunistic, calculating, shabby at times to a point of revulsion. Who will justify his conduct at Jotapata? But the second half of his life, as a freeman and protegé of imperial favor, he devoted himself to the prodigious task of establishing the record of his people, striving to effect a better understanding between Jew and Greek, answering the anti-Jewish writers, and giving the world the only comprehensive description of the Judaism of his day. And he wrote as a proud, believing Jew, for all his assimilation to Roman paganism.

Did he counsel his people to knuckle under to Rome and surrender their country and their shrine?

Two considerations must be borne in mind in any attempt at rethinking the case of Josephus before the bar of justice.

First, in the long run of history, he held out the wisest course for his people to follow. This is proven by subsequent history. Times come to most nations when surrender is the only sane measure to take. John of Gishchala looms as a heroic figure; he draws our admiration while Josephus shrivels into a nauseating opportunist. But what did John's course achieve? Heaps upon heaps of corpses and absolute defeat. Judea might have saved itself as a Roman province; Rome did grant its conquered people a good measure of religious liberty.

Second, others gave Israel similar advice and have been enshrined as heroes in Jewish annals. Johanan ben Zakkai too turned his back on flaming Jerusalem and took refuge in the comparative safety of academic life in a lonely village far from the scenes of combat. We revere Johanan ben Zakkai as the builder of rabbinic Judaism. Back in the seventh century B.C.E. Isaiah told his hard-pressed people that Assyria was "the rod of His anger;" God was chastising His people for their sins. Jeremiah in the sixth century urged surrender to the Babylonians. We revere Isaiah and Jeremiah. The later rabbinic masters agreed with Josephus' theology that the Holy One had gone over to the side of Rome. In their daily prayers, continued to the present day, is the confession: "Because of our sins were we exiled from our land."

Granting all his faults, Josephus still stands as a tragic son in the household of Israel in an evil hour, witnessing to the heroic record which he personally snatched from the burning.

The time has come to salvage Josephus from the limbo of Jewish history, exhume him from the tomb of technical scholarship, and place him in our schools and synagogues for the book of remembrance he holds for us. Let Jewish children in our religious schools read Josephus and give the ancient historian the reward of the glint in their eyes as they read his awesome story; let religious Jewry read from his writings on the Ninth Day of the Month of Ab along with Scriptural *Lamentations,* or read selections from his chronicle on Hanukkah, when we recall the Maccabees.

The time has come to drop the curtain of charity on Josephus the man and reclaim him as a son and builder in Jewish history.

12

Yohanan Ben Zakkai: Builder of the Portable Fatherland

Jerusalem Under Siege

Vespasian and his victorious legions were heading toward Jerusalem. It was the winter of the year 68 C.E. Josephus' armies—60,000 footmen, some 4500 mercenaries, his ill-conceived, bungled cavalry—had fallen apart; the traitor-general had abandoned his people and his armies and perpetrated his blackest perfidy at Jotapata, literally walking over the corpses of his trusting comrades whom he had betrayed. Jerusalem was under siege, chocked with heaps of rotting humans. Starvation, disease, and insanity, no doubt were rampant. The Zealots—John Gishchala, Eleazar bar Simon, Simon bar Giora, each commanding his own army—were in the grip of insane zealotry and endless slaughter. The holy city was in its death-throes.

A pattern was taking form.

One approach to the oncoming catastrophe of the year 70—the complete destruction of the Temple, the state, the nation, and the dispersion of the Judean remnants—was the road chosen by Josephus: surrender, collaboration with the enemy. Rome was invincible. Had not the Holy One of Israel Himself abandoned His people once again, even as He had in the days of Jeremiah, and moved his abode to Italy as Josephus was proclaiming? It was the road of the "practical" man, the way of prudence. A bargain could be struck with the Romans. After all, they were permitting their conquered peoples to worship their gods as they wished. The Hellenists, the Romanizers, the vested Temple Sadducees, the business men, could follow this road with profit.

A second approach to the impending doom was the opposite road taken by the Zealots, the dagger-men, the devout Pharisees turned terrorists under the outrageous harassment of Roman military: no compromise with Caesar. To "render to Caesar the things that are Caesar's and to God the things that are God's," meant surrendering to Caesar this world and all that was in it, including freedom and all that was holy. Every Zealot carried his stubby dagger under his cloak and moved swiftly and relentlessly, striking down pagan Romans and compromising Jews alike.

A third road was that taken by the Messianists, the apocalyptists, the Essenes: abandon this doomed world and retire to the desert and wait for the Lord to come "in the end of days." In the end of days He will bring a new heaven and a new earth, even as John the Baptist had proclaimed in words borrowed from the prophet Isaiah:

> Clear ye in the wilderness the way of the Lord,
> Make straight in the desert a highway for our God.
> Every valley shall be lifted up,
> Every mountain shall be made low;
> And the rugged shall be made level,
> And the rough places a plain;
> And the glory of the Lord shall be revealed . . . .[1]

God, in His own good time, will raise up a *Redeemer*, or *Messiah*, or *Teacher of Righteousness*, and "gird him with strength, that he may shatter unrighteous rulers, and that he may purge Jerusalem from nations that trample her down to destruction.''[2] He will bring to suffering mankind a new heaven and a new earth. Death itself will be vanquished and "sorrow and sighing will be no more."

A fourth road was emerging: the way of the Pharisees who sought salvation in Torah. The destined leader was Yohanan ben Zakkai. Just as Josephus was under the spell of Rome, and the Zealots were in the grip of direct action and terror, and the apocalyptists, messianists, and Essenes were entranced with ecstatic visions of supernatural redemption, Yohanan ben Zakkai and his segment of the Pharisees—the so-called "peace party"—were under the spell of Torah. The way of Torah, with its vision of Israel as "a kingdom of priests and a holy people," as understood by these Pharisees and expounded by Yohanan and his colleagues, proved to be the "eternal life" for Jewry and Judaism.

Father of the Future

We have only scant information of Yohanan's personal life and little of his specific teachings and juridical decisions. Josephus does not mention him. The scraps of information we do have are scattered throughout rabbinic literature. These notes are recollections and idealizations of an adoring posterity. Reverence and adulation replaced prosaic facts.[3]

We do know that Yohanan came in succession to Hillel and Shammai as teacher and expounder of the law. His dates, it is estimated, are from the turn of the first century to a decade or so after the fall of the Temple and state in the year 70. He is endowed with a legendary lifespan, in a traditional formula based on the life of Moses: one hundred and twenty years. The same 120-year formula is applied to Hillel before him and Akiba after him. Again in a fixed traditional formula, he is reported to have devoted forty years of his life to business, forty to scholarship, and forty to the service of his people.

That Yohanan did have some business experience is a reasonable assumption. It was good practice for scholars to earn their livelihoods by engaging in trade, in some craft, or farming. Hillel, as we have noted, was a humble water carrier. Some revered personalities in rabbinic tradition were carpenters, charcoal burners, tailors or cobblers. Perhaps he gained his business knowledge, at least in part, from his father, who had engaged in business in the wake of the Herodian period. Herod had opened avenues of trade and extended the markets. Roman conquests had opened trade routes and created markets in vast areas of the Mediterranean world and gave Judea a measure of economic stability. Many took advantage of these opportunities. It was a period of stable currency, commercial rivalry, and high taxation. Yohanan was familiar enough with the business life of his day not to be a cloistered scholar only. He left a reputation for sharp cross examination of witnesses. In the spirit of Hillel, he learned the importance of concerning himself with pressing social problems.[3]

Posterity draped Hillel's cloak on Yohanan's shoulders. On his death bed, surrounded by several of his intimate students and disciples, Hillel asked for Yohanan. "The youngest of you is father of wisdom and father of the future," he is supposed to have said.[4]

Yohanan was a man of extensive learning and singlemindedness in his devotion to Torah. It is recorded in the Talmud—again, by an adoring posterity—that

> he never in his life engaged in idle conversation, and he never went four cubits without words of Torah and without phylacteries, either winter or summer, and none ever preceded him into the house of study, either accidentally or intentionally, and

he never left any one in the school house, and none ever found
him slumbering there, and none ever opened the door to his
students but he himself, and he never made a statement which
he had not first heard from his master, and he never said, "The
hour has come to arise from our studies," except on the after-
noon before Passover and before the Day of Atonement [to
prepare for the holy day] . . .[5]

It is the personification of a tradition that idealized
the consecrated scholar in pious surrender to every dis-
comfort:

> . . . a morsel of bread with salt you must eat, and water by
> measure you must drink; upon the ground you shall sleep, and
> live a life of trouble while you toil in the Torah.[6]

The highest good—the only good—is Torah. And the
scholar must ever remember before whom he will have
to stand in judgment at last: "before the Supreme King
of kings, the Holy One, blessed be He."[7] His life-long
motto was "If you have learned much of the Torah, do
not claim special credit for it; for this was the purpose
of your creation."[8]

After Hillel's death, in the first decade of the first
century C.E., Yohanan moved to Galilee, settling in a
village near Sephoris. The territory was supposed to
have been defended by Josephus. Vespasian's armies had
no difficulty overwhelming the land. Sephoris itself was
a prosperous Jewish center of considerable commerce,
dominated by Hellenists and Romanizers, following the
Sadducean emphasis on the literal interpretation of Bible
text. The Pharisaic masters were in the minority. Yohanan seemed to have labored under frustrating circumstances. There was sharp cleavage between the majority
that followed the Sadducees, consisting mainly of those
who had vested commercial and Temple interests, and
the minority of Pharisees with their emphasis on the

Oral tradition as well as the Written. The Oral, they were convinced, was as authoritative as the Written, for God had revealed both to Moses himself on Mount Sinai, and the rabbinic masters were the authentic custodians of the tradition.

Yohanan seemed to have served as teacher and magistrate. The cases he adjudicated, as reported in the sources, were primarily of a ritualistic nature. The modern mind can hardly appreciate the reality and the urgency the ritualistic issues had in the life of the time. They were direct applications of God's word.

We have a glimpse of a personal tragedy at this period in Galilee. A son—perhaps his only one, though there is a vague reference that leads some scholars to conjecture that he had another son—died at the age of eighteen. We have a touching report of his students seeking to comfort their revered master.

Did Yohanan in his youth hear of Jesus? Had any report of Jesus and his preaching and miracle-working reached him? They were contemporaries; both were active in Galilee. Did he hear of Jesus when he returned to Jerusalem? We have no reports whatsoever.[9]

Yohanan did leave behind him in Galilee a disciple by the name of Hanania Ben Dosa—mystic, faith healer, ascetic—who heard heavenly voices. Several of his sayings have been preserved in rabbinic lore:

He, in whom the fear of sin takes precedence over wisdom, his wisdom will endure; but he in whom wisdom takes precedence over sin, his wisdom will not endure.

He whose deeds exceed his wisdom, his wisdom will endure; but he whose wisdom exceeds his deeds, his wisdom will not endure.

He in whom the spirit of his fellow creatures takes delight, in him the spirit of God takes delight; he in whom the spirit of his fellow creatures takes no delight, in him the spirit of God takes no delight.[10]

How much of this basically Pharisaic spirit reflects Yohanan's influence can only be conjectured.

Teaching in Jerusalem

Yohanan ben Zakkai returned to Jerusalem about the year 40 C.E., after eighteen years in Galilee. That he had been frustrated in Galilee as Pharisaic expounder of the law we may gather from the sigh attributed to him on leaving for the Holy City: "Galilee, Galilee, you hate the Torah!" Yohanan, classic Pharisee, interpreted the Torah in the light of the divinely revealed Oral tradition; the Galilee authorities were literalists, or "fundamentalists," recognizing the Written Torah only. Conflict was inevitable.

In Jerusalem too he encountered the literalistic Sadducean tradition, with its loyalty to the cultic religion of the Temple. By no means did the Pharisaic masters ignore the Temple and its sacrificial cult; but they did give it a broader, what in our time we would consider "liberal," interpretation.

Yohanan opened an "academy," and gained a modest following. The word "academy" brings to mind an organized school, a building, a staff, a curriculum. It had a much more restricted meaning in Yohanan's experience. He met with his few fellow scholars "in the shadow of the Temple," as it is usually designated. Perhaps the sessions were in the immediate proximity of the Temple, perhaps in some corner of the Temple itself. He had no organization, and only a personal following. Any Jew might present himself and propound his views, as we read in the gospels in the activities of Jesus. His teaching center, known as "the great house," became the center of much rabbinic legendry. For a time he was a member of the chief legislative-judicial body, the Great Sanhedrin; he may have served as its head for a short period. His title *Rabban* testifies to that.

At one time he had five distinguished scholars, revered in rabbinic tradition. The Talmud affords us a glimpse of the master and his method of teaching:

> Rabban Yohanan ben Zakkai had five disciples . . . He used to recount their praise: Eliezer ben Hyrcanus, is a cemented cistern, which loses not a drop; Joshua ben Hanania—happy is she that bore him; José, the priest, is a pious man; Simeon ben Nathaniel is a fearer of sin; Elazar ben Arach is like a spring flowing with ever-sustained vigor.
>
> He said to them, Go forth and see which is the good way (the highest good) to which a man should cleave. Eliezer said, a good eye [kindly disposition]; Joshua said, a good friend; José said, a good neighbor; Simeon said, one who forsees the fruit of an action; Elazar said, a good heart [unselfish love in word and action]. Thereupon he said unto them, I approve the words of Elazar . . . for in his words yours are included.[11]

Yohanan's method of teaching seems to have been a twofold one: questions and answers, seeking to elicit the individual judgments of the students; and dealing with specific cases. These involved matters of ritual, the status of women, tithing, calendation, the privileges of priests. Basic principles were involved in each area. Ritual meant reexamination of basic beliefs and theologies. The status of women led Yohanan to abrogate, for all practical purposes, the primitive "bitter waters" test of a woman's fidelity as legislated in Mosaic law.[12] Calendation presented a serious problem in determining the dates of holy days and festivals. Tithing and the privileges of priests brought Pharisaic law into conflict with priestly prerogatives and the natural desire to seek more and more fringe benefits. Yohanan is quoted as warning the people: "Guard your steps when you go to the house of God. [The Temple, under the authority of the Sadducees.] To draw near to listen [to the Pharisaic interpreters of the law, such as he was] is better than to offer the sacrifices of fools, for they do not know they are doing evil."[13]

Again, he urged parents: "Keep the children away from the proud, and separate them from the householders [that is, the privileged upper classes, and they were Sadducees], because the householders draw a man far from words of Torah . . . . "[14]

In the spring of the year 68 Vespasian clamped his siege on Jerusalem. Yohanan counselled submission. He sent for the men of Jerusalem and said to them: "My children, why do you destroy this city and why do you seek to burn the Temple? For what is it that he asks of you? Only one bow or one arrow [tokens of subjection], and he will go off from you."[15] His primary aim was to spare the city and its population and save the Temple. His influence upon the immediate turn of events was nil. Jerusalem was in the grip of fratricide.

He made his way somehow to Vespasian's quarters, greeted him with a submissive *Vive Imperator,* and foretold his impending elevation to Emperor. (The same prophecy is attributed to Josephus.) To a superstitious man such as Vespasian such a prophecy was most impressive. Another holy man was foretelling his elevation to the purple.

"Ask what I may grant you," Vespasian is supposed to have said to Yohanan. Yohanan replied, according to this one report, "Give me Yavneh and its sages [so that he might establish an academy there], and the family chain of Rabban Gamaliel . . . " [that is, spare the dynasty of the house of David].[16]

This was granted. Vespasian, evidently, considered Yohanan a friend of Rome. We may well imagine the sneer of contempt on the pagan warrior's lips. What obscurantists these fanatic Jews were! Some three decades later a sage, perhaps the more zealous Akiba, sneered: "God turneth wise men backward and maketh their knowledge foolish." Scholars turn senile with age. Yohanan should have asked that all Jerusalem be spared. Akiba was burned at the stake, as we shall see; his zeal brought Jewry to a new calamity.[17]

A more romantic report of how Yohanan made his way through the military guards of Jerusalem to the general's quarters is cherished in rabbinic lore:

> Now after Rabban Yohan ben Zakkai had spoken to them one day, two, and three days, and they would still not listen to him, he sent for his disciples, Rabbi Eliezer and Rabbi Joshua. My sons, he said to them, Arise and take me out of here. Make a coffin for me that I may lie in it. Rabbi Eliezer took hold of the head end of it, and Rabbi Joshua took hold of the foot, and they began carrying him as the sun set, until they reached the gates of Jerusalem. Who is this? the gatekeepers demanded. It is a dead man, they replied, do you not know that the dead may not be held overnight in Jerusalem? If it is a dead man, the gatekeepers said to them, take him out. So they took him out, and continued carrying him until they reached Vespasian. They opened the coffin, and Rabban Yohanan stood up before him. Art thou Rabban Yohanan ben Zakkai? Vespasian inquired. Tell me what I may give you? I ask nothing of thee, Rabban Yohanan replied, save Yavneh, where I might go and teach my disciples, and there establish a prayer-house, and perform all the commandments. Go, Vespasian said to him. By your leave, may I say something to you? Speak, Vespasian said to him. Said Rabban Yohanan to him, Lo you are about to be appointed king.[18]

Yavneh

With Jerusalem and the national shrine reduced to rubble, the remnants of Jerusalem's population sold into slavery or carried off to slave labor—thousands were

forced to build the Roman Colosseum, for instance—
Yavneh, under the studious, persistent efforts of Yohanan's leadership, replaced Jerusalem; the Pharisaic court
became the new national tribunal. We may take Yohanan
ben Zakkai as the representative of the Pharisaic masters
who ultimately transformed Temple and state into Torah
and synagogue, thus laying the foundations of the Jew's
"portable fatherland" that has sheltered Jewry throughout the centuries to our own day.

Yavneh,* on the Mediterranean shore, was a thriving
commercial center. It was one of the towns in the area
that the Romans had developed as a military base. The
climate was warm and conducive to outdoor living. It
held a Jewish community of considerable size. Many
were merchants, some were craftsmen. Jerusalem refugees—among them many rabbis—augmented the population. It came to be known in Jewish tradition as "the
Vineyard of Yavneh." The scholars were supposed to
have sat on the floor in rows, "like vines in the vineyard."
Here, about the end of the first century, the Bible canon
was established; here too was started the Talmudic
literature. For the most part the populace was friendly
to Rome. Yohanan found here the comparative security
and the scholars he needed to help him forge the new
authority.

They built perhaps better than they knew. They
searched the Scriptures—God's word—for the answers
to their problems, many and complicated: social, legal,
ethical, theologic, ritualistic, liturgic. The liturgic problems were particularly urgent, since these involved setting the dates of the holy days and the festivals from a
center other than Jerusalem.

In classic Pharisaic tradition, they operated with two
levels of Torah: the Written, dictated by God Himself

---

*Present-day Yavne, or K'far-Yavne, on the coastal road between
Rishon-Letsiyon and Ashdod.

to Moses on Mount Sinai, and the Oral, equally authoritative. The Oral enabled them to keep the Written alive and responsive to life and its stresses. In the crucial hour of national-religious reconstruction it was the saving power. The saying of one of the sages became standard coin: "Turn the Torah and turn it over again, for everything is in it, contemplate it and grow gray and old over it; you can have no better rule than this."[19] In time of crisis correct understanding of God's word held salvation in this world and redemption in the world to come. Eschewing allegorizing and the eschatologic, the juridic scholars aimed at the practical application of God's word to the daily life of the individual and the community.

This does not mean that Yohanan and his colleagues did not share in the eschatologic notions of the time and placed no credence in miracles. What we consider esoteric was urgently practical in their day. They heard heavenly voices, saw Ezekiel's chariots and heard them rumbling in the heavens, knew ecstasy and were on tip toe for the coming of the Messiah. They took Bible theophony in dead earnest. They transmitted this tradition from the generations before them to the synagogue and the emerging church. In days of crisis such notions always gain power and urgency.

However, in adjudicating immediate, every-day problems of an uprooted people in days of radical reconstruction, the Pharisaic masters sought the practical. They had a healthy skepticism of messianism and miracles. Decisions in law were not permitted on the basis of heavenly voices; human basic needs only were the deciding factors in the application of God's word. Yohanan is reported to have said: If you have a sapling in your hands and some one announces, "Look! The Messiah is approaching!" go on with your planting. Only after you have planted go out to receive the Messiah.[20]

Prepare a Throne for Hezekiah

Johanan died within the decade after the disruption in the year 70. His disciples have placed a crown of legends on his last hours. He is believed to have been surrounded by his students. The report, lovingly embellished, is that he wept as he reflected on his impending confrontation with the Holy One. Asked what his last words to his disciples would be he again spoke in terms of the practical and immediate.

> They said to him: Master, bless us! He said to them, May it be God's will that the fear of Heaven be upon you as much as the fear of flesh and blood. They said to him, "Just so much?" (that is, *only* so much?) He said, Would that it were so! Knew ye that when a man sins a sin, he says, I hope no *man* sees me.
>
> As he breathed his last, he said, Clear the house of uncleanness of vessels which can receive corpse uncleanness (that is, his corpse would render certain utensils ritualistically unclean, in keeping with rabbinic law) and prepare a throne for Hezekiah, King of Judah, who cometh . . . .[21]

The laws of ritual purity had to be obeyed, and he rehearsed his faith in the coming of the Messiah and a better world. King Hezekiah, it would seem, is himself deemed the Messiah. Thus on his death-bed he reaffirmed his conviction that the Holy One had not abandoned His people; redemption was on the way. All his work as teacher and expounder of the law was only a preparation for the coming Messianic redemption.*

Yohanan planted a sapling that through the centuries has continued to grow into a tree of life for his people and their faith.

---

*One recalls the last words spoken by Socrates, a far different type of man, in a radically different tradition: "Crito, I owe a cock to Asclepius; will you remember to pay the debt."

Talmudic Masters and Apostolic Fathers

PART V

Talmudic Masters and
Apostolic Fathers

Akiba: Fortress of the Law

Akiba and Paul—a Contrast

While Paul was on his missionary travels, driven relentlessly by his passion to make Jesus the Christ of all the earth, at whose name "every knee should bow in heaven above and on the earth and under the earth," founding congregations, appointing leaders, cajoling and pleading and quarrelling with disciples and rearing by brilliant dialectics a towering system of creeds, an illiterate shepherd was tending the sheep of his rich master in the environs of Lydda, present-day Lod, in the low-lying plain near the Mediterranean coast. The two never met. They had nothing in common. Akiba, at this stage in his life, had nothing but disdain for the scholars and the preachers. The two men, however, were destined to rear two opposing fortresses, the law set against the creed, from the battlements of which the millennial spiritual warfare has been waged to this day, and will continue as long as there are Christians and Jews loyal to their respective traditions.

From a personal standpoint the two men represented as sharp a contrast as can be found in history. Paul was a volcanic personality, an ascetic bachelor, probably epileptic; Akiba was a patient jurist who knew love and romance and family life, with all its attendant joys and sorrows. Paul's vision was eschatologic, seeking salvation in the hereafter; Akiba's aim was to hold together a crushed people, enduing them with strength to carry on as the "Chosen People," and forging the instruments of survival. Paul came of a privileged family, Roman freemen; Akiba was the child of the submerged masses and was born into extreme poverty. Paul was a Diaspora Jew, reared in a family of culture; Akiba remained illiterate well into middle age. Paul was a deeply disturbed personality psychiatrically; we know of no such disturbances in the personality of Akiba. Paul was transfixed by a vision of a heavenly Messiah; Akiba, eventually finding his way to the academies, was a sure-footed, practical jurist, agreeing or disputing with his colleagues, shunning visions and searching for the meanings of texts and the logic of the law. Paul was basically antinomian; Akiba sought to regulate every detail of every-day life, of the individual and his community, within the law. Both men, in the fullness of their years, died martyr's deaths, and both died at the hands of the Romans.

One tremendous aspect of their personalities in common: relentless zeal for their conflicting interpretations of their ancestral faith. Paul's passion was the resurrected Christ; Akiba's was the divine Law given to Moses on Mount Sinai and entrusted to the authoritative rabbinic masters. Paul travelled on his fantastic missionary journeys propagating his faith among the gentiles, cutting himself off from "the rock whence he was hewn;" Akiba worked all his life among and for his own people. The few journeys with which he is credited were for the purpose of fortifying his own people and "building a fence around the Torah."

Facts and Legends

Once more we must declare that the facts of our hero's life are hidden in clouds of legends. Scholars draw their inferences from scraps of texts and folk traditions

—and scholars have their creative imaginations. Again we must remind the reader: proceed with caution.

Akiba ben Joseph was born in the middle of the first century, between the years 40 and 50, to a poor family in the general area of Lydda. Until he approached his middle age, he remained a shepherd tending other men's sheep, and having only disdain for scholars and all their works.

Enormous happenings were taking place during these years. One Rabbi, Saul of Tarsus turned into Paul the Apostle, was travelling from Jerusalem to Damascus, to Antioch, to Ephesus, to Athens, to Corinth, to Rome propagating an enormous heresy, cutting all historic ties with his people and their ancestral faith, transfixed by the vision he had seen on the road to Damascus. Roman conquest had reduced the Temple and the State to ashes and bitter national memories. Josephus was writing his histories in Rome; Yohanan ben Zakkai's academy at Yavneh replaced Jerusalem as the seat of authority. Akiba was, evidently, totally unaware of all these enormous events; he was tending his sheep.

And then he fell in love with the daughter of a rich man.

Tradition delights in weaving a romance. The ancients needed a bright spot to relieve the lamentations and the drabness into which Judean life had sunk. Rachel's father was indeed a rich man, and of course hard-hearted. He forbade his beautiful daughter to see the illiterate peasant. But love knows no obstacles, especially in folk fancy. They met in secret. Rachel influenced her lover to turn from sheep-tending to the academies. The country rustic had serious misgivings. How could he, a man approaching middle age, whose mind had never been opened to the sharp dialetctics of the schoolmen, hope to hold his own in the academies? One day, brooding over this, he found himself observing a drop of water falling on a slab by the well; he noticed that the drop, by sheer persistence, had created a cavity in the rock. If a drop of water could do that why might not the words of the Torah, by persistence, make an impression even upon his untutored brain? By nature he was optimistic, convinced that whatever God does He does for the best. A yarn that has delighted countless generations of Jewish children is spun in rabbinic literature to illustrate this.[1]

At the age of forty, the father of several children, he presented himself at a school and applied for admission, along with his five-year-old son. He joined these very young children, and thus began his distinguished career as scholar, jurist, leader, and finally martyr. The sharp transfiguration of his personality, unlike Paul's on the road to Damascus, had nothing of the supernatural about it. It was the calm, deliberate decision of a middle-aged man.

The spinning wheel of legendry continues to weave the double strand of fact and fancy.

Akiba and his bride were desperately poor. All they had to sleep on was some straw matting, and even that they shared with a wayfarer who was still poorer than they, only to discover that this destitute wanderer was none other than Elijah the prophet. Rachel, like Ruth many centuries before, captivated the imaginations of the folk preachers, many of whom were poets at heart. She sold her lovely hair to help finance her husband's schooling, a most serious sacrifice for a young woman of that day. For some dozen years he studied at the feet of Yohanan ben Zakkai's most distinguished disciples, Eliezer ben Hyrcanus and Joshua ben Hananiah.

Thus the golden chain of tradition was forged. Akiba in his day carried forward the teachings of the aging— or late—Yohanan ben Zakkai at Yavneh. For a time he sold himself out as a day laborer. Eventually he returned to his beloved Rachel—"the crown of her husband," in the language of the rabbinic romantics trapped in their academies—only to leave her for another extended number of years to sharpen his wits with the distinguished masters of the age. On his final return home he was accompanied by a huge throng of students. Pointing to his ragamuffin wife, grown old before her time, he is reported to have said to them, "for what I am, and for what all of us are, to this noble woman thanks are due."

He opened his own school at Benei Berak, in what is today the environs of Tel Aviv. It is a historical fact that the leading masters of the century came from Akiba's school. To this day Benei Berak is revered as a seat of scholarship and piety.

Akiba's is a romance in the "from rags to riches" tradition. Not only did he become famous as the revered master of his generation, but he also became rich. His skinflint father-in-law relented and dowered him with an ample fortune. The bearded rabbinic masters weave a yarn of an aristocratic Roman lady leaving him a fortune in the form of a casket of jewels washed up by the sea, and another wonder-tale of a rich Roman aristocrat, converted to Judaism under Akiba's influence, leaving him another fortune. Rags to riches romances require happy endings. Any more pleasant way of acquiring wealth than through inheritance?

Frequently Akiba was involved in good-natured disputations with Roman intellectuals; always he bested these pagan simpletons. From these exchanges come some of his most famous aphorisms, which we shall note when we turn to his religious teachings and legal decisions.

A Mighty Harvest

Victorious Roman legions plowed the Holy City and planted it with salt so that nothing might ever grow in it; defeated Jewry nurtured it with blood and tears and prayers, and produced a mighty harvest which has continued to sustain the generations of Israel for almost two millennia. Akiba ben Joseph's sure hand helped to bring forth this harvest.

During his inordinately long lifetime—he lived well into his nineties—the Hebrew Bible (the Old Testament) was completed. The oral traditions were systematized. This produced the foundations upon which Akiba's successors based their Mishnah, now in our hands. The Synagogue finally replaced the Temple. The prayer book acquired a new development, which, like the Bible and the Mishnah, became a powerful force in the hands of every Jewish community. The calendar was regulated into an automatic system and honed into an effective instrument for the new circumstances. Akiba labored in all these areas and sealed his testimony with his martyr's blood.

Old Testament Canon

Scholars point with some certainty to Akiba's part in completing the Old Testament canon. It is known that he was instrumental in excluding the book of Ecclesiasticus, now in the Apocrypha, and that he was responsible for including the Scrolls of Esther and, especially, the Song of Songs. Akiba's allegoric interpretation of the love songs of the Shulammite and her lover in the vineyards of Israel as the love embrace between God and Israel was not a truly Pharisaic mode of Bible interpretation. The Pharisees avoided the allegoric method; it gave every pagan an easy way out of the disciplines of the law and could send him off into wild vagaries of the mystery cults. But, fortunately for us, Akiba was enamored of the God and Israel relationship in terms of tender love. "I am my beloved's and my beloved is mine"[2] he expounded as God and Israel in holy embrace. And since the notion that King Solomon had written it was a belief at the time, the song of love became a song of faith and thus was accepted into the holy scriptures.

The Hebrew Bible in its final form—begun with the first edition of the Pentateuch in the year 444 B.C.E. by Ezra—is the rock of immortality on which Jewry built its new life. "I shall not die but live and declare the works of the Lord."[3] The later rabbinic masters, determining the ritual of the synagogue, composed a special benediction to be recited after reading from the Pentateuch: "Blessed art Thou, O Lord our God, King of the universe, who has given us the law of truth and hast planted everlasting life in our midst."[4] Everlasting life it has been. The Temple that had gone up in flames now was only a memory and a vision that comforted and sustained the devout; but the folk synagogue was the functioning every-day sanctuary.

Synagogue

The synagogue thus came into its own as the replacement for the Temple. The Temple was the nation's central authoritative shrine established in the laws of Moses; it was the aristocratic, vested institution of a hereditary and privileged priestly class and its subservient functionaries. These had constituted the Sadducees. Priests were at times arrogant; vested hereditary interests do not breed piety. The sons of Eli were always greedy for their fringe benefits. They were the rich and represented the interests and the thinking of the rich. The common people, faithful to the laws of Moses, dutifully paid their tithes and offered their sacrifices; but their religious homes, their comfort and their satisfactions, they found in the little unofficial folk meeting houses formerly ancillary to the Temple. These folk meeting places had originated back in Babylon when the refugees of those days met for mutual assistance and comfort.

The Synagogue was thus born out of the loneliness and dire need of the masses. Returning to Jerusalem in the days of the Second Commonwealth and the rebuilt Temple the folk synagogues functioned off-the-record as places for worship, for study and for prayer. Thus we hear of Jesus and Paul meeting their fellow-Jews in the synagogues and there expounding their views, which they drew from the Pentateuch canon. By the time of Yohanan ben Zakkai and Akiba ben Joseph, with the Temple no more, the Synagogue came into its own and has functioned ever since as Jewry's school, chapel and social center.

Systematizer of the Law

By the time of Akiba the oral traditions, which represented the unique, revolutionary creation of the Pharisees in their persistent effort to make the Torah cover every living need of a growing community under steadily varying circumstances, had become an enormous and amorphous mass. The Oral law started back in Bible days. Ezra not only "read" the laws of Moses but "expounded" them to the people and the Judean masses officially accepted and confirmed their eternal covenant with their God.[5] Centuries passed and this oral tradition expanded under the new circumstances. Hillel and Shammai and Yohanan ben Zakkai, as we have noted, gave it further expansion in the crises of their times. By Akiba's time the vast amount of interpretation and reinterpretation became unworkable. It needed systematization; Akiba was the great systematizer. He arranged the basis for subsequent codification, indispensable to a living law. His colleagues compare his work to a man who goes to market and buys whatever attracts him. He puts it into his basket. At home he places each item in its place. That was Akiba's true genius and his major contribution to the survival of Jewry in its most critical stage.

A most respected scholar of the Talmud of our own time testifies on this point:

> Akiba no doubt perceived that the intellectual bond uniting the Jews—far from being allowed to disappear with the destruction of the Jewish state—must be made to draw them closer together than before. The Bible could never again fill the place alone; for the Christian also regarded it as a divine revelation. Still less could dogma serve the purpose, for dogmas were always repellent to rabbinical Judaism, whose very essence is development and susceptibility to development.

Thus it was Akiba who "marked out a path for rabbinical Judaism for almost two thousand years."[6]

Hermeneutics and Law

Akiba developed an elaborate—to us artificial—system of Bible interpretation in applying the abstract word of God to the daily life of the people. He saw special meanings in every word, every particle, every meaningless stroke of the Law of Moses as he found it in the sacred scrolls. When Jesus affirmed his absolute fidelity to every letter, iota and dot of the law, he spoke in the same Pharisaic tradition that made Akiba suspend mountains of legal interpretations on every word and syllable, however obscure and superfluous it may have been. One scholarly wag has observed that Moses did not know all that was in his laws until Akiba expounded them.[7]

Everything Akiba needed to make the law viable and vital was in the Torah. All that was needed was to render explicit what was implicit. The laws were immutable while life was making new demands. Akiba, following the Pharisaic tradition, was under compulsion to harmonize the two into a way of life. The striking aspect is that though working with particular laws meant for a separate and separatistic people he nevertheless achieved a universalistic reach. Akiba anchored what was literalistic and separatistic in the universal. Capital punishment, for example, is not only permitted in the Bible but is required in some twenty-five instances. The rabbinic masters practically outlawed capital punishment altogether. Akiba and a colleague declare, "Had we belonged to the Sanhedrin no man would ever have been executed."[8]

Akiba insisted on subordinating the individual to the law; no man, no scholar, however deeply revered, was above the letter and logic of the law. And he insisted on subordinating class interests to the demands of the same law, though he himself, scholars aver, was strongly influenced by the poverty of his youth and leaned toward the disinherited masses. "Within his wide range of sympathies he included the struggle of the shepherd against the farmer, the highland against the valley, the town against the country, the artisan against the noble, and the Levite against the priest."[9] Behind some of the finely spun dialectics and arguments based on every obscure word of the sacred text were vested economic interests, political prestige and social status of the landless peasantry and the patrician landowners, and all the class and group interests in-between. Akiba was on the side of the disinherited. "The vigilance of Akiba was quick to perceive the implications of opposed class interests behind the academic façade. When, for instance, Eliezer made the innocent remark that the honey, which Scripture enumerates as one of Palestine's blessings, must mean the honey of dates, Akiba vigorously objected. He saw in this interpretation an attempt to enhance the prestige of the oasis of Jericho, the ancient home of the aristocracy and the only part of Palestine where date palms grew. 'No, it means the honey of the bees,' he said; 'for that could be found in the plebeian upland country in even greater quantities than in the lowlands.' "[10]

A practical man, Akiba was not beyond employing the tricks of the lawyers of our own day. A rich priest by the name of Eleazer, for example, was receiving tithes from a certain field. This practice, in the opinion of Akiba, was not lawful. The man was greedy. More, the whole matter of tithing for the priests was at issue. Akiba noticed that this particular field had two approaches. One of these led into a cemetery. Akiba had the other approach closed, leaving open only the cemetery entrance. The law prohibited a priest from entering a cemetery, and Eleizer could not enter the field to collect his tithe.[11]

Religious Teaching

Man, Akiba insisted, was made, as Genesis affirms, "in the image of God." "Beloved [of God] is man, for he was created in the image of God." His colleagues enlarged on this declaration: man is created in the image of God potentially. All the divine capacities and potentialities are in man; what man needs do is to develop them and thus achieve for himself the divine image. He has the freedom and the capacity—yes, the mandate— to do this. Akiba brooked no opposition on this point. Perhaps he was motivated in part by the growing emphasis of the rising Christian sect on the depravity of human nature and the need for a supernatural redeemer.

His teaching on this point has come down to us in a
popular pronouncement and metaphor:

> He used to say, Beloved is man, for he was created in the
> image of God; but it was by a special love that it was made
> known to him that he was created in the image of God; as it
> is said, "For in the image of God made he man." Beloved are
> Israel, for they were called children of the All-present; but
> it was by a special love that it was made known to them that
> they were called children of the All-present; as it is said, Ye
> are children unto the Lord your God. Beloved are Israel, for
> unto them was given the desirable instrument; but it was by
> a special love that it was made known to them that that de-
> sirable instrument was theirs, through which the world was
> created; as it is said, 'For I give you good doctrine; forsake
> ye not my Law.'
> Everything is forseen, yet freedom of choice is given; and the
> world is judged by grace, yet all is according to the amount
> of work.
> He used to say, Everything is given on pledge, and a net is
> spread for all the living: the shop is open; and the dealer gives
> credit; and the ledger lies open; and the hand writes; and
> whosoever wishes to borrow may come and borrow; but the
> collectors regularly make their daily round; and exact payment
> from man, whether he be content or not.[12]

Perhaps in direct and conscious opposition, too, to the
developing Christian belief of God's redemptive love,
Akiba and his colleagues taught that this belief was an
arbitrary and gratuitous conception: man needed to do
nothing to merit salvation. All he needed to do was
affirm his belief. Akiba insisted on God's retributive
justice; every man was required to *merit* his salvation.
Justice, however, is not God's sole attribute; He is also
a God of "compassion, gracious and merciful, long suffering, abounding in mercy and ever true."[13] God rules
the world by justice *and* by loving kindness; the mixture
of good and the bad in human conduct determines the
combination. "I have set before you life and death,

blessing and curse; therefore choose life . . . "[14] Man has the capacity and the duty to make the choice and live or die accordingly.

Mortal man is endowed with a divine deposit. Life is sacred. "He who sheds the blood of a fellow man is to be considered as committing a crime against God's original pattern set for man."[15] The emphasis is on *man*, the human being, not only on an Israelite.

With all his particularistic and separatistic emphasis Akiba affirms Leviticus 19.18 to be the root principle of the entire Law of Moses: "You shall love your neighbor as yourself."

Calendar

Perhaps the last project with which Akiba was concerned was establishing the calendar for the synagogue and for scattered Jewry. He was now in his nineties, imprisoned in Caesarea, as we shall note. From his prison cell he continued forging the instruments of survival for his people and their faith, in flat defiance of Hadrian's decrees. The fixing of the calendar was crucial.

The Synagogue calendar is lunar, borrowed from ancient Babylon. To this day the Hebrew months are known by their Babylonian names. The beginnings of the months were determined by the primitive method of stationing watchmen at appointed places to observe the first signs of the new moon and report it to the Sanhedrin in session at Jerusalem. When the reports were accepted, the new month was proclaimed officially; heralds—or fires at lookout points—carried the news to the Jewish communities all through Palestine and to the Diaspora. The observance of the holy days as ordained in the Pentateuch depended on these reports. Religious Jewry was paralyzed without a functioning calendar.

But in the days of Akiba, Jerusalem was no more; the Sanhedrin was no more. No authorized watchmen could bring reports; no authorities were there to receive them. Yohanan ben Zakkai struggled with this problem in Yavneh. The lunar calendar was most inaccurate. Even back in Babylon it had been necessary to regulate it by the solar. It had to be converted into an automatic system. Following only the lunar calendar meant that the holy days and festivals could not be observed in their seasons. Passover, for instance, which is a spring festival, might come in the middle of the winter, and Sukkot, which is a fall harvest festival, might come in the middle of summer. While the Sanhedrin, or the deputed courts, were in session in Jerusalem, before the year 70, the authorities had been adding an intercalary month from time to time and thus bring the lunar calendar into line with the solar, and place the holidays in their proper seasons.

Akiba, in prison, concentrated on this problem. He was convinced that a fixed, realistic calendar was Jewry's lifeline. He met with his disciples in defiance of the Hadrianic laws and paid for it with his life. A fixed automatic calendar was finally achieved.[16]

Zealotry and Messianism Again

For some fifteen years following the fall of the Temple and State in the year 70 the Roman rulers followed a policy of quiescence. The Jews, at least in theory, were granted equal rights with their non-Jewish neighbors. The emperors Domitian, Nerva and Trajan were reasonable men. As long as the conquered Jews paid their taxes they were left to their own devices. We hear of Roman converts to Judaism, and of rumors that Trajan had promised to permit the Jews to rebuild their Temple.

In the year 115 Trajan was involved in a far-flung war with the Parthians, a most stubborn enemy. While he was in the field news reached him of flaming rebellion all over the western Mediterranean, Armenia and Mesopotamia. The Jews also rebelled with vengeance. The smouldering fires of zealotry and messianism burst into vast fires among the Jews of Palestine, Egypt, Cyrene and Cyprus. A Roman historian reports that before these rebellions had run their courses some 220,000 men, Jews and non-Jews, were killed in Cyrene alone; 240,000 in Cyprus. We do not know how accurate these figures are, but there is no doubt that the devastations and slaughter were vast.[17]

In the year 117 Trajan was assassinated by Arabs in Cilicia. Succeeding him was his nephew, one of the most glamorous and one of the most able of the Roman emperors, Publius Aelius Hadrianus. A "philospher king," he was among the most brilliant of the Roman rulers. A highly sophisticated man and a superb administrator, he was devoted to the arts and to a fantastic building program, and was also bent on pacifying his rebellious subjects in the far flung empire. In addition, he determined to pursue a Hellenizing program and to placate his restless Christian subjects. But he was astonishingly stupid in dealing with the Jews. The brief period of toleration which Hadrian himself had encouraged for a short time was reversed, and was replaced by persecutions that pitilessly crushed Jewry. Yavneh, with its promise of religious rebirth, was suppressed. Circumcision, Sabbath observance, the teaching of Torah in any form was outlawed; every form of Jewish organization was banned. Ordination of scholars was made a capital offense. Hadrian, like the Antiochuses before him and long after him, knew the secret of Jewish survival: study and fulfillment of the law.

The new upsurge of zealotry and messianism found

its leader in a man known in history as Bar Kokba. His real name was Simon. The name by which he is distinguished in history was given him by Akiba, who saw in his fantastic person the fulfillment of Scripture.

> A star (*kokov*) shall come forth out of Jacob
> And a sceptre shall rise out of Israel.[18]

The name Bar Kokba ("Son of a Star") stuck to the man. Phenomenal he was. His personality, radiating enormous physical prowess, was fearless, dauntless, magnetic; he gained a vast following. A prayer attributed to him affords us a glimpse into his personality. "We pray Thee, O Lord, do not give assistance to the enemy; us Thou needest not help."[19]

In the year 132 the insurrection burst into full fury. Bar Kokba fought from his headquarters at Bethar, a fortress southwest of Jerusalem.* Next to Masada, Bethar acquired a legendary character. The zealots fought from every fortified place, from every cave, every tunnel available to them. They succeeded for a time, and even captured Jerusalem. Flushed with victory, they struck a coin celebrating their triumph. The Christian sect would not join in the rebellion; Bar Kokba was being hailed as the new Messiah, and the followers of Jesus could not concur in that.

The victories were short lived. Hadrian, after initial defeats, recalled his most able general from Britain, and equipped him with a powerful army. On the ninth day of Ab in the year 134, the insurrection was finally crushed. Bethar, like Masada earlier, held out in fanatic futility. A year later it fell to the Romans; Bar Kokba was slain on the walls of his fortress. Half a million Jews are believed to have been slain in the course of the insurrection; fifty fortresses and a thousand villages

---

*Now under excavation.

were wiped out. The Holy City was plowed as a symbol of Roman conquest. Upon its site rose the new Aelia Capitoliana, replete with temples to Bacchus, Serapis, Venus; on the site where the Temple once stood, dedicated to the Holy One of Israel, a temple to Jupiter was erected. Once again the daughter of Zion sat in ashes and wept with none to comfort her.

Martyrdom

What part did Akiba play in this tragic uprising? Some historians have sentimentalized his role in the heroic but utterly futile tragedy. It is claimed that he was "the soul of the insurrection," that his travels for the welfare of his people—not only visiting communities in Palestine but also in Rome, Parthia, Asia Minor, Capadocia, Africa—were motivated primarily with the purpose of rousing and organizing rebellion against Rome. There is nothing in the sources to document this claim. All we know is that the rabbi hailed Bar Kokba as the new Messiah, thus undoubtedly encouraging the rebellion.

Sometime before Jerusalem finally fell to Hadrian's forces Akiba was incarcerated at Caesarea. The charge against him was not political or nationalistic; it was claimed that Akiba was in defiance of Hadrian's decrees against the practice of Judaism. From his prison cell he directed his students and disciples, against Roman orders, to stand true to their religious duties as Jews. His disciples were teaching and ordaining scholars in secret, "even as the Lord had commanded." All of them paid with their lives. The martyrdom of Hananiah ben Teradion may be considered symbolic.

They then brought up R. Hanania ben Teradion and asked

him, "Why hast thou occupied thyself with the Torah?" He replied, "Thus the Lord my God commanded me." At once, they sentenced him to be burnt, his wife to be slain, and his daughter to be consigned to a brothel.[20]

The aged scholar was wrapped in a scroll of the Law and burnt at the stake. His weeping disciples caught his voice and his vision: scholar and scroll were going up in flames, but the letters of the Law soared upward, a defiant vision.

Sometime during these black days a clandestine rabbinic conference was held at Lydda. A desperate question confronted these rabbinic masters. How far might they encourage their people to save themselves, their families and their communities, by violating their religious duties? Or were they to preside at the extermination of their people? An historic pronouncement came out of this conference:

> By a majority vote, it was resolved in the upper chambers of the house of Nithza in Lydda that in every (other) law of the Torah, if a man is commanded: "Transgress and suffer not death," he may transgress and not suffer death, excepting idolatry, incest (which includes adultery) and murder.[21]

The existence of God, the sanctity of life and the purity of family must never be compromised.

We have no documentary proof that Akiba was at this conference. It is reasonable to assume that he was, unless he was incarcerated in Caesarea at this time. However, the decision was in complete accord with his lifelong teachings. The purpose of the Law was that "man should live by it."

The Talmud contains the report of his martyrdom. It is the report of revering disciples. The words may be charged with legendry added later. The event they record is historically accurate:

When R. Akiba was taken out for execution, it was the hour for the recital of the *Shema,* and while they combed his flesh with iron combs, he was accepting upon himself the kingship of heaven (i.e. reciting the *Shema*). His disciples said to him: Our teacher, even to this point? He said to them: All my days I have been troubled by the verse, *with all thy soul,* [which I interpret] "even if He takes thy soul." I said: When shall I have the opportunity of fulfilling this? Now that I have the opportunity shall I not fulfill it? He prolonged the word *ehad* (One) until he expired while saying it.[22]

The most distinguished talmudic scholar of our generation has testified: "Pure monotheism was for Akiba the essence of Judaism; he lived, worked and died for it."[23]

14

Apostles and Martyrs—
The Church Triumphant

From Synagogue to Church

They met and worshipped in their obscure chapels, even as they had in their folk synagogues; they sought mutual consolation and prayed in their accustomed Judaic manner. Hovering over them, beckoning and mesmerizing them, was the vision of the risen Christ, their Redeemer, consoling them in their sorrows, fortifying them in their faith, inciting them with fervid expectations of the Kingdom of Heaven. These Nazarenes were devout Jews, desperately in earnest. Their prayers and their blood seeded the Church.

As the century advanced, their meetings diverged in the direction of their apocalyptic vision of the resurrected Christ. From pondering the Torah of Moses and rearing a fortress of *mitzvot*—commandments, ordinances, anchored in the covenant their fathers had sealed at Sinai with the God of Israel—they were absorbed with and enthralled by a creed.

They were lowly, God-fearing folk, maligned by some historians—as their Pharisaic brothers were—as the scum of society. Rather, they were a community of grim believers, meticulously observant in their religious devotions, puritanical in personal morals, communistic in social relationships, bound by powerful ties in the resur-

rected Christ who was returning to judge the living and
the dead. They were his elect; he would bring redemption to them and, in his own time, would raise them with
him into the heavenly realm whence he had come.

They were predominantly proletarian. They welcomed
the fellowship of slaves, though they made no effort to
liberate them. That was left to the will of God. They
were industrious and shared all their possessions among
themselves. Convinced that the world was coming to an
end and that they, personally, would stand before the
throne of the Last Judgment, what reason was there
for them to amass wealth? They followed their Master
faithfully. Jesus had taught them that a rich man had
as much chance of entering heaven as a camel had to
pass through the eye of a needle. His brother James
expressed this conviction in graphic terms:

> Come now, you rich, weep and howl for the miseries that are
> coming upon you. Your riches have rotted and your garments
> are moth eaten. Your gold and silver have rusted, and their
> rust will be evidence against you and will eat your flesh like
> fire . . . . Be patient, therefore, brethren, until the coming of
> the Lord. Behold, the farmer waits for the precious fruit of
> the earth, being patient over it until it receives the early and
> the late rain. You also be patient . . . . Has not God chosen
> those who are poor in the world to be rich in faith and heirs
> of the kingdom which he has promised to those who love him?[1]

They refreshed their faith with periodic love feasts—
agapé—prayers, hymns, Scriptural readings, a practice
carried over from their synagogues; they partook of
bread and wine properly blessed by the priests. Some
concluded these *agapé* meetings with an Amen of a holy
kiss. To the more imaginative and excitable the bread
and the wine were the transubstantiated body and blood
of their Master, even as he had indicated at the Last
Supper. Thus developed, in time, the doctrine of transub-

stantiation.[2] The Sabbath they observed strictly, as Moses had prescribed and the Pharisees had interpreted. It was not until the second century that the Jewish Sabbath was transferred to Sunday.

Women they treated in the manner to which they had been conditioned in the faith of their fathers: respected, man's helpmeet as ordained in Scripture. Woman must be modest, properly subservient to man. Had not Paul taught: "I want you to understand that the head of every man is Christ, the head of a woman is her husband, and the head of Christ is God?" Woman must be properly veiled; man need not for he is the glory of God; "but woman is the glory of man. For man was not made from woman, but woman from man. Neither was man created for woman, but woman for man."[3]

We may assume that since women were feminine they had the rights, liberties and prerogatives they wanted. If, to sophisticated moderns, this attitude to women is objectionable, lacking in freedom and rights, we need but recall the debauched attitude towards women that permeated the surrounding pagan society. The Judaic Christians were repelled by the continuing pagan immorality—canine sex promiscuity, abortions, infanticide.

Thus the Nazarenes were devout and observant Jews. They treasured their Hebrew Scriptures as the infallible word of God, discharged their Temple obligations dutifully—that is, as long as the Temple functioned—paid their tithes, observed the dietary laws, circumcised their sons, wore their garments properly fringed, even as Moses had commanded: that they might see and "remember and do all my commandments, and be holy to your God."[4] Their vernacular was Aramaic; their prayers they spoke, at least in part, in Hebrew.

All the while they were enthralled by the vision of Christ the Redeemer.

Three beliefs in particular separated these Judaic

Christians from their fellow Jews; and the gulf widened
and deepened as the decades advanced: A) The Messiah,
in the person of Jesus, had come, was martyrized as
Scripture had foretold, and had risen from the tomb on
the third day, returning to his Father in heaven. B) He
would surely return—in a Second Coming—speedily, in
their own time, and would terminate the present world
order and establish his Kingdom of Heaven on earth.
C) They, personally and physically, would be resurrected
from their graves for the awesome hour of the Last
Judgment. Devoutly and grimly they believed in these
three dogmas. The apostle assured them: "Children, it
is the last hour; and as you have heard that antichrist
is coming, so now many antichrists have come; therefore
we know that it is the last hour."[5] Had not Nero, Vespasian, Domitian, Hadrian already come and done their
evil works? Was not the Temple already destroyed?
"So we may be sure it is the last hour." Perhaps his
Second Coming might be delayed; perhaps He would
return in a millennium; but return He will and at that
time He will take the elect back with him to eternal
glory.*

When, in the year 70 and again in 135, the rebellion
against Rome broke and their fellow Jews were dying
by the thousands—ghastly figures could be seen on
crosses all around Jerusalem—these Nazarenes dis-
engaged themselves from the Jewish community. They
took refuge in Pella, a pagan pro-Roman center far from
the fires of war, and waited for their Messiah to return

---

*It is a Christian adaptation of conceptions of the "Messianic Kingdom
on earth, such as were popular in late pre-Christian Jewish apocalyptic
speculation, especially in Daniel, 2 Esdras, Book of Enoch." *(Oxford
Dictionary of the Christian Church)*
A potent root of Church anti-Semitism is latent in the doctrine that
Christ would not return until the Jews had accepted Him and were
extinct as a separate, heretical people. Hence the stiff-necked Jews were
preventing His Second Coming.

from his heavenly heights. Thus they violated a basic principle of their Pharisaic brethren: "Separate not yourself from the community," especially at a time of crisis.[6] They concentrated on their personal redemption in the Hereafter, and ceased being Jews. The tides of their times swept them farther and farther away from their ancestral moorings. To their Jewish brethren—fighting and dying by the thousands in defense of their faith, their Temple, their Holy City—these Nazarenes must have been deluded apocalyptists, or worse, cowards and traitors. How could an embattled Pharisee understand the Nazarene's hailing the destruction of the Temple as a fulfillment of God's prophecies? How could they condone their deserting their brethren at a time of crisis? Zealous Pharisees could no more understand them on this point than they could understand Josephus' haranguing the embattled defenders of the Temple to the effect that the Holy One of Israel had abandoned them, their city and their shrine, and moved to Italy.

Much of the New Testament came out of this heat and hatred, of this war and pious fratricide. The anti-Semitism, so deeply embedded in the New Testament, can be explained historically.

The Blood of the Martyrs

Tertullion's oft-quoted dictum, "The blood of the martyrs is the seed [of the church]"[7] is a true expression of the passions, the zeal and the woes that gave birth to the Church and sustained it in the agonies of its infancy.

Jesus on the cross, his blood drawn by a centurion's sword in sheer horseplay; his brother James dying a martyr's death in 110 under Trajan, sanctifying God's name, whose laws he would not compromise; Peter and

Paul, their quarrels settled and their devotions sealed with their blood at the hands of the purple beast of Rome—these were but the beginnings of the vast host of Christian martyrs. The tragedy of history is that in time the sons of the crucified themselves turned crucifiers, and in the name of the Crucified Christ tortured their own brothers in the faith who differed with them in fine interpretations of the creed.

Nero, the infamous fiddler, turned the blame for the fire that devastated Rome on July 18, 64, on the Christians. He found the Christians obnoxious. Their outlook on life, their demeanor, their stiff-necked refusal to engage in Emperor worship, infuriated him. Christians were seditious, it was charged; they practiced black magic, engaged in immoral practices; they drank human blood at their Paschal feast and worshipped the head of an ass.* In the book of Revelation Nero is depicted as the monstrous antichrist, the very messiah of Satan, who forced the faithful Christians to drain to the full "the seven bowls of the wrath of God." His Rome was "the great harlot who is seated upon many waters, with whom the kings of the earth have committed fornication, and with the wine of whose fornication the dwellers on earth have become drunk."[8] And the excited apostle John, presumably the author of Revelation, adds: "Babylon the great [that is, Rome] mother of harlots and of earth's abominations . . . drunk with the blood of the saints and the blood of the martyrs of Jesus."[9]

In the year 95 St. Clement of Rome wrote: "To these men [Peter and Paul] whose lives were holy, there is joined a great multitude of elect ones who, in the midst of numerous tortures inflicted for their zeal, gave amongst us a magnificent example."[10]

Under each of Nero's successors to the time of Con-

---

*The very same charges Christians later levelled against the Jews.

stantine, the bestial circuses, the gladiatorial combats, the Augustalis festivals dedicated to the worship of deified emperors, went on and on—under some emperors more than under others: suppression of the Christian faithful, burning their chapels, vilification of all they were and all they represented, torturing, burning, beheading. We recall but a few of the honored names of the martyrs who endowed the Church with an awesome heritage. Nero's ghost went rampaging on.

Ignatius, Bishop of Antioch and successor to Peter, and who was the first of the Apostolic Fathers, pleaded with his friends not to intercede with Rome and deprive him of the opportunity to sanctify the name of his Master with his blood. He considered himself the "wheat of God, and I must be ground by the teeth of wild beasts to become the pure bread of Christ."[11] He was executed in Rome about the year 110. In the year 165, at Smyrna, eleven Christians were butchered in the amphitheater to the drunken revelry of a mob. Bishop Polycarp, in his eighty-sixth year, on "the Great Sabbath," faced the Roman executioners with the dignity worthy of his faith. To the demand that he renounce his Christian faith and bow to Roman Emperor worship, he is reported to have said: "For eighty-six years have I been his servant, and he has done me no wrong; how can I blaspheme my King who saved me?"[12] His words and conduct are reminiscent of the words and conduct spoken by the father of the Maccabees at Modin, by Eleazar in his response to the Syrian persecutors, of Hananiah ben Teradion and of Akiba as they faced the Roman executioners.[13] Justin Martyr, philosophic convert from Paganism, enamored of Plato, was executed for his heretical ideas in the year 165; the same year, in Rome, Justin of Samaria, along with eleven disciples, was martyrized. Bishop Pothinus of Lyons, ninety years old, died in jail after merciless torture. The Augustalis festival was celebrated with the execution of forty-seven devoted Christians. In Carthage and in Smyrna, in 250, hundreds of Roman Christians were beheaded or burned at the stake, or thrown to the beasts in an orgy of holiday celebrations. Pope Sixtus II was seized as he was conducting a service and, along with four of his deacons, was beheaded. The Bishop of Carthage and the Bishop of Tarragona were put to death; one was beheaded and the other burned. Throughout the third century, ban followed ban, burning followed burning; congregations were outlawed, their properties confiscated. Rome was determined on unity, obedience. The black waters of persecution reached their crest in the reign of Diocletian (284-305). In a fury over the burning of his palace, a crime which he attributed to the Christians, he pressed a savage program of forcing the stiff-necked believers into submission. Eusibius recalls the gory details. For eight years the persecutions raged relentlessly, and 1500 Christians are believed to have been put to death in every conceivable diabolic manner. "There is no greater drama in human record," writes Will Durant, "than the sight of a few Christians, scorned or oppressed by a succession of emperors, bearing all trials with a free tenacity, multiplying quietly, building order while their enemies generated chaos, fighting the sword with the word, brutality with hope, and at last defeating the strongest state that history has known. Caesar and Christ had met in the arena, and Christ had won."[15]

Preaching the Gospel, Schisms, More Blood

Christian chapels dotted Judea by the turn of the century and were multiplying rapidly. The apostles were zealots. Their mission to preach the word of Christ was a fire in their bones. Conversion to Christ was their primary dynamic. Jesus was "the way, and the truth, and the life."[16] His words had to be amplified to all the world and speedily fulfilled. Jewish dispersion and Roman roads and commerce prepared the way. In Jerusalem itself James, brother of Jesus, presided in absolute devotion to the established Jewish ceremonial traditions, true as he was to the vision of the Messiah. Philip made converts in Samaria and Caesarea; John gained a following in Ephesus, a commercial center whose cultural life was dominated by the goddess Artemis, a city that had given Paul so much distress. Peter proclaimed the Gospel in Syria. A vision instructed him to accept non-Jews as converts. Circumcision was a serious impediment to proselytizing, as Paul had found; baptism was more pleasant and more saleable. Peter, as well as James, it will be recalled, had opposed Paul on this point. Peter vacillated for a time. Finally he chose to follow Paul's practice. The apostles broke with their Lord at this point. Jesus had charged them originally: "Go nowhere among the Gentiles, and enter no town of the Samaritans, but go rather to the lost sheep of the house of Israel."[17] They stretched his vision and by doing so converted him from the particularistic to the universal. In the same Gospel (Matthew), towards the end of his career, Jesus is quoted as charging the same disciples: "Go therefore and make disciples of all nations, baptizing them in the name of the Father and the Son and of the Holy Spirit, teaching them to observe all that I have commanded you; and lo, I am with you always, to the close of the age."[18]

From the long-range standpoint, the apostles shifted Jesus from the racial and narrow to the broadest, embracing all humanity. They changed their movement from a separatist cult to a universal religion. However, flinging the gates wide open to all peoples, there poured into the nascent church many Greeks bearing strange gifts: beliefs, rites, practices of all the mystery cults in that part of the world. A bold illustration of this pagan penetration and transmutation may be seen in the pagan backgrounds to Christmas. The feast of the Nativity was transmuted by the Saturnalia rites. Christianity was turning into one more mystery cult.[19]

Peter preached in the very precincts of the Temple, then proceeded to Galilee, Lydda, Sharon, Joppa, performing miracles and winning followers. His reputation as healer was sensational.

> And more than ever believers were added to the Lord, multitudes both of men and women, so that they even carried out the sick into the streets, and laid them on beds and pallets, that as Peter came by at least his shadow might fall on some of them.[20]

Eventually Peter found his way to Rome, where he played a leading role in expanding, if not founding, the Christian community, and where he met a martyr's death. Tradition has it that he was crucified head down so that he might drain the cup of bitter wine in sanctifying the Lord's name more fully—or, perhaps, give up the ghost more readily. He was forced, further, to watch the martyrdom of his wife, who had travelled with him.* On the spot where Peter was crucified, according to tradition, today stands the central shrine of Catholicism, which bears his name.

Paul, as we have recalled when we traced his life and amazing travels, outstripped all the apostles and won his place in history as "the Apostle to the Gentiles," the relentless proselytizing and organizing genius of the Church, and the man who gave the Church its theologic foundations.

Dissent and schism were inevitable. They issued from the very nature of the Gospel.

---

*Cf. martyrdom of Hananiah ben Teradion in the days of Hadrian.

The Gospel was apocalyptic. Unlike the covenant sealed at Sinai, it knew no barriers, no restraints, no disciplines, no limitations imposed by a text, nor by law, nor by life's circumstances. The monstrous visions of the books of Daniel, Enoch and Esdras, as amplified in the book of Revelation, incited aberrations and sent men off into wild flights from reality. When Hillel and Shammai disagreed they disagreed within the law, and within the community; they disagreed as jurists. Life's circumstances and a written law forced a measure of consensus. No such restraints controlled the frenzied preachers, enthralled as they were by an other-worldly Gospel. The authority of emotional doctrine replaced the authority of law. The New Testament canon had not yet been formulated. The allegorical method of Bible interpretation, favored by the apostles and spurned by the rabbis, encouraged the preachers to see whatever they wished to see in Old Testament texts. Further, the preachers differed wildly in their personal temperaments and in the general biases of their personalities. Still more, the native cultures the apostles found throughout Judea, Syria, Asia Minor, Greece, Rome—from the Jordan to the Tiber—were enormously diversified; each had its own native religions, rites, rituals, magic. The Christian missionaries come to convert were themselves converted. Cultural osmosis is subtle and persistently pervasive; schism followed schism. By the last decade of the second century Iranaeus, Greek Bishop of Lyons, listed some twenty varieties of Christianity.

Gnosticism, which had antedated Christianity, was a persistent and brilliant competitor for the souls of men. Marcion, a rich, young Greek, assumed the mantle of St. Paul and opposed every vestige of Judaism, only to have himself and his followers excommunicated by Rome. Montanus attacked the nascent Church as too worldly and corrupt and demanded a return to its primitive

purity. He attracted a wide following of zealots who
were not only ready but eager to sacrifice themselves for
their version of the Gospel. Heresies were inevitable;
they sprouted from the nature of nascent Christianity.*

All along primitive Roman paganism was resisting
the encroaching Christianity, and Greek philosophy was
a persistent and brilliant challenge. By the time Constantine the Great established "unity" in Christian ranks,
with the iron fist of Rome, some hundred creeds were
competing as the true exponents of the Gospel and warring among themselves. Each had its zealots and
martyrs.

The Keys to the Kingdom

The Church of Rome moved into the welter of competition and contention and grasped authority. Peter is
the rock in whom the Lord himself had recognized special grace. In the hour of decision Jesus had turned to
his disciples to ascertain if they had the true understanding of him:

> He said to them, "But who do you say am I? Simon Peter
> replied, "You are the Christ, the Son of the living God. And
> Jesus answered him, "Blessed are you, Simon Bar-Jonah! For
> flesh and blood has not revealed this to you, but my Father
> who is in heaven. And I tell you, you are Peter, and on this
> rock I will build my church, and the powers of death (or *hell*)
> shall not prevail against it. I will give you the keys of the
> kingdom of heaven, and whatever you bind on earth shall be
> bound in heaven, and whatever you lose on earth shall be loosed
> in heaven.[21]

Supreme authority was thus vested in the church of
Rome, supreme authority on earth as in heaven. Roman

*See *Heresy, Sects* in Oxford Dictionary of the Christian Church; New
Catholic Encyclopedia; Encyclopedia Britannica.

organizing efficiency, wealth, ecumenical charities gained and held for it an ever-growing following.

The Church had much to learn from Rome and it did. It refused to waste its energies and opportunities in the revolving doors of theologic disputations. It let others do it. It learned from mighty Rome the secret of efficient organization; it made general concessions to the religious forms and traditions of pre-Christian Rome and would not quibble about theologic niceties; it accepted Roman canon law as the basis for its own codes; it adopted the Roman title of supreme authority, *Pontifex Maximus;* and, in time, it adopted the Roman vernacular as the sacred tongue of the conquering Church. Thus it grasped the keys to the kingdom of heaven and of earth, and the lives and destinies of every man in the Here and in the Hereafter by following the Roman patterns of government and power.

Constantine (Flavius Valerius Constantinus) was appointed Caesar in 305. A year later he was proclaimed *Augustus* by his troops, a title that he was compelled to defend against powerful forces. In 312 he was "converted" to Christianity, though his baptism did not take place till the very last hours of his life. He sought unity; the warring Christian sects were creating chaos and were weakening him against his rival, Lincinius, and his mighty legions in the East. Constantine made himself the leader and defender of the Christian West.

The Meletian schism and the outbreak of Arianism in Alexandria seriously threatened the military and political unity the Emperor needed. In 324 he convoked a synod of Oriental Bishops at Antioch, extracted from them a confession of faith, and banished the opposition. Constantine then summoned a general council of Bishops to meet at Nicaea (June 325); he presided over this ecclesiastical assembly as if it had been a session of his Senate, settled their theological and administrative problems in his own efficient way, and declared the decisions of the Council of Nicaea as "the will of God," with himself as the *Pontifex Maximus*. Within the year he had banished the leading heretics. Henceforth his armies marched under the banner bearing a strange emblem: the initials of Christ interwoven with a Roman cross. The symbol had come to him in a vision at a crucial hour in his conquests (October 27, 312): a flaming cross in the sky bearing the command (in Greek): *by this sign conquer*. This banner he transmitted to the Church. Henceforth the Church went forth as a mighty, conquering power, Jesus in the web of Roman might. The persecuted turned persecutor.

With the keys to the kingdom in the iron fist of Rome, it offered men salvation or eternal damnation as they accepted or rejected the official Apostolic creed:

> We believe in one God, the Father Almighty, maker of all things visible; and in one Lord Jesus Christ, the Son of God, begotten from the Father, only-begotten, that is, from the substance of the Father, God from God, light from light, true God from true God, begotten not made, of one substance with the Father, through Whom all things came into being, things in heaven and things on earth, Who because of us men and because of our salvation, came down and became incarnate, becoming man, suffered and rose again on the third day, ascended into heaven, and will come to judge the living and the dead; and in the Holy Spirit.[22]

15

Quo Vadis? Issues and Vision

Peter, according to an ancient Christian tradition, in flight from Rome during the persecutions of Nero, met Jesus on the Appian Way. "And when he saw him he said *Domine, quo vadis?* 'Lord, whither goest thou?' And the Lord said to him, 'I go into Rome, to be crucified.' And Peter said to him, 'Lord, art thou being crucified again?' He said to him, 'Yes, Peter, I am being crucified again.' "[1]

To the sensitive Christian, lured by the vision of his Redeemer—(the personification of all that is sacred—infinite compassion, atonement, salvation) trapped in the demonic evils of our age (apocalyptic slaughter in every land, the earth groaning under the traffic of diabolic weapons, the heavens rent with orbiting satellites on-the-ready to annihilate cities and nations and continents), the question is a painful, pressing reality: *Domine, quo vadis?* "Lord, art thou being crucified again?" To the sensitive Jew, chanting his ancient lamentations over six million martyrs gone up the chimneys of the crematoria, while official Christendom looked the other way and kept silent, the prophetic visions of justice, peace, loving kindness, a bitter mockery, the same question, in different words, is a pulsating pain: "How long, O Lord, how long?" "Whence comes my help?"[2] To too many sons of Israel the Psalmist's answer "My help comes from the Lord," is a Satanic joke, for the Heavenly Father is no longer in the heavens. The heavens are only infinite black emptiness. God, if there is one, if there ever was one, has turned his back on his children.

Quo vadis? "Whence comes my help?"

We must face reality. The faithful shepherd of the Exile who faced the same question in his day by the waters of Babylon—"How shall we sing the Lord's song in a foreign land?"[3]—speaks to us: "Stand on your feet, son of man, and I will speak unto you."[4] If we stand on our feet, face the facts of our moral civilization faithful to our ancient vision of a rainbow arching over our sinful world, perhaps the Holy One will grant us a glimpse of Himself.

The True Religion

Addressing himself to his cardinals, bishops and through them the millions of his faithful the world over —one-fifth of the world's population—Pope Paul VI said,

"Indeed, honesty compels us to declare openly our conviction that there is but one true religion, the religion of Christianity. It is our hope that all who seek God and adore Him, may come to acknowledge its truth."[5] The Holy Father is faithful to the apostle whose name he bears: " . . . at the name of Jesus every knee should bow in heaven and on earth . . . "[6]

Has no progress in insights, in freedom of mind and conscience, been achieved since the days of the first Paul?

Honesty compels the Pope to reaffirm the ancient dogma that Christianity is the only true religion; honesty compels us to ask him, and all those whose conviction he voices, "Which version of Christianity? The Holy Father means, of course, his version. What of the non-Roman Catholics? What of the millions of

Protestants? Implied in his dogma is the belief that all truth, grace, wisdom, salvation is the exclusive possession of his Roman Catholic Church. Honesty compels us to ask, further, "What of the millions upon millions of non-Christians of every creed, every race, every nation, every continent—untold millions who too 'seek God and adore Him'—each cherishing its own spiritual treasures?"

By what standards do men assert the unyielding and cruel dogma that theirs is the one and only true religion?

Is it true by virtue of its fidelity to a heavenly Messiah? If so, by whose revelations? Who interprets the oracle? Is a doctrinaire eschatology the final test of the true religion?

Is it by virtue of its fidelity to an ancient text? If so, which text and what makes the text sacred and infallible? Are we confusing antiquity with sanctity? And who expounds the pure divinity of the text's words? What shall we do with the enormous scholarship in Old and New Testament exegesis made by brilliant, devout Jews and Gentiles alike, in every generation and in every land? And what shall we do with the non-Biblical texts— the Koran, for example?

Is it true by virtue of its fidelity to a canonized tradition, "the right doctrine?" If so, which tradition and whose "right doctrine"—the tradition from Mount Sinai? Calvary? Mecca? And what shall we do with the non-Biblical traditions?

Is it true by virtue of its fidelity to a social vision— righteousness, compassion, love, the Kingdom of Heaven on earth? If so, what shall we do with the wide and deep differences of interpretation as to what spells justice, what makes for love and compassion, what is meant by the Kingdom of Heaven? What of the vested worldly interests that blind us to God's truth and ensnare us into sanctifying the status quo? The prophetic fires of one generation may be the ashes of the subsequent centuries.

Is it by virtue of fidelity to the "scientific spirit," with all its vaunted objectivity? If so, what shall we do with the reality that areas in life there are—primary concerns, without which we would not be human enough to have any sort of religion: a sense of awe, reverence, compassion, self-sacrifice for an ideal, duty, honor, loyalty—sentiments that are not amenable to clinical analysis? "Yea, though He slay me, yet will I believe in Him." Life is not a laboratory, not a clinic; it points to a morning star that is utterly different from a dead body in the heavens, and summons men to greatness.

Is it by virtue of the emotional satisfaction our respective religions give us? If so, is anesthetizing the mind an ideal to be desired and smug complacency to one may be an irritant—even a repellent—to another. No one prescription will fit every patient in the hospital.

What do men mean when they affirm that theirs is the one true religion?

The harp of faith has many strings. No one string is the only true one. It is the music the skillful artist produces by playing on all the strings that gives us an intimation of the true religion. And here, too, highly intelligent and gifted men will have preferences and seek variations. Religion is an art. Truly religious men are artists in religion instinctively.

Ultimately the true religion is determined by the integrity of the vision that guides the faithful, and even then it may be true for that particular communion only and for those who prefer it out of personal conditioning from childhood or out of personal disposition, or out of intellectual conviction.

Issues

Dividing Judaism and Christianity are basic issues. That is why they are two separate religions. Their distinctiveness and their special contributions to moral civilization are among the factors that divide them. There can be no peace between mother and daughter faiths till the issues are understood and appreciated.

First is the proclivity to arrogate to one's own faith the claim to be the one and only true religion. By the mercy of God and human intelligence this dogma must be expunged from our religious life. The time is long past due.

Second, the passion to convert, to "save souls," especially of the young and credulous, is a grievous issue between Judaism and Christianity. In an open society, affirming the freedom of the mind and conscience, we have every right to propagate our own particular beliefs and notions, to propagandize as we see fit; but this propagandizing and proselytizing must occur in the market places of ideas in a free exchange, according to the rules of free intellectual pursuit. Why shall there not be a decent sportsmanship in interreligious communication even as in all other spheres of intellectual exchange?

Third, the Church must purge itself of the canonized anti-Semitism which is at its very heart. We have pointed to this in our study of Saint Paul, in the Gospel reports of the Crucifixion, in the preachments of the apostles. The Second Ecumenical Council took a long step forward in its revision of the Crucifixion reports, lifting the eternal guilt from universal and contemporary Jewry, and fixing it in part on the particular group of that fateful day; but there is an appalling gap between the official pronouncements of the Vatican and the preachments and

prayers of the village churches the world over. That gap
is ominous. The Ecumenical Council was enmeshed in
sanctified anti-Semitism and could not entirely extricate
itself from it. Even the report of so faithful and skillful
a prince of the Church as Cardinal Bea testifies to that.[8]

The historic fact is incontrovertible: The New Testament issues from the heat and hatred of a holy war; all
the passions and frustrations of the civil religious war
and its fratricide color its pages. Salvation at this point
is in an historic, critical approach to the New Testament,
as well as to the Old. Scholars of integrity have long
been pointing the way. We must break with dogmatic
theologians and seek to disengage ourselves from sanctified bad scholarship.

Other issues between Judaism and Christianity run
through the entire spectrum of theologic beliefs and
disbeliefs. These beliefs are debatable, and are of benefit
to both religions. It would be desperately tragic were
these theologic differences to be suppressed by an ecclesiastic body or by the State. A black pall would ex-
tinguish the lights in the Church and in the Synagogue.
Would we have a monolithic ethic, or a totalitarian
philosophy? The histories of Judaism and of Christianity are histories of inner conflict. Perhaps the most tragic
word in the vocabulary of religion is the word "heresy."
It connotes evil, sin, rebellion against God Himself and
His supposed representatives on earth. The word "heresy" should be banished forever to the limbo of human
horrors; and in its stead the proper terms should be
used: "Differences of belief," "variant views," "diver-
gent opinions." It is the "heresies"—however bizarre
some of them may have been, or appeared to have been
to the entrenched self-rightous authorities of the time—
that have made for progress out of the dark tunnels
towards the light in Judaism and in Christianity. Spinoza

made a far more precious contribution to the intellectual life of mankind and to the glory of Judaism than did the pious rabbis who excommunicated him.

The rabbinic masters spin a yarn about Moses being deeply perplexed as he was writing down God's dictation at the supreme hour of revelation on Mount Sinai. The power of prophecy flashed over him; the ages unrolled; he heard the scholars in their academies the world over expounding the words in his name: "These are the words the Lord hath spoken to Moses"; but they were slanting them. He turned to the Holy One and complained: "O Lord, the words are as I have communicated to them in Thy Name; but they are giving them strange meanings." The Holy One comforted Moses: that is as it should be. Every generation, every community, must interpret Scripture in keeping with its own special needs, and with its own peculiar capacity to understand.

Vision

Religion is primarily a vision and a dedication. It is a vision that lifts men out of the depths and impels them to lift their eyes unto the hills in awe and aspiration. It motivates them to accept duties, cherish loyalties, fight for justice, truth, love, seek peace and pursue it. It is a search for inner harmony and inner peace that passeth understanding in our adjustment to the inexorable forces that play upon our mortal little lives. "While the earth remains, seed-time and harvest, cold and heat, summer and winter, day and night, shall not cease." Thus have we been taught in Sacred Scripture.[9] And it is more than a matter of climate and the moving seasons. Birth and death, hope and despair, good and evil, joy and sorrow, bereavement, frustrations, cruelty, love, demonic evil in the human breast and infinite compassion—all these shape our destinies. The mind persists: Why? Why? Whence do we come and whither do we tend? A medieval philosopher reminds us that the spans of our years are like bridges anchored in the unknown at both ends. Out of the unknown we come and into the unknown we go, inevitably, inexorably. "And who shall say, what doest Thou?" The mind seeks answers, and the heart will not adore what the mind disowns.

Our respective religions give us our traditional answers, expressed in a wide diversity of text, symbols, chants, rites. These are expressive of a wide diversity of personalities, times, climates. Who shall say that there is only one true pattern of beliefs, symbols, rites, sacred days? How shall we think of absolute answers to the eternally unknown?

The Hebrew prophet gives us the only sane answer: "Let every people walk in the name of the Lord its God; but we will walk in the name of the Lord our God forever and ever."[10] It is an affirmation born not of mere dissent, not an answer from so-called "liberalism," most assuredly not from indifference. Micah was an intensely religious man, and he avows determination for himself even as he grants freedom to others: " . . . but we *will*—[we *shall*]—walk in the name of the Lord our God forever and ever."

Overarching all our differences is the vision and the hope voiced by the prophet Isaiah: "There shall be a highway and a way and it shall be called the way of holiness."[11]

Appendixes

Appendixes

Appendix I

Letters of Saint Paul

"Of the nine letters of Paul which are generally recognized as authentic, the most important are undoubtedly *Romans,* I and II *Corinthians* and *Galatians;* and of these four the letter to the Romans can lay claim to a certain preeminence . . . It is the principal source book for the study of Paul's gospel, and in consequence it is unquestionably the most important theological book ever written."[1] Doubt of Paul's authorship is associated with all the rest of the writings traditionally attributed to him, in part or in toto.

The Acts of the Apostles is a secondary source. The problems in text the book presents are "unique in the New Testament."[2] Involved are two basic texts; various portions of the book are based on different literary sources. It underwent much editing by several writers, who had special interests to advance. Luke, it has been affirmed by scholars, was the companion of Paul and wrote this book—or portions of it—from his notes or recollections. There is no unanimity among scholars as to the date when the book was written, nor when it was completed. The dates advanced range from the year 63–64 as the earliest, to the year 110–125 as the latest. "A date between 80–90 seems most probable. It underwent much editing before it received its final form in the latter part of the second century. Where the book was written is a subject for speculation. Rome seems to be the most probable place.

Acts must therefore be read with much caution. Each writer and editor, from the earliest to the latest, had a special theologic interest to promote. These ancients were not writing history, as we have noted, not biography, but propaganda: promotion of the new faith as they cherished it. The aim was to gain converts and establish congregations, not the preservation of historic data as such. They were preaching the good news of Jesus the Lord Christ; hence their reports of Paul—as of Jesus—must be understood in the light of their basic interests.

Bibliography

The lay student should consult a reliable study of New Testament sources by sympathetic but critical scholars. The present author recommends the following: *The Interpreter's Bible* (Cokesbury) to the *Epistles,* and *The Acts of the Apostles,* the Introductions and Exegesis; Donald Wayne Riddle, *Paul, Man of Conflict* (Cokesbury Press), 1940; Arthur Darby Nock, *St. Paul* (Harper and Brothers), 1948; Joseph Klausner, *From Jesus to Paul,* tr. Wm. F. Stinespring, (N. Y., Macmillan), 1943; Samuel Sandmel, *A Jewish Understanding of the New Testament* (Hebrew Union College Press), 1956, and *The Genius of Paul;* Hugh J. Schonfield, *A History of Biblical Literature,* Mentor Book, Am. Library of World Lit., N. Y. 1962; Peake's Commentary on the Bible, (N. Y.: Nelson), 1962.

Notes

1. Knox, John. *Interpreter's Bible,* Int. to Romans.
2. *Ibid.*

Appendix II

Deicide

The charge of Deicide, that "the Jews killed Christ," has plagued Jewry for the past 1900 years. Its origin is the crucifixion account, in Matthew especially, and the verse, "His blood be upon us and our children."[1] It was the official policy of the Church all through history; it instigated mobs to violence against the Jewish people in every Christian country; it is still a menacing force, despite the efforts made by various lay and clerical bodies.

The theologic formula, and an intimation of the emotions involved, may be had from the pronouncements of the Medieval Popes. Innocent III, for instance, addressing the Bishops of Sens and Paris (July 15, 1205), ordering stricter enforcement of the restrictions on the Jews, writes: "While Christian piety accepts the Jews who, by their guilt, are consigned to perpetual servitude because they crucified the Lord, although their own prophets had predicted that He would come in the flesh to redeem Israel . . . " Again, "The Jews' guilt of the crucifixion of Jesus consigned them to perpetual servitude, and like Cain, they are to be wanderers and fugitives."[2]

Pope Gregory IX rehearses the tragic story with emphasis: "Since their own sin consigned them to eternal slavery when they nailed Him to the cross Who, as their own prophets had predicted, would come to redeem Israel . . . "[3] (May 18, 1233).

Even so good a man as Robert Grosseteste (Robert of Lincoln) —Prince of the Church, humanist, Hebraist, religious and political reformer who stood up to Pope and King, builder of the University of Oxford—vigorously preached the same doctrine: because the Jews killed Christ they are cursed of God, and, like Cain, they are branded fugitives forever. In a letter written in 1231 to the Countess of Winchester, who was thinking of

235

giving asylum to Jewish refugees driven from their homes, he warns her:

> For word has come to me that Your Excellency has arranged to gather together on your domain the Jews whom Lord Leicester expelled from his town to prevent their pitiless and usurious oppressing the Christians dwelling there.

> If you so arrange, give careful attention to the manner in which the Christian lords are to settle them and guard them. Being guilty of murder, in cruelly killing by crucifixion the Savior of the world, our Lord Jesus Christ . . . because of this sin they did lose their standing unhappily at the hands of Titus and Vespasian, and having themselves entered into captivity, were scattered as captives through all lands and peoples, and they shall not be restored to freedom until the very end of the world.

> In regard to Cain, who stands as a type of the Jews, when he had murdered his brother, who stands as a type of Christ, who was slain by the Jews for the safety of the world, it is said: "And now shalt thou be cursed from the earth, which hath opened her mouth and received thy brother's blood from thy hand; when thou tillest her she shall not henceforth yield unto thee her strength; a fugitive and a vagabond thou shalt be upon the earth."[4]

The Second Vatican's Council, convoked by Pope John XXIII grappled with this problem. Augustus Cardinal Bea, primary architect of this Council, next to the Pope, summarizes its final decision, adopted on October 28, 1965:

> Briefly stated, the indictment runs thus: as a consequence of the unjust condemnation of Jesus, extorted from Pilate at the instigation of the Sanhedrin, which was the legitimate representative authority of the Jewish people, the people became guilty of "deicide" and lost all its privileges; the chosen people of God is no longer Israel but the Church, the 'new Israel according to the Spirit.' God's past bounty to Israel rendered it all the more worthy of grave punishment. Israel was rejected by God and cursed, as is shown by the great tribulations, pre-

dicted by Jesus, which fell upon the Jewish people in the decades following the crucifixion and culminated in the destruction of Jerusalem and the scattering of the nation under the emperor Hadrian . . .

As a result, the Jewish people is to be regarded as frankly inferior to all other peoples from a religious point of view, precisely because it is a deicide people, rejected and cursed by God.

Cardinal Bea adds the following footnote

A recent author has expressed himself as follows: "It can be legitimately said that the whole Jewish people at the time of Jesus [i.e. all those who professed the religion of Moses] was collectively responsible for the crime of deicide, although it was only their leaders, together with a small professional group, who were materially involved in its preparation." From this he concludes that "Judaism" should hold itself as "rejected and cursed by God, in the sense and with the reservations detailed above." This pronouncement is also extended to the Judaism of later times. In this specific sense, and taking into account the biblical mentality, Judaism after the time of Christ also shares in the responsibility for deicide, in so far as it constitutes a free and voluntary prolongation of the Judaism of former times.[5]

The Result of the Inquiry as formulated and reported by Cardinal Bea:

1. The Jewish people can not be said to be guilty of deicide.

2. Where the New Testament speaks explicitly of responsibility for the crucifixion of Jesus, it refers either to the Sanhedrin or to the inhabitants of Jerusalem . . .

3. The severity of the judgment on Jerusalem neither presupposes nor proves the existence of a collective guilt for the crucifixion attributable to the whole Jewish people.[6]

Cardinal Bea reveals, further, the thinking of the Second Vatican Council:

It is stated plainly that the events of Christ's passion can not be indiscriminately imputed to all the Jews alive at the time and still less to the Jews of our own day. Consequently, the Jews should not be represented falsely as under a curse and rejected by God.[7]

If we examine the historical records we shall find that on many occasions Christians have become so far blinded and that they have arbitrarily set themselves up as the avengers of Christ, discriminating against the Jews, whom they brand as outcasts cursed by God.[8]

Nowhere does Cardinal Bea take note of the historic-critical studies of the Crucifixion made by Protestant or Jewish scholars. The Council ignored these studies officially. Every word of the New Testament reports is assumed as divine truth; their efforts at revision are in terms of interpretation and reinterpretation of an authoritative text.

Bibliography

For the persistence of the "Christ killing" charge in Protestant churches on the American scene, the reader is referred to the following: *Christian Beliefs and Antisemitism,* Charles E. Glock and Rodney Stark, Harper and Row, N. Y., 1967; on the European level, *The Foot of Pride,* Malcom Hay, Beacon Press, Boston, 1950; paperback edition, *Europe and the Jews,* 1960. For more comprehensive historic backgrounds, Charles Guignebert, *The Early History of Christianity,* N. Y. Twayne, 1962; Dominic M. Crossman, "Anti-Semitism and the Gospel," *Theologic Studies,* XXVI, 2 (Jan. 1965).

Notes

1. 27.65
2. Grayzel, S., *The Church and the Jews in the XIIIth Century,* Philadelphia, Dropsie College, 1933
3. *Ibid.,* p. 205

4. Gen. 4.11–12; L. Freedman, *Robert Grosseteste and the Jews,* Cambridge, Harvard Press, p. 13
5. Bea, Augustus Cardinal, *The Church and the Jewish People:* A Commentary on the Second Vatican Council's Declaration on the Relation of the Church to non-Christian Religios. Tr. Philip Lorenz, S. J. N. Y. Harper and Row, 1966, p. 67–68. See also Gilbert, Arthur, *The Vatican Council and the Jews,* World Publishing, N. Y., 1968
6. *Ibid.,* p. 87–88
7. *Ibid.,* p. 52
8. *Ibid.,* p. 66

Appendix III
The Works of Josephus

Jewish War

Josephus' first work, *The Jewish War,* in seven books, is his most famous. He wrote it under the commission of Vespasian. The first draft was in his native Aramaic, the language of Galilean Jewry, but this edition is lost. The book has come down in history in an enlarged Greek version, which Josephus prepared for the Greek-speaking public, with the assistance of literary collaborators. He admits this quite frankly in his *Against Apion,* written late in life.

During the siege of Jerusalem he kept a record of events. "No incident escaped my knowledge. I kept a careful record of all that went on under my eyes in the Roman camp, and was alone in a position to understand the information brought by deserters. Then, in the leisure which Rome afforded me, with all my materials in readiness, and with the aid of some assistance for the sake of the Greek, at last committed to writing my narrative of the events."[1]

A nice literary problem presents itself. Are these the writings of Josephus' own pen or the work of his literary assistants we are reading? Josephus, of course, was not alone in engaging talent for his writings. It was common practice in his day, as it is in ours. The polishing done by editors is particularly pertinent to his *Jewish War,* since it is the first book he wrote. Josephus could not have achieved such elegant literary Greek in so short a time. He displays considerable knowledge of Homer, the Greek poets, Sophocles and others. Where and when could he have acquired this?

His imperial masters and the aristocracy, whom he presents in glowing colors, were highly pleased with his chronicle. This, he asserts, proves the integrity of his work.

The history was completed towards the end of Vespasian's reign, between the years 75 and 79.

The purpose is practical: a warning to the East* against rebellion, and to the conquered Jewish communities against revenge. Roman might is invincible. "If I have dwelt at some length on this topic," he notes in describing the invincibility of Roman armies, "my intention was not so much to extol the Romans as to console those whom they have vanquished and to deter others who may be tempted to revolt."[2] Subjugated Jewish communities should not expect aid from the outside.

He begins the *Jewish War* with the history of the Maccabees and narrates the story of the Jewish insurrection in which he figured personally. Always the Romans were invincible and generous; always the Jews were fanatic and rash, led by extremists. The aristocracy and the Jewish masses in general were not to blame; the Zealots—always termed "brigands," "assassins," "robbers"—were truly the guilty ones responsible for the enormous catastrophe that befell Judea. They rejected the generous terms offered by Titus. Because of the blind intransigence of the Zealots, God Himself permitted the Romans to reduce His City and His Temple.

The book was accepted with complete satisfaction by Josephus' imperial patron; it was given the official imprimatur and placed in the royal library.

Scholars who have delved deeply into his writing, examining minutely his facts and figures, charge him with distorting some basic data and suppressing facts, and exaggerating much. Long speeches put into the mouths of heroes twist the historic facts for propagandistic purposes.**

The work testifies to enormous industry, and to a gift for narrative. H. St. John Thackeray, after a lifetime of study and

---

*"Parthians and Babylonians and the most remote tribes of Arabia were our countrymen beyond the Euphrates and the inhabitants of Adiabne." (*J. W.*, I.2)

**The student is referred to the words of Benedictus Nisei and H. St. John Thackeray.

astute analysis, testifies: "After all reservations have been made, the narrative of our author in its main outlines must be accepted as trustworthy. Considered as a work of art, it takes high rank in literature; the reader's appreciation of its merits, for which the author is largely indebted to his skilled assistants and constant revision, grows on closer acquaintance. The poignant story is told with pathos worthy of the theme and with all the resources of vivid and dramatic description."[3]

The Jewish War is indispensable for an understanding of the history of the first century; it delineates the beliefs and practices of the Pharisees, Sadducees and Essenes, the three "Sects" as Josephus designates them. It illumines the background to the New Testament as no other historic work does, and is thus invaluable to an understanding of emergent Christianity. Christendom has rewarded Josephus by preserving his work.

Jewish Antiquities

About sixteen years after the completion of *Jewish War,* Josephus finished his second major work, *Jewish Antiquities.* He labored over it for twenty years, completing it in the year 93 or 94. The enormous materials he had to gather, systematize and assimilate, the weariness that induced him to lay the work aside from time to time, the lack of encouragement from the imperial authorities that had aided him in the writing of the *Jewish War* may explain the long interval between the two works. The Emperor Domitian, brother of Titus (who died in 81), was hostile to literature. Josephus found a new patron in a Greek man of learning and wealth by the name of Epaphroditus. He is reported to have had a library of 30,000 volumes. To him Josephus dedicates the *Antiquities, Life,* and *Against Apion*—that is, all his writing subsequent to the *Jewish War.*

The *Antiquities* chronicles the history of the Jews from the earliest times to the year 66, which marks the beginning of the revolt against Rome, in which Josephus participated in such anguish, and which story he reported in his first book. The two works thus complement each other, with considerable repetition of the Greco-Roman period, and with much contradiction at crucial points.

The work is in twenty volumes, and unlike *Jewish War* was originally written in Greek. We make special note of this because it suggests the primary motive for the writing of *Antiquities,* and which Josephus explains: he had an inner compulsion to clear the record of his people, which was badly perverted by biased, ignorant and self-seeking historians. "The majority of these authors have misrepresented the facts of our primitive history," he declares, "because they have not read our sacred books."[4] He undertook the burden of exposing their ignorance. In our time we may speak of Josephus as a public relations historian. He did not hesitate to bend the material to the special purposes he had set for himself.

The Jews have a divinely glorious history going back to the very beginning of times. The Greco-Roman world has much to learn from the history of Josephus' Jewish people. "If in his *Jewish War* the author had offended Jewish susceptibilities by recommending submission to the conqueror, he would now make amends by showing that his race had a history comparable, nay in antiquity far superior, to that of the proud Roman."[5]

Had Josephus known long nights of soul-searching? Was he writing as a penitent? Was he, perhaps, disillusioned in the society of the Roman aristocracy?

He writes as a believing Pharisee: a just God presides over the destinies of men and nations, ultimately rewarding the righteous and punishing the wicked. He draws heavily on the Greek translation of the Bible and its Aramaic interpretations. Scholars identify many phrases from these Bible versions. He draws, further, on rabbinic lore and on *First Maccabees.* When he reaches the period where Bible records cease, he resorts to the pagan historians, especially to the writings of Nicholas of Damascus, intimate friend of Herod, who had written from personal experience, and on Strabo. Unfortunately he only paraphrases or summarizes these non-Jewish historians; he does not use them critically enough, does not analyze them in depth. When he reaches the Roman period after the year 70 he employs official Roman state papers, and incorporates portions into his text. Writing as he does for the Greek-speaking intellectuals, he draws on Hellenistic ideas and traditions to make himself intelligible, and make Jews and Judaism acceptable. In striving for this effect he forces the Hebraic into an alien mold and thus seriously misrepresents the Hebraic at vital points.*

In form he is believed to have modeled himself after a history of Rome by Dionysius, an Asiatic historian who had settled in Rome and in the year 7 B.C.E. produced a history of Rome in twenty books, entitled *Roman Antiquities*. Josephus may have written his *Jewish Antiquities,* in twenty books, as a sort of counterpart to it.[6]

As in all his writings, Josephus is an apologist; but in *Antiquities* he is not defending himself, as he does in *Life,* and not the Romans, as he does in *Jewish War;* he is defending his people. He takes serious liberties with Bible text and rabbinic tradition. He resorts freely to the Greek method of allegory in expounding Biblical portions when it suits his purpose. He had ample warrant for it, from his standpoint; further, Philo of Alexandria had interpreted Judaism in the Hellenistic tradition by the use of allegory. Josephus draws heavily on fanciful, often wild, midrashic material, even the apocalyptic; he resorts freely to rhetorical embellishments, in good Greek style of the period and in emulation of the pagan historians after whose writings he modeled himself. He omits and enlarges. He stresses those aspects of the Bible which he thought held special interest for the Hellenistic intellectuals, and touches lightly on what he felt would reflect unfavorably on his people, their religion, their history. Thus, for example, he hardly mentions the Hebrew prophets, but enlarges on the pomp and splendor of the priestly vestments. "He had a pride of caste and a love of the pomp and circumstance of the Temple service; and the national ceremony could be more easily conveyed to the Gentile than an understanding of the spiritual value of Judaism."[7] He is non-committal at points he considered embarrassing—such as the crossing of the Red Sea, the revelation at Mount Sinai—by resorting to the formula, so dear to the hearts of modern liberals, "Let every one judge as he will." He has been described as "a wavering rationalist."[8]

For all its shortcomings, *Jewish Antiquities* is an invaluable

---

*The student is again referred to the writings of Benedictus Niese and H. St. John Thackeray. The fine article on Josephus in the *Jewish Encyclopedia* by Samuel Krauss, and Norman Bentwich's, *Josephus,* Philadelphia, 1914, are especially helpful in rabbinic backgrounds.

work. It reflects honor on the author. At least two considerations must be fully appreciated.

First, it was written to meet a sore need. It aimed at countering vicious libelling of the author's people, religion and history—malicious perversion which was poisoning the minds of generations of Greco-Roman intellectuals. No other writer had assumed the burden. Josephus was the only historian who strove to set the record straight, and he wrote as an avowed Jew proud of his heritage. Thus he rendered his maligned people a precious service. And he had no encouragement from any quarter in this labor of twenty years.

Second, if he took liberties with the records, as he did, we can not adjudge him by our modern standards of presumed objectivity in the writing of history. Ours is a modern ideal, and it is by no means fully established. Any eighteenth- or nineteenth-century English historian's account of the American Revolution and the delineation of George Washington, or any Confederate account of the American Civil War and the portrayal of Abraham Lincoln, may serve as ample warrant for our observation.

Josephus sought objectivity in the light of his time—or, shall we say, in the darkness of his time, a darkness which has not yet lifted. In his own judgment he was following the standards of the best of his age and before.

THE PASSAGE ON JESUS

In *Jewish Antiquities* is a passage referring to Jesus, embodied in Book XVIII, Chapter 3. It has been a scholar's battlefield. Devout Christian historians, since the fourth century, have read it confidently as Josephus' witnessing to Jesus the Christ; equally devout Christian scholars, perhaps more critical, more under the influence of modern analytic scholarship, have challenged it. Some have repudiated it entirely and branded it as pious forgery; a number have sought to salvage a portion of it. For a fair presentation of the issues involved the reader should turn to two masters in this field: B. Niese and H. St. John Thackeray. Niese gives us a generous summary of his findings and conclusions in an article on *Josephus* in Hastings' *Encyclopedia of Religion and Ethics.* Thackeray summarizes his lifelong research in a series of lectures published under the title *Josephus—The Man and the Historian.*[9] The Jesus passage, in Thackeray's translation, is as follows:

> Now about this time arises Jesus, a wise man, if indeed he should be called a man. For he was a doer of marvellous deeds, a teacher of men who receive the truth with pleasure; and he won over to himself many Jews and many also of the Greek (nation.) He was the Christ. And when, on the indictment of the principal men among us, Pilate has sentenced him to the cross, those who had loved (or perhaps rather 'been content with') him at the first did not cease; for he appeared to them on the third day alive again, the divine prophets having (fore) told these and ten thousand other wonderful things concerning him. And even now the tribe of Christians, named after him, is not extinct.

Two incidental references to Jesus are also found in the *Antiquities:* (1) XVIII, 5 lines 116–119, where Josephus refers to John the Baptist and James "the brother of Jesus who was called the Christ;" and (2) XX, lines 197–203, where we find an account of the death of James "the brother of Jesus who was called Christ."

Niese dismisses the first of these passages as part of the Jesus paragraph which he rejects as spurious. The second reference "is altogether beyond suspicion, and we are unable to agree with scholars who regard it likewise as an interpolation. The manner in which Jesus is here mentioned coincides exactly with what we should expect from Josephus. Thus, while Josephus had undoubtedly heard of Jesus, he did not deal with him in his history, and the passage in *Jewish Antiquities* XVIII, which we have discussed, must be pronounced spurious."[10]

Thackeray sees historic validity in both these incidental references to Jesus and accepts them as genuine.

The scholars who have challenged the authenticity of the passage in XVIII base themselves on two considerations: external evidence, and evidence from context and style.

From the external standpoint the basic fact is that the earliest church historians were unaware of any such passage in *their* editions of Josephus. The earliest reference to it is by Eusibius, ecclesiastic historian and Bishop of Caesarea. His dates are 260–

340. But a century earlier an Alexandrian writer and teacher by the name of Origen indeed found allusions in Josephus to John the Baptist and James, but not only does he not quote the "Christ passage, but he uses such language as makes it practically impossible to suppose that he knew it *in its present form.*"[11]

Further, from the external standpoint, had Josephus written anything about Jesus he would have done it in his first work, *Jewish War,* where it belongs; but no mention of Jesus is found there. The *Jewish Antiquities,* written years later, is only a restatement of the earlier work.

From the internal standpoint, Niese summarizes the evidence as follows: It is not a narrative "as we should expect from a historian, but is, in the main a eulogy, and a kind that only a Christian could have written."[12] Josephus was too proud a Jew to write in this eulogistic manner. Therefore, the conclusion is that it is an interpolation by a Christian editor or copyist.

Thackeray, however, writing some three-quarters of a century after Niese, and benefiting from the subsequent exhaustive studies, believes that the passage in its present form is a Christian revision of the original passage written by Josephus. "The criterion of style, to my mind," he writes, "turns the scale in favor of the authenticity of the passage considered as a whole . . . The paragraph in the main comes from Josephus or his secretary, but the Christian censor or copyist has, by slight omissions and alterations, so distorted it as to give it a wholly different complexion."[13]

This view advanced by Thackeray with impressive learning and logic is not new; it had been argued by renowned scholars before him. Niese, in his day, countered it: "This view appears to the present writer untenable; the whole chapter forms so obviously an indivisible unity that, if any part of it is a fabrication, the whole of it must be so, and ought to be removed from the text altogether."[14]

The fact—if it is a fact—that this passage does not come to us from Josephus' own pen can not be used to prove the non-existence of Jesus. That is an entirely different matter. Further, there is at least one unchallenged reference to Jesus, if not two, as we have noted. We must bear in mind that Josephus was interested only in those events that had repercussions outside

Judea. Jesus' activity in his own lifetime attracted very little attention within Judea and none outside his country. He was only one of untold numbers of wandering preachers who met with the same fate at the hands of the Roman authorities, who feared popular uprisings. Josephus had no reason to include him in his chronicles.[15]

The passage—forgery or authentic—made the writings of Josephus enormously important to the Church and has assured the author's immortality.

The scholars cited in the above paragraphs on both sides of the debate were Christians. The consensus of opinion among Jewish scholars may be summarized in the following, by Norman Bentwich. Though published in 1914, the judgment still expresses the overwhelming majority opinion: "The uncompromising Christian character of the text, the discrepancy between Origen, Eusibius, and the notorious aptitude of early Christian scribes for interpolating manuscripts, and especially the manuscripts of Hellenistic Jewish writers, with Christological passages, make it well nigh certain that the paragraph was foisted in between the second and third century. That was a period when, as has been said, 'faith was more vivid than good faith.' "[16]

Life

In recalling the life of Josephus we drew on his autobiography and called attention to several aspects of this pamphlet. It must be remembered, as we have noted, that it is an apologetic work; the author is defending himself against charges leveled against him by a rival historian and soldier, Justus of Tiberias. Josephus smarted under the charges of treason and treachery against both, his native Judea and Rome, even while he was enjoying the Emperor's favor. His autobiography details only six months of his life, but these six months were the most crucial—the tragic and ignominious campaign in Galilee.

Justus' work is lost. Presumably, not flattering the Roman authorities, contradicting the favorable report Josephus had written in his *Jewish War,* attacking their favorite protege, the imperial authorities never placed the book in the royal archives, or

library; and it is therefore lost to us. We know it only from
the answer Josephus makes in his defensive autobiography. He
wrote it towards the end of his life and appended it to the second,
or later, edition of *Jewish Antiquities*. He omits and slants what
he himself had written. The shameful story of Jotapata, for
example, is omitted altogether. He dismisses it with a brief
reference to the account in *Jewish War*. The date of its appearance, it is believed, is shortly after the year 103. Hence, it
is the work of his advanced years, and the result of long brooding.
Meant to clear himself of hated charges, and to safeguard his
favor with the imperial authorities, he wrote it in Greek and
dedicated it to his chief patron, Epaphroditus. "The work, in
which the author indulges his vanity to the full, is, alike in
matter and in manner, the least satisfactory of his writings. The
weakness of his boasted strategy is on a par with the crudity
of the style."[17]

Against Apion

It is an intriguing fact to contemplate: Pagan and Christian
historians preserved for Jewry one of the best—if not the very
best—defense of Judaism in history. By universal consent Josephus' *Against Apion* is so considered.

The tract first appeared in the writings of Eusibius, the third-
century Bishop of Caesarea. It is repeated by Jerome, fourth–
fifth-century father of the Church, considered the best non-Jewish
Hebrew scholar of his time. From Jerome it found its way into
the editions of Josephus then in circulation and down through
history to our own time.

Dedicated to his patron Epaphroditus, who died in the year
95, the tract must have appeared before then, or very shortly
thereafter.

Josephus gives a complete head-on answer to the distortions of
the anti-Jewish writers. He had refuted them in *Antiquities;*
here he gives a more concentrated reply. This he follows with
an exposition of the laws, beliefs and practices of Judaism.

Writing as Josephus did for the Roman intellectuals, he could
make all the attacks he felt like making against the Greek

writers. He brands them as ignorant, scurrilous, malicious and mendacious. He is fighting the intellectual Jew-baiters with ammunition from their own writings, and from the records of "the Phoenicians, Chaldeans and Egyptians."

They are a conceited, arrogant lot; intellectually they are upstarts and vulgar pretenders. Only *they* know; only *their* people have all the good qualities. Our modern term "racism" carries the evil freight weighing down their writings.

Apion was a leader of the Stoic school of philosophy in Alexandria of the first pre-Christian century. Considerable rivalry for converts obtained between the Stoics and the rabbinic masters. In his five-volume history of Egypt Apion included a violent attack on Jews and Judaism. Josephus wrote his answer a half century after Apion's work had appeared. What the immediate occasion was we do not know; there may have been a resurgence of hostilities between the Syrians, Greeks and Jews of Alexandria, which harbored the largest Jewish community in the world of that time.

In the year 39 anti-Jewish excesses rocked Alexandrian Jewry and these were tolerated by the Roman Governor. In the year 66 as many as 50,000 Jews were killed. The Palestinian revolt against Rome probably sparked this massacre. Behind the hoodlums were intellectuals with their malicious distortions of Jewish history and culture—the same sickening phenomenon that has been repeating itself in history time without end. In the fifth century, for example, the Patriarch of Alexandria stirred riots against the Jews; the Nazi crematoria were the logical consequences of Aryan racism perpetuated by German professors in college classrooms. On and on courses the black river.

After disposing of these ignorant intellectuals Josephus concentrates his fire on Apion and his successors in the evil guild. (Apion's work, unfortunately, is lost; we know it only from the detailed answer Josephus makes.)

Hitler's charges against Jews and Judaism are anticipated in astonishing detail. There is hardly anything the Nazi dictator's professors and propagandists added to the list.

The Jews are represented as a diseased people, lepers who had been expelled from Egypt—as a degenerate race wedded to a degenerate religion. They were infiltrators, congenitally aliens, incapable of civic virtue and true patriotism, totally lacking in capacity for self-government; they were guilty of barbaric religious practices, such as circumcision, slaughtering a Greek annually and devouring him in religious rites, worshipping the golden head of an ass, teaching their children hatred for non-Jews. These are charges that have plagued Jewry throughout history.

Outraged, Josephus wrote his specific denials with conviction. He had dealt with these matters in the *Antiquities* in a general manner; in *Against Apion* he is more thorough. His purpose was not, he made clear, "to find fault with the institutions of other nations nor to extol our own, but to prove that the authors who have maligned us have made a barefaced attack on truth itself."[18]

He dwells on the beliefs and practices enjoined by Mosaic law, on the exemplary virtues in Jewish living: wholesome family life and sex relations, emphasis on education, honoring parents, respecting non-Jews and aliens. By comparison—including the overrated Greek—the Jewish religion, under the genius of Moses the Lawgiver and his disciples, is superb. History has proven all that.

Now, since Time is reckoned in all cases the surest test of worth I would call Time to witness to the excellence of our lawgiver and of the revelation concerning God which he has transmitted to us. An infinity of time has passed since Moses, if one compares the age in which he lived with those of other legislators; yet it will be found that throughout the whole of that period not merely have our laws stood the test of our own use, but they have to an ever-increasing extent excited the emulation of the world at large.

Josephus concludes his defense with verve:[19]

I would therefore boldly maintain that we have introduced to the rest of the world a very large number of very beautiful ideas. What greater beauty than inviolable piety? What higher justice than obedience to the laws? What more beneficial than to be in harmony with one another, to be a prey neither to disunion in adversity, nor to arrogance and faction in prosperity; in war to despise death, in peace to devote oneself to crafts or agriculture; and to be convinced that everything in the whole universe is under the eye and direction of God?[20]

Josephus stands revealed in *Against Apion* as a proud Jew and convinced Pharisee in the noblest sense of the word.

1. *Against Apion,* 50
2. Ibid., II.345; III, 108
3. H. St. John Thackeray, *Josephus—the Man and the Historian,* Jewish Institute of Religion, N. Y. 1929, p. 49
4. *CA,* above, I.218
5. Thackeray, above, p. 56
6. See Thackeray, above; Williamson, G. A., *The World of Josephus,* Boston, Little Brown, 1964
7. Bentwich, N. *Josephus,* Philadelphia, JPS, 1914, p. 149
8. *Ibid.*
9. Jewish Institute of Religion, N. Y., 1929, p. 136-7. B. Niese's research is embodied in a 7 volume work issued in Berlin, 1885-95, reprinted in 1955. Thackeray's impressive work is embodied in the Loeb Classical Library edition of Josephus (with the cooperation of Ralph Marcus, in part. G. P. Putnam's Sons, N. Y.)
10. *Hastings Encyclopedia of Religion and Ethics. art. Josephus*
11. Thackeray, *Josephus—Man and Historian,* above, p. 139
11. H.E.R.E., above
13. Thackeray, p. 142, 148
14. H.E.R.E., above
15. Considerable excitement was created among scholars in the 1920s by an alleged reference to Jesus in a Slavonic version of *Jewish War.* The claim has been pronounced spurious by most of the researchers in the field. For a digest of the issues and literature in this highly technical matter, see Louis H. Feldman, *Scholarship on Philo and Josephus,* Yeshiva U., N. Y.,; S. W. Baron, *A Social and Religious History of the Jews,* 2nd ed. Vol. II, p. 379, Phila. JPS, 1952
16. *Josephus,* above, p. 242
17. Thackeray, *Life,* p. XIV
18. II. 40
19. II. 38
20. II. 41

Appendix IV

The Martyrdom of Rabbi Akiba

A Page from the Talmud

Our Rabbis taught: Once the wicked Government issued a decree forbidding the Jews to study and practise the Torah. Pappus b. Judah came and found R. Akiba publicly bringing gatherings together and occupying himself with the Torah. He said to him: Akiba, are you not afraid of the Government? He replied: I will explain to you with a parable. A fox was once walking alongside of a river, and he saw fishes going in swarms from one place to another. He said to them: From what are you fleeing? They replied: From the nets cast for us by men. He said to them: Would you like to come up on to the dry land so that you and I can live together in the way that my ancestors lived with your ancestors? They replied: Art thou the one that they call the cleverest of animals? Thou art not clever but foolish. If we are afraid in the element in which we live, how much more in the element in which we would die! So it is with us. If such is our condition when we sit and study the Torah, of which it is written, *For that is thy life and the length of thy days,*[1] if we go and neglect it how much worse off we shall be! It is related that soon afterwards R. Akiba was arrested and thrown into prison, and Pappus b. Judah was also arrested and imprisoned next to him. He said to him: Pappus, who brought you here? He replied: Happy are you, R. Akiba, that you have been seized for busying yourself with the Torah! Alas for Pappus who has been seized for busying himself with idle things! When R. Akiba was taken for execution, it was the hour for the recital of the *Shema,* and while they combed his flesh with iron combs,

253

he was accepting upon himself the kingship of heaven.[2] His disciples said to him: Our teacher, even to this point? He said to them: All my days I have been troubled by this verse, *"with all thy soul,"* [which I interpret,] "even if He takes thy soul." I said When shall I have the opportunity of fulfilling this? Now that I have the opportunity shall I not fulfill it? He prolonged the word *ehad*[3] until he expired while saying it. A *bath kol*[4] went forth and proclaimed: Happy art thou, Akiba, that thy soul has departed with the word *ehad!* The ministering angels said before the Holy One, blessed be He: Such Torah, and such a reward? [He should have been] *from them that die by Thy hand, O Lord.*[5] He replied to them: *Their portion is in life.*[6] A *bath kol* went forth and proclaimed, Happy art thou, R. Akiba, that thou art destined for the life of the world to come.

—Berakoth 61b
Soncino Translation

Notes

1. Deut. 30.20
2. I.e., recited the *Shema*.
3. *One* in "Hear, O Israel, the Lord our God, the Lord is One."
4. Heavenly voice
5. Ps. 17.14
6. *Ibid.*

Notes and Bibliography

All Bible citations are from the Oxford Annotated Revised Standard Version, ed. Herbert G. May and Bruce M. Metzger, Oxford University Press, New York, 1962.

Chapter 1—Herod

1. Josephus, *Ant.* XIV, 14.3-5.
2. *Ibid.* XIV. 9.
3. *Ibid.*, XIV, 2 ff.
4. *Ibid.*
5. *Ibid.*
6. *Ibid.* XIV. 16.4.
7. Perowne, S., *Life and Times of Herod the Great,* N. Y., Abingdon Press, pp. 45–46.
8. Gen. 25.21-23.
9. Deut. 23.8-9.
10. *Ant.* XV. 7.4-7.
11. *Ibid.*
12. *Ibid.* XVI. 11-18.
13. Josephus, *War* I. 24-2.
14. *Ibid.* I, 33.2-4.
15. *Ibid.* I. 33.5-9. Herod's disease has been diagnosed as arterio-sclerosis of an aged person. See Perowne, *Life* (above), p. 186.
16. Josephus, *War,* I. 33.9.
17. Roth, C., *Short History of the Jewish People,* London, 1948, p. 93.
18. Perowne, *Life* (above), p. 115.
19. Josephus, *Ant.* XIV-XV; *War,* I, II, IV, VII. See Yigal Yadin's *Masada,* an absorbing description of the amazing fortress and its excavation. Josephus' report, with its fantastic number of suicides, is suspect—as are practically all figures stated by him.
20. *Ant.* XV. 15-1 ff
21. *Abot* 1.10

Chapter 2—Hillel and Shammai

1. *Abot.,* 1.1.
2. *Yoma.,* 35b.

255

3. *Abot.*, 1.12.
4. *Sab.*, 31a.
5. *Abot.*, 1.14.
6. Matt., 7.12.
7. *Abot.*, 2.5; Matt., 7.1.
8. *Ibid.* 2
9. *Shab.*, 31a.
10. *Abot.*, 5.25.
11. See *arts.* *"Bet Hillel"* and *"Bet Shammai"* in *Jewish Encyclopedia.*
12. *Sheb.*, 10.3
13. Gen. R., Wayera, LIII, 7.
14. Matt., 22.21.
15. I *Macc.*, 2.5.

Chapter 3—Sadducees, Pharisees

1. 13.9-27.
2. Is. 52.7.
3. The word *Pharisee* is derived from the Aramaic *perisha,* "one who
   separates himself from the religiously impure." In the days of the
   Maccabees, in the second century, the Pharisees constituted an official brotherhood. With the fall of the Temple in the year 70 they
   lost their official organization and became the majority of the Jewish
   population; the designation *Pharisee* then passed out of common use.
4. See Chapters on Hillel and Shammai, Yohanan Ben Zakkai, Akiba.
5. Exod., 19.6.
6. *Ibid.*, 24.3, 7.
7. Matt., 5.17–20.
8. Lev., 18.5.
9. *Abot,* 1.1.
10. *Ibid.*, 5.25.
11. 3.12.

Chapter 4—Essenes

1. Since their discovery in 1947, an extensive—at points polemic—
   literature has been produced. The following are selected works for
   the layman.

TRANSLATIONS

Dead Sea Scrolls in English, G. Vernes. Penguin Books, 1962.
Dead Sea Scrolls, Thanksgiving Hymn, with Introduction by Menahem Mansoor, Grand Rapids, Eerdman, 1961.

Dead Sea Psalm Scroll, J. A. Sanders, Cornell U. Press, 1968.
Dead Sea Scriptures, Th. H. Gaster, Garden City, New York, 1956.

DISCOVERY AND CONTENTS

Burrows, Millar, *The Dead Sea Scrolls, With Translations* New York, Viking, 1955.
———*More Light on the Dead Sea Scrolls,* With Translations and Important Recent Discoveries, *Ibid.,* 1958.
Cross, F. M., *The Ancient Library of Qumran and Modern Biblical Studies,* Doubleday Anchor Book, New York, 1961.
Stendahl, Krister, *The Scrolls and the New Testament,* New York, Harper & Row, 1957.
Mansoor, Menahem, *The Dead Sea Scrolls: A College Text Book and a Study Guide,* Grand Rapids, Eerdman, 1964.
Yadin, Yigal, *The Message of the Dead Sea Scrolls,* New York, Simon and Schuster, 1957. (A lucid and dramatic account of the discovery and significance of the scrolls.)
A competent, and more recent, survey of the data and issues involved in *The Dead Sea Scrolls* is by Edmund Wilson. Oxford University Press, 1969.
2. Deut. 18.15.
3. *Ant.* XIII. 5-9.
4. Cited by Kohler, K. art. *"Essenes,"* Jewish Encyclopedia.

Chapter 5—Zealots

1. Josephus, *Ant.* XIV; XV; *War,* I; II; IV. Yigal Yadin's *Massada* is a vivid report of the recent excavation, under his guidance. New York, Random House, 1966

Chapter 6—Apocalyptists and Messiahs

1. Considerable apocalyptic writing is in the Hebrew Bible, produced centuries earlier; the little book of Joel, portions of the books of Isaiah, Ezekel, Zechariah, especially the book of Daniel. But the apocalyptic literature flowered most luxuriantly at this time; hence the New Testament embodies much of it. Much of it was excluded from both the Hebrew Bible and the New Testament; they are collected in the Apocrypha and the Pseudepigrapha. See edition by Charles, Oxford Press. See any competent introduction to the New Testament.
2. Is., 11.4.
3. Ps., 121.3; 35.10.

Chapter 7—Procurators, Pilate

1. Margolis, M. L., and Marx, A., *A History of the Jewish People,* Philadelphia, Jewish Publication Society of America, 1927, p. 190.
2. Durant, Will, *Christ and Caesar,* N. Y., Simon and Schuster, 1944, p. 543.
3. John 18.33–38.

Chapter 8—John The Baptist

1. Luke 1.5-25; 57-80; 3. 1-20; Parallel passages: Matt. 3; Mark 1; John 1.
2. *Ant.* XVIII, 5.2.
3. Luke 1.15-17.
4. Mal. 4.5.
5. Mark 1.6.
6. 40.3-5.
7. John 1.29.
8. Mark 6.21-28.

Chapter 9—Jesus

1. Josephus, *Ant.* XVIII, III.3. For a masterly presentation and analysis of all the sources the student should study Joseph Klausner's *Jesus of Nazareth* (tr. Danby), N. Y., Macmillan, 1926, Sections I and II for the Hebrew, Greek and Latin sources. See also Jacob Z. Lauterbach, *Jesus in the Talmud* in *Rabbinic Essays,* Cincinnati, Hebrew Union College Press, 1951.
2. Enslin, M. S., *The Prophet From Nazareth,* N. Y., McGraw-Hill, 1961.
3. *Quest of the Historical Jesus,* London, 1954, 3rd ed., p. 396.
4. The present writer leans on the following: *Interpreter's Bible,* N. Y. Abingdon Press, 1951; C. G. Montefiore, *Synoptic Gospels,* 2 Vol; London, 1927; Feine, Behm, Kummel, *Introduction to the New Testament,* N. Y. Abingdon Press, 1966; the standard Encyclopedias; *Peake's Commentary on the Bible,* N. Y. Nelson, 1962.
5. *Jesus,* p. 167.
6. Is., 11.1-6.
7. *Ibid.,* 9.2-6.
8. Ps. 2.7.
9. Is., 61.1.

10. Mk., 1.7.
11. *Ibid.*, 1.10.
12. Ps., 2.7.
13. Ps., 22.1.
14. Matt., 5.17-20.
15. Montefiore, C. G. *Rabbinic Literature and Bible Teaching,* London, 1930, p. 38
16. Enslin, above, p. 111.
17. Matt., 7.6; Mk. 7.27-30.
18. Matt. 22.36; Mk. 12.30.
19. 6.8.
20. 6.8.
21. Jer. 7. See Enslin, above; Henry Cadbury, *The Perils of Modernizing Jesus,* N. Y. Macmillan, 1937. "It is not irreverent to suppose that the modern ethical problems—of chattel slavery, war, competitive business—no more entered Jesus' head in the modern form than they did the heads of his contemporaries and his followers for many centuries." (p. 96) "I have tried in vain to find in our Synoptic gospels a single injunction to social service based explicitly on the neighbor's need for love and service." (p. 104)
22. Is., 5.8*ff.*
23. Matt., 5.1 *ff.* Cf. Luke, 6.20 *ff.*
24. Matt., 5.29-30; 38-42
25. Klausner, above, p. 388.
26. Cohon, B. D., *Jacob's Well,* N. Y., Bookman's Associates, 1956, p. 79 *ff.*
27. Matt., 5.21 *ff.*
28. Klausner, above, p. 7, 17
29. See on Matthew 23 the works listed under 4, above.
30. Mk., 3.22.
31. Deut. 30.12. A famous passage in the Talmud reports a disputation among scholars in an academy; some resorted to miracles to validate their argument. One scholar dissented. He dismissed all proof adduced from miraculous manifestations. The Torah "is not in heaven;" it has been entrusted to man on earth for him to interpret it in keeping with his understanding and needs. We pay no attention, he insisted, to heavenly voices, but rely on the scholars and their rational understanding. (See *Baba Mezia* 59 b: Soncino Tr.)
32. Mk., 1.14-15.
33. *Ibid.,* 1.45.
34. *Ibid.,* 3.31-35.
35. *Ibid.,* 6.3; Matt., 13. 53-58; Luke, 4.16-30.
36. Deut., 16.16.
37. Mk., 11.10.
38. 9.9.
39. Mk., 11.15-16.
40. Jer., 7.
41. Mk., 11.17; Matt., 21.13; Zech., 14.20.

42. Mk., 12.13-17.

43. The specific evening when the Last Supper took place is difficult to determine. The Synoptic Gospels and John differ. All four gospels agree that the crucifixion took place on Friday. According to the Synoptics, Friday was the 15th of Nisan, which is the first day of Passover; according to John it was the 14th. John considers Jesus as the Paschal lamb sacrifice, which was slain on the Passover. The Last Supper, in such an event, could not have been the *seder* at all. Considerations from rabbinic law governing cases such as Jesus represented complicate the problem further. For the purposes of the present chapter this technical problem is of no consequence. The reader is referred to the chapter in Klausner's *Jesus,* p. 324. Any reliable N. T. commentary will present the main points to consider.

44. Mk., 14.32.

45. Matt., 10.16.

46. 50.6.

47. 53.7.

48. 22.18; 69.21.

49. Matt., 27.25.

50. 18.31.

51. See Note 43 above.

52. Matt., 27.11; Mk., 15.2; Lk., 23.3; John, 18.33.

53. Matt., 27.37; Mk., 15.2; Lk., 23.38; John, 19.19.

54. Mk., 7.27.

55. Matt., 19.14.

56. *Ibid.* 5.21-26

57. See Schweitzer, Albert, *The Quest of the Historical Jesus,* London, 1926; Walker, Th. *Jewish Views of Jesus,* New York, Macmillan, 1931; Cohon, S. S., *The Place of Jesus in the Religious Life of His Day,* Journal of Biblical Literature, Vol. XLVIII, p. 82–108.

58. Parkes, James, *Judaism and Christianity,* University of Chicago, 1948, p. 31.

59. Klausner, *Jesus,* p. 7, 17, etc.

60. John, 1.10-13.

61. Mk., 9.2-8; Matt., 17.1-9; Lk., 9.28-36.

62. Mk., 14.49.

63. Matt., 2.18-23; Is., 7.14.

64. Matt.

65. 15.7.

66. John 1. 1-5.

67. *Ibid.,* 14.6.

68. Hab., 2.4.

Chapter 10—Paul

1. Phil., 1.21.
2. *Ibid.*, 2.10-11.
3. Nock, A. *St. Paul*, Harper & Brothers, N. Y., 1948, p. 246. See Hatch, Wm. H. P., *Interpreter's Bible*, Vol. 7, p. 187.
4. Cited by K. Kohler, art. "Saul of Tarsus," *Jewish Encyclopedia*.
5. Nock, above, p. 13 ff.
6. *Ibid.*
7. Knox, John, *Interpreter's Bible*, Introduction to *Romans*.
8. *Life of Appolonius of Tynna* (Loeb Classical Library), Book I, Chpt. VIII, Cited by Schonfield, *The Jew of Tarsus*, p. 18.
9. Phil., 3.5.
10. Lev., 18.23; Deut., 6.14.
11. Phil., 3. 4-6; Acts, 22.3.
12. Acts, 5. 34-39.
13. Gal., 1.14.
14. Romans, 7.15.
15. II Cor. 12.7. See Donald Wayne Riddle, *Paul, Man of Conflict,* Nashville, Cokesbury Press, 1940.
16. 6.5-11; 12-14; 7.54-60.
17. Lev., 19.7.
18. Acts, 7.58-8.1-3.
19. Gal., 1.13.
20. See art. "Stripes" in *Jewish Encyclopedia*.
    This persecution of Saul—and later by him—was not on the basis of belief or disbelief in Jesus or the Messiah. Rather, it was for conduct in violation of the law, and was in accord with biblical legislation. "Its administration was carefully supervised, and hedged about with due process of law. It is possible that when Paul so radically reversed his loyalties, and became an advocate of the cause which he had formerly opposed, he suffered exactly the same punishment which he himself meted out in the days of his zeal for the faith of his fathers.
21. Acts, 9.1-9. *See also* 22.4-16; 26.9-18; Gal., 1.13-17.
22. Acts, 9.21-22.
23. Is., 6.5; Acts, 9.21-22.
24. Tresmontant, Claude, *Saint Paul and the Mystery of Christ*, N. Y. Harper Torch Books, 1957.
25. II Cor., 11.24-27.
26. Establishing the specific dates in the activities of Paul presents a difficult problem. Historians are not always in agreement. The following dates of the three missionary journeys may be the most reasonable: The first, about 45-49; the second, about 50-53; the third began in 52 or 53.
27. I Cor., 15.3-4.

28. Gal., 5.6.
29. *Ibid.*, 5.1.
30. Acts 17. 16-32.
31. Thes., 1.1
32. Gal., 5.1.
33. *Ibid.*, 1.8-9.
34. Klausner, *From Jesus to Paul*, p. 559.
35. I Cor., 13.
36. *Ibid.*, 16.21–22.
37. Acts, 26. 9-18.
38. *Ibid.*, 25.12.
39. *Interpreter's Bible*, Acts, p. 349.
40. II Cor., 3.12-14.
41. 17.1.
42. *Abot*, 6.
43. Gal., 3.13.
44. Eph., 2.14.
45. Klausner, above, p. 593.
46. Eph., 4.6-8; I Cor., 8. 4-6.
47. Klausner, above, p. 469.
48. *Ibid.*, p. 453.
49. Acts, 17.6-8.
50. I Cor., 3.14, etc.
51. Rom., 9.22.
52. Kohler, K., art. "Saul of Tarsus," *Jewish Encyclopedia*.

Chapter 11—Josephus

1. Baron, Bentwich, Graetz, Roth, etc.
2. Thackeray, H. St. John, *Josephus—the Man and the Historian*, p. 3; N. Y. Jewish Institute of Religion, 1929.
3. *Ibid.*, p. 95.
4. *Life*, 1.
5. *Ibid.*, 2.
6. *Ibid.*
7. *Ibid.*, 3.
8. *JW*, II, XVII, 1–2.
9. *Ibid.*, II, 531.
10. *Life*, 4.
11. *JW*, II, 5; *Life*, 7.
12. *Life*, 4.
13. *Ibid.*, 9.
14. See Farmer, Wm. R., *Maccabees, Zealots and Josephus*, N. Y., Columbia University Press, 1956.
15. *JW*, II, XXI, 1.

16. *Ibid.*, IV, 13.
17. *Ibid.*, III.7.
18. *Ibid.*, III, 6-7.
19. *Ibid.*, VII, 6.
20. *Life*, 75. "Gentle Titus" killed thousands upon thousands of Jewish prisoners in city after city in an endless series of Roman holidays of slaughter, in celebration not only of victories but of family birthdays. Josephus cites one sickening incident after another of untold numbers of men thrown to the lions or burnt alive by "gentle Titus," his patron and personal friend.
21. *Apion*, 50.
22. *JW*, II, 345; III, 108.

Chapter 12—Yohanan ben Zakkai

1. Is., 40.3-5.
2. Ps. of Solomon, 17.24.
3. The most complete study in English of the sources is Jacob Neusner's *A Life of Rabban Yohanan Ben Sakkai,* a doctoral dissertation, published by E. J. Brill, Leiden, 1962. The author strains for the historic facts by analyzing the fragments of texts available. *Rabban* —"our teacher," "our master"—is a title given at the time to patriarchs, or presidents of the Sanhedrin.
4. He is credited with having studied under Hillel in his youth, but chronology makes it highly dubious.
5. *Suk.*, 28a.
6. *Abot.*, 6.4.
7. *Ibid.*, 3.1.
8. *Ibid.*, 2.9.
9. R. T. Herford, in his *Christianity and the Talmud,* London, 1902, suggests that there is a good possibility that Yohanan had seen and heard Jesus.
10. *Abot.*, 3.11-13.
11. *Ibid.*, 2.10-13.
12. *See* Numb. 5.11-31.
13. *See* Neusner, above, p. 45.
14. *Ibid.*, p. 48.
15. *Abot d'R. Nathan* (ed. Golden), p. 35.
16. Gittin 56b.
17. See Neusner, above, p. 120.
18. *Ibid.*, above, 109ff.
19. *Abot.*, 5.25.
20. Neusner, above, p. 174.
21. Ber. 28b.

Chapter 13—Akiba

1. These legends are rabbinic legendry (Haggadah or Agada, Midrash). A good sampling for the layman, in English, is C. G. Montefiore and H. Loewe, *Rabbinic Anthology*, N. Y., London, Macmillan, 1938.
2. S of S, 6.3.
3. Ps., 118.17.
4. *Authorised Daily Prayerbook*, ed. Singer, p. 147, etc.
5. Ezra, 8.8.
6. Ginzberg, L. art. "Akiba," *Jewish Encyclopedia*.
7. Cited by Finkelstein, L., *Akiba*, Philadelphia, Jewish Publication Society, 1936.
8. *Mak.* 1.7a. Cited in art. "Capital Punishment," *Jewish Encyclopedia*.
9. Finkelstein, *Akiba,* above, p. 30-31.
10. *Ibid.,* p. 102, Note 21.
11. *Ibid.,* p. 84.
12. *Abot.,* 3. 18-20.
13. Exod., 34.6.
14. Deut., 30.18.
15. *Gen. R.,* XXXIV. 14.
16. See art. *Calendar* in *Jewish Encyclopedia*.
17. See Durant, Will, *Christ and Caesar,* N. Y. Simon and Schuster, 1944, p. 548.
18. Numb., 24.17.
19. Cited, art. "Bar Kokba," *Jewish Encyclopedia*.
20. *Abodah Zarah* 17a (See Soncino tr.)
21. *Sanh.* 74a (See Soncino tra).
22. *Ibid.,* See Appendix IV, The Martyrdom of Akiba.
23. Ginzberg, L. art "Akiba," *Jewish Encyclopedia*.

Chapter 14—Apostles and Martyrs

1. James, 5.1-3; 25.
2. See *Transubstantiation* in Oxford Dictionary of the Christian Church, or The New Catholic Encyclopedia. Similar beliefs were held by the followers of Dionysus, Attis, Mithras, and by the Indians of Mexico and Peru.
3. I Cor., 11.3, 7-8.
4. Numb., 15.37-40.
5. I John, 2.18.
6. *Abot.,* 2.5.
7. Cited by Will Durant, *Caesar and Christ,* N. Y. Simon and Schuster, 1954, p. 652.

8. Rev., 17.1-2.
9. *Ibid.*, 17.1-2.
10. Cited in art. "Peter," *New Catholic Encyclopedia.*
11. "Ignatius," *New Catholic Encyclopedia.*
12. *Polycarp,* above.
13. II Macc., 6.24-30.
14. *New Catholic Encyclopedia.*
15. Durant, above, p. 652.
16. John 14.16.
17. Matt. 10.5-6.
18. *Ibid.*, 28. 19-20.
19. See Blau, Joseph, *On the Celebration of Christmas,* N. Y. Columbia University Press, *Rapport* for 1964–65, p. 3ff. See, also, on Resurrection, Salvation, Virgin Birth, dying and rising gods, etc. in Guignebert, Charles, N. Y., Twayne, 1962
20. Acts, 5.14-15; 9.36*ff.*
21. Matt., 16.17-19.
22. See "Creed," *New Catholic Encyclopedia.*

Chapter 15—Quo Vadis?

1. James Apoc. N. T., 333; *New Catholic Encyclopedia,* "Quo Vadis."
2. Ps., 121.1.
3. Ps., 137.4.
4. Ezek., 2.1.
5. *N. Y. Times,* August 11, 1964, p. 21.
6. Phil., 2.10-11.
7. Job, 13.15.
8. See Appendix, Deicide, and literature cited.
9. Gen., 8.22.
10. Micah, 4.5.
11. Is., 35.8.

Index

Abtalion, 38

Abyssinian Church, 67

Acropolis, 135

Acts, 143

Acts of the Apostles, 83, 233

Aelia Capitoliana, 205

Against Apion (Josephus), 249, 252

Agrippa, 157

Akiba, 12, 176, 182, 189 ff, 253

Albinus, 67

Alexander the Great, 51

Alexandria, 220

Ananias, 130

Antioch, 133, 220

Antiochus, 203

Antipater, 20

Anti-Semitism, 148

Antonia, 157

Apion, 250

Apocalyptists, 63, 90, 174

Apostolic creed, 221

Arabs, 25

Aramaic language, 87, 92, 127, 154, 210

Archelaus, 30, 34, 35

Arch of Titus, 167

Arianism, 220

Aristobulus, 20, 22, 27

Armenia, 203

Asia Minor, 124, 125, 133

Athenians, 136

Athens, 135, 136

Attis, 145

Augustalis festivals, 214

Baal-Tarz, 124

Babylon, 33, 54, 200

Baptism, 57, 77

Bar Kokba, 204

Barnabas, 132, 134

Benei Berak, 193

Bentwich, Norman, 244 *n*, 248

Berea, 135

Bethar, 204

Bet Hillel, 42

Beth-horon, 157

Bethlehem stories, 86 *n*

Bet Shammai, 42

Bible interpretation, 41, 51, 197, 218

Bible stories, 99

Bishop of Tarragona, 215

Caesar, 32, 44, 45, 50, 106, 142, 146, 174

Caesaria, 32, 68, 104, 139, 140, 156

Calvary, 112, 116

Capernaum, 100, 101

Capitoline hills, 62

Cardinal Bea, 227, 236–238

Carthage, 215

Cestium Gallus, 157

Christianity, 226 ff

Christian martyrs, 213

Christian missionaries, 218

Christian monasticism, 56

Christians, 189

Church of Rome, 100, 219–220

Circumcision, 133–134, 145, 216

Colosseum, 166, 183

Colossians, letter to, 142

Constantine, 213–214, 219, 220

Corealius, 167

Corinth, 136, 137

266

Corinthians, epistle to, 137, 138
Crete, 143
Crucifixion, 108, 109
Crusaders, 119
Cyprus, 132

Dagger men, 60, 160, 166, 174
Damascus, 20, 130, 133, 141, 156
Daniel, 64–65, 88, 90, 218
Dead Sea, 55
Dead Sea Scrolls, 55, 75, 108
Deicide, 235 ff
Deuteronomy, 58
Diocletian, 215
Dionysius, 244
Domitian, 168, 202, 242
Durant, Will, 215

Ecclesiastes, 194
Ecumenical Council, 226–227
Edom, 25
Egypt, 164
Elazar ben Jair, 62
Eleazar, 165, 199, 214
Eleazar bar Simon, 61, 62, 173
Eli, sons of, 195
Eliezer, 198
Eliezer ben Hyrcanus, 192
Elijah, 74, 75, 76, 98, 99, 102, 192
Elisha, 98, 102
Enoch, 90, 218
Enslin, Morton Scott, 78 n, 86 n, 91
    n, 94 n
Epaphroditus, 249
Ephesus, 137, 139, 143, 216
Epistles of Paul, 122 ff
Esau, 25
Esdras, Book of, 218
Essenes, 47, 55 ff, 76, 90, 155, 174
Esther, Scrolls of, 194
Eusibius, 215, 246, 248, 249
Ezekiel, 54, 98
Ezra, 195, 196

Felix, 155
Festus, 67
Flood, the, 99
Florus, 67, 157
Francis of Assisi, 119

Gabara, 159
Galatians, epistle to, 134, 137
Galileans, 68
Galilee, 99, 104, 111, 157, 163, 179
Galilee, Sea of, 100
Gamaliel, 38, 39, 126–127
Gethsemene, 107
Gishchala, 161
Gnosticism, 218
Golden Rule, 95
Golgotha, 90, 103
Gospels, 81, 83
Gregory IX, 235
Grosseteste, Robert, 235

Hadrian, 201, 203, 204
Haggadah, 127
Halacha, 127
Hanania ben Dosa, 178
Hananiel ben Teradion, 205, 214
Hanukkah, 172
Hasmonean dynasty, 24
Hebrew Bible, 195
Hebrew months, 201
Hellenism, 51, 124, 160
Hellenistic law, 44
Herod, 17, 19 ff, 22
Herod Agrippa, 140, 154
Herod Antipas, 78
Herodian Period, 176
Hezekiah, 185
Hillel, 17, 34, 36 ff, 96, 155, 176, 218
Hill of Mars, 135
Hitler, Adolf, 250
Holy Communion, 57
Homer, 240
Hyrcanus, 20, 21, 22, 23, 27, 28

Idumeans, 25, 60, 162

Ignatius, 214

Innocent III, 235

Iranaeus, 218

Isaac, 74

Isaiah, 64, 76, 94, 98, 109, 131, 174, 229

Isis, 145

Israelites, 25

Jacob, 25

James, 86, 144, 216

Jason, 146

Jeremiah, 64, 98, 100, 106, 172

Jerome, 249

Jericho, 30, 199

Jerusalem, 21, 23, 60, 104, 139, 140, 164, 167, 179

Jerusalem, Temple at, 32

Jesse, 88

Jesus

baptized, 77; birth, 117; crucifixion, 11, 23, 69, 111 ff; in the desert, 76; ethics, 95; image of persecution, 85 ff; "King of the Jews," 112 ff; life, 115; miracle-worker, 97, 101; Palestinian rabbi, 80 ff; and Pilate, 111; and rabbinic law, 106; and salvation, 83; son of God, 82; teacher, 40, 50, 53, 100; transfiguration, 115 ff; tried before Roman governor, 32

Jewish Antiquities (Josephus), 242 ff

Jewish calendar, 201–202

Jewish War (Josephus), 152 ff, 240 ff

Jews, 110, 189, 202, 203, 216

Johanan ben Zakkai, 164, 169, 172, 202

John, 96, 213

John the Baptist, 35, 65, 68, 73 ff; 100, 154

John of Gishchala, 61, 153, 159, 160, 161, 169, 171, 173

John XXIII, 236

Jordan, 33

Jordan River, 75, 90

Jose, 86

Joseph (father of Jesus), 96, 117

Joseph ben Caiaphas, 112

Joseph ben Matthias (Josephus), 153

Josephus, 11, 21 ff, 28 ff, 58, 61, 62, 74, 151 ff

Joshua, 36, 53

Joshua ben Hananiah, 192

Jotapata, 159, 162, 163

Judah, 86

Judah Maccabeus, 26, 157, 161

Judaic Christians, 210–211

Judaism, 54, 65, 145, 146, 175, 226 ff, 249

Judas Iscariot, 106, 108

Judea, 19 ff, 66, 154, 159, 171, 215, 241

Judean people, 75

Justin Martyr, 214

Justin of Samaria, 214

Justus of Tiberia, 153, 248

Kaddish, 95

King David, 26

Klausner, Joseph, 111

Krauss, Samuel, 244 *n*

Lamentations, Book of, 172

Levites, 49

Leviticus, 201

Luke, 65, 74, 82, 118, 142

Lydda, 189, 206

Maccabees, 20, 21, 27, 55, 60, 157

Macedonia, 139, 143

Machaerus, 78

Malachi, 75

Manual of Discipline, 55

Marcion, 218
Mariamne, 26, 27, 29
Mark, 82, 90, 106, 107, 118
Mary, 86, 103, 117
Masada, 33, 61, 62, 166, 204
Mattathias, 60
Matthew, 82, 102, 118, 216
Meletian schism, 220
Mesopotamia, 203
Messiah, 47, 56, 63
Messianists, 90, 174
Micah, 93, 229
Miracles, 98
Mishnah, 97, 194
Mithra cult, 99
Mithraic processions, 124
Mithras, 145
Montanus, 218
Moses, 36, 52, 53, 58, 76, 98
Mount Gerizim, 69
Mount of Olives, 107
Mount Scopus, 157

Nativity, feast of, 217
Naturai Karta, 94 n
Nazarenes, 76, 208, 210, 212
Nazareth, 86, 102
Nebuchadnezzar, 98
Nero, 123, 143, 155, 213, 222
Nerva, 202
New Testament, 84, 212, 227
Nicaea, Council of, 220–221
Nicanor, 157
Niese, Benedictus, 244 n, 246, 247
Noah, 99

Old Testament, 194
Oral Torah, 52, 54, 196
Origen, 247, 248

Palestine, 199
Palestinian Jewry, 84
Palestinian revolt, 250
Pappus ben Judah, 253

Parables, 101, 118
Passover, 103–104, 202
Patriarchs of the Bible, 73
Paul, 50, 81, 83, 96, 108, 189, 213, 216, 233 ff
Paul VI, 223
Paul of Tarsus, 121 ff
Pella, 211
Pentateuch, first edition of, 195
Peter, 143, 144, 213, 216, 222
Pharisaic Judaism, 91, 93
Pharisees, 21, 29, 47 ff, 69, 87, 92, 96, 113–114, 144, 162, 177, 194, 212
Philemon, 142
Philip, 216
Philippi, 135
Philippians, letter to, 142
Philo, 55, 58, 127, 244
Phrygia, 142
Pilate, 35, 65, 69, 110, 112, 154
Plato, 214
Polycarp, 214
Pompey, 19, 21, 22
Pontifex Maximus, 220, 221
Pothinus of Lyons, 214
Procurators, 35, 63, 64, 66 ff, 88
Psalms, 64, 109
Publius Aelius Hadrianus, 203
Puteoli, 156

Queen Alexandra, 26, 28
Qumran, 55, 58, 76

Rachabites, 76
Rachel (wife of Akiba), 191–192, 193
Revelation, Book of, 213
Roman Catholic Church, 224
Roman legions, 52, 55
Roman oppression, 88
Romans, 81, 100, 163, 165, 202, 204, 241

Rome, 19, 142, 155 ff, 168, 169, 173, 213, 217

Sabbath, 57, 210
Sadducees, 21, 47 ff, 105, 155, 160, 177, 195
St. Clement of Rome, 213
Samaria, 158
Samson, 74
Sanhedrin, 23, 27, 31, 38, 50, 67, 113
Saturnalia, 217
Saul of Tarsus, 11, 39, 191
Schweitzer, Albert, 84, 119
Scypholis, 156
Sepphoris, 158, 159
Sergius Paulus, 132
Sermon on the Mount, 94
Shabuot, 140
Shammai, 36 ff, 96, 175, 218
Shemayah, 38
Shulamite, songs of, 194
Sicarii, 166
Silas, 134, 135
Simeon, 87
Simeon ben Yohai, 97
Simon, 166
Simon bar Giora, 61, 62, 162, 173
Simon called Peter, 100-101, 107, 108
Simon the Leper, 105
Sixtus II, 215
Smyrna, 214, 215
Solomon, 49, 195
Song of Songs, 194
Sophocles, 240
Spain, 143
Spinoza, 227
Stephen, 129, 144
Stoics, 250
Strasbourg cathedral, 147

Synagogue, 51, 147, 196
Synoptic Gospels, 82, 100, 111
Syria, 124, 157, 216
Syrian Greeks, 20

Tacitus, 67
Talmud, 42, 54, 176-177, 253
Tarichea, 159
Tarpeian Rock, the, 62
Tarsus, 123-124, 126, 128
Tel Aviv, 193
Temple, the, 52, 195
Tertullion, 212
Thackeray, H. St. John, 153, 241, 245, 247
Thessalonica, 135
Tiberia, 158-159
Tiberius, 68
Timothy, 134
Titus, 33, 164, 165, 167, 241
Torah, 41, 198
Torquemada, 119
Trajan, 202, 203, 212
Trinity, the, 146

Vespasian, 162, 163, 164, 168, 173, 177, 181, 241

Wailing Wall, 11
Western Wall, 33
Whiston, William, 152

Yavneh, 182, 183, 203
Yohanan ben Zakkai, 11, 97, 173 ff

Zadock, 49
Zealots, 45, 47, 50, 58, 60 ff, 157, 159, 166, 174, 241
Zechariah, 64, 65, 74, 105
Zerabbabel, 33